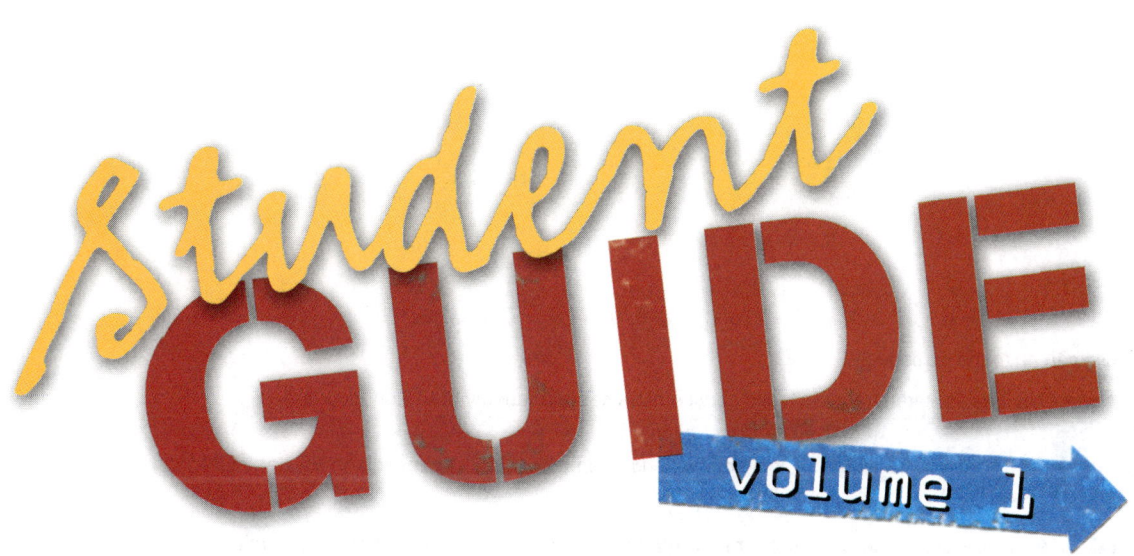

Program Consultant
William F. Tate
Edward Mallinckrodt Distinguished University Professor
Washington University, St. Louis

Image credits can be found on page 262.

Academy Awards® is the registered trademark and service mark of the Academy of Motion Picture Arts and Sciences.

Use of the trademark implies no relationship, sponsorship, endorsement, sale, or promotion on the part of Pearson Education, Inc. or its affiliates.

Copyright © 2009 by Pearson Education, Inc. or its affiliate(s). All rights reserved. Printed in the United States of America. This publication is protected by copyright, and permission should be obtained from the publisher prior to any prohibited reproductions, storage in a retrieval system, or transmission in any form or by any means, electronic, mechanical, photocopying, recording, or likewise. For information regarding permission(s), write to: Pearson School Rights & Permissions Department, One Lake Street, Upper Saddle River, New Jersey 07458.

Pearson® is a trademark, in the U.S. and/or in other countries, of Pearson Education, Inc. or its affiliate(s).

ISBN-13: 978-0-7854-6506-5
ISBN-10:   0-7854-6506-5
2 3 4 5 6 7 8 9 10 12 11 10 09

1-800-992-0244
www.pearson.com

CONTENTS

UNIT 1

Tools for Solving Math Problems

LESSON 1	**The Four-Step Problem-Solving Plan**	2
LESSON 2	**Problem-Solving Strategy** Draw a Picture or Use a Model	4
LESSON 3	**Problem-Solving Strategy** Find a Pattern	6
LESSON 4	**Problem-Solving Strategy** Make a List	8
LESSON 5	**Graphic Organizers** Venn Diagram, Concept Map, Flowchart, Three-Column Chart	10
LESSON 6	**Problem-Solving Strategy** Try a Simpler Form of the Problem	12
LESSON 7	**Problem-Solving Strategy** Make a Table or a Chart	14
LESSON 8	**Problem-Solving Strategy** Guess, Check, and Revise	16
LESSON 9	**Graphic Organizers** Bar Graph, Circle Graph, Coordinate Grid	18
UNIT 1 REFLECTION		20

UNIT 2

Multiplication and Division

READING STRATEGY	**Summarizing**	22
LESSON 1	**Learn the Skill** Multiplication	24
LESSON 2	**Choose a Strategy**	27
LESSON 3	**Learn the Skill** Properties of Addition and Multiplication	31
LESSON 4	**Choose a Strategy**	34
LESSON 5	**Application**	38
LESSON 6	**Learn the Skill** Place Value and Expanded Notation	42
LESSON 7	**Choose a Strategy**	45
LESSON 8	**Application**	49
LESSON 9	**Connections** The Breaking-Apart Algorithm	53
LESSON 10	**Review and Practice**	57
LESSON 11	**Learn the Skill** Division	61
LESSON 12	**Choose a Strategy**	64
LESSON 13	**Learn the Skill** Multiplication and Division as Inverse Operations	68
LESSON 14	**Choose a Strategy**	71
LESSON 15	**Application**	75
LESSON 16	**Learn the Skill** Tables, Bar Graphs, and Pictographs	79
LESSON 17	**Choose a Strategy**	82
LESSON 18	**Application**	86
LESSON 19	**Connections** Working Right-to-Left or Left-to-Right	90
LESSON 20	**Review and Practice**	94
UNIT 2 REFLECTION		98

(Contents continues)

UNIT 3

Fractions

READING STRATEGY Questioning	100	
USE THE STRATEGIES	102	
LESSON 1 Learn the Skill	104	
Proper Fractions		
LESSON 2 Choose a Strategy	107	
LESSON 3 Learn the Skill	111	
Improper Fractions and Mixed Numbers		
LESSON 4 Choose a Strategy	114	
LESSON 5 Application	118	
LESSON 6 Learn the Skill	122	
Comparing Fractions		
LESSON 7 Choose a Strategy	125	
LESSON 8 Application	129	
LESSON 9 Connections	133	
Fractions in Measurements		
LESSON 10 Review and Practice	137	
LESSON 11 Learn the Skill	141	
Benchmark Fractions and Common Numerators or Denominators		
LESSON 12 Choose a Strategy	144	
LESSON 13 Learn the Skill	148	
Equivalent Fractions and Simplest Form		
LESSON 14 Choose a Strategy	151	
LESSON 15 Application	155	
LESSON 16 Learn the Skill	159	
Ordering Fractions		
LESSON 17 Choose a Strategy	162	
LESSON 18 Application	166	
LESSON 19 Connections	170	
Accuracy and Precision		
LESSON 20 Review and Practice	174	
UNIT 3 REFLECTION	178	

UNIT 4

Decimals

READING STRATEGY Previewing/Predicting	180	
USE THE STRATEGIES	182	
LESSON 1 Learn the Skill	184	
Decimals		
LESSON 2 Choose a Strategy	187	
LESSON 3 Learn the Skill	191	
Fractions and Decimals		
LESSON 4 Choose a Strategy	194	
LESSON 5 Application	198	
LESSON 6 Learn the Skill	202	
Ordering and Rounding Decimals		
LESSON 7 Choose a Strategy	205	
LESSON 8 Application	209	
LESSON 9 Connections	213	
Using Decimals to Find Equivalent Fractions		
LESSON 10 Review and Practice	217	
LESSON 11 Learn the Skill	221	
Comparing and Ordering Decimals and Fractions		
LESSON 12 Choose a Strategy	224	
LESSON 13 Learn the Skill	228	
Estimating Decimal and Fractional Amounts		
LESSON 14 Choose a Strategy	231	
LESSON 15 Application	235	
LESSON 16 Learn the Skill	239	
Decimals in Graphs		
LESSON 17 Choose a Strategy	242	
LESSON 18 Application	246	
LESSON 19 Connections	250	
Decimals and Stem-and-Leaf Plots		
LESSON 20 Review and Practice	254	
UNIT 4 REFLECTION	258	

Glossary 259

UNIT 1
Tools for Solving Math Problems

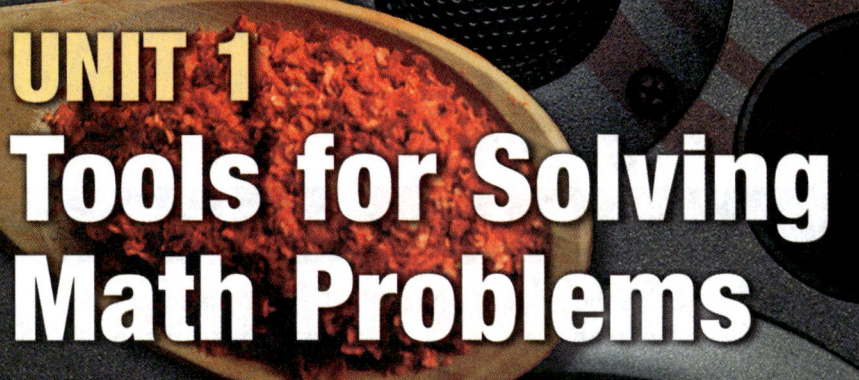

MATH STRATEGIES
Learn **PROBLEM-SOLVING STRATEGIES** and how to apply them to solve real-world problems.

VOCABULARY

PROBLEM-SOLVING WORDS:
Know them!
Use them!
Learn all about them!

The Four-Step Problem-Solving Plan
1. Read 3. Solve
2. Plan 4. Check

The Four-Step Problem-Solving Plan

The Four-Step Problem-Solving Plan

Step 1: Read	Step 2: Plan	Step 3: Solve	Step 4: Check
Make sure you understand what the problem is asking.	Decide how you will solve the problem.	Solve the problem using your plan.	Check to make sure your answer is correct.

When you are given a problem to solve, having a plan makes the task easier. The Four-Step Problem-Solving Plan is a useful tool to help you solve math problems.

Step 1: Read

It is very important to read the problem carefully. Try to answer the following questions once you have read the problem.

- What do you know about the problem?
- What is the question in the problem?
- What facts are given in the problem?

If you do not understand some of the words in the problem, you can look them up in a dictionary or the glossary of your textbook.

Read the problem below. Restate the problem in your own words on the lines below. Underline the question and circle any facts that could help you answer it.

1. Sam works 20 hours a week and earns $9 an hour. How much will he earn in two weeks?
   _____
   _____
   _____

Step 2: Plan

Once you know what the problem is asking, you need to plan how to solve it. Ask:

- Have you solved a similar problem before?
- What problem-solving strategies can you use?

Problem-solving strategies are ways you can set up and solve a problem. In this example, you might want to look for words that can tell you what operation to use.

2. Write your plan for solving the problem. Make sure you have explained all the steps you will take to get your answer.
   _____
   _____
   _____
   _____

The Four-Step Problem-Solving Plan

Step 3: Solve

To solve the problem, follow the plan you made in Step 2. As you solve, ask:

- Are you following each step of your plan?
- Do you need to change your plan?
- Do you need to try another problem-solving strategy?

It is okay to change your plan if it does not solve the problem.

Make sure to keep a record of everything you did as you solved the problem. This is also known as showing your work. It can help you identify what you did wrong and what you did right as you move on to the next step.

3. Show your work in the space below. Circle your final answer.
   _____

Step 4: Check

After you have solved the problem, check your answer. Think about the following questions while you check your answer.

- Have you answered the right question?
- Did you make any mistakes as you followed the steps of your plan?
- Does your answer make sense? Is it reasonable?
- Can you solve it another way and get the same answer?

Reviewing your work once you have finished can help catch any simple mistakes you may have made.

4. What is another way you could solve this problem? Use your plan to check the answer you found in Step 3.
   _____
   _____

Use the Four-Step Problem-Solving Plan to solve the problem below. Follow the steps in this lesson. Write your plan on a separate sheet of paper. Write your answer below.

5. Maria made three beaded bracelets. She used the same number of beads for each bracelet. If Maria started with 86 beads in all, how many beads did she use for each bracelet? How many more beads will she need for another bracelet?
   _____
   _____

Problem-Solving Strategy

Draw a Picture or Use a Model

VOCABULARY

expression: a mathematical statement including numbers and symbols

physical model: a real-life representation of an object

strategy: a plan or way of doing something

A **strategy** is a plan or a way of doing something. Problem-solving strategies help you organize the information you need to solve a problem. A useful strategy is **Draw a Picture or Use a Model.**

Drawing a picture can help you better understand the problem. For example, drawing out the following problem can help you "see" all the bumper cars.

Read: Miguel and Joel want to ride the bumper cars at the county fair. They see four red cars and five blue cars. How many total bumper cars do they see?

What do you know? There are four red cars and five blue cars.

What do you need to find out? How many cars are there total?

Plan: Draw a picture to show the cars. Count the cars.

Solve: There are nine cars.

Check: $4 + 5 = 9$

This drawing also shows the **expression** $4 + 5$.

1. **Read:** Pam had eight fish in her fish tank. Then she added nine more fish to the tank. How many fish are in the tank now? Use the Draw a Picture or Use a Model strategy to solve this problem.

   What do you know? _____

   What do you need to find out? _____

   Plan: _____

   Solve: _____

   Check: _____

Unit 1, Lesson 2

Problem-Solving Strategy

The Use a Model strategy can either refer to a **physical model** or a model on paper. One example of a physical model is base ten blocks. Base ten blocks come in single blocks, rods of 10, and flats of 100.

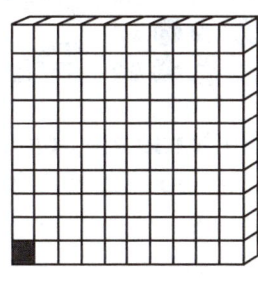

1 single block   one rod of 10 blocks   one flat of 100 blocks

2. **Read:** Wong had 300 marbles in a bag. He took out 245 marbles. How many marbles are still in the bag? Use a physical model to help solve the problem.

   What do you know? _____
   What do you need to find out? _____
   Plan: _____
   _____
   Solve: _____
   Check: _____

3. Draw a picture and write a story problem about your picture. Give the problem to a classmate to solve.
   _____
   _____
   _____

4. Write one question you have about this strategy.
   _____
   _____
   _____

Problem-Solving Strategy

 ## Find a Pattern

VOCABULARY

pattern: objects, designs, or numbers that change in a specific way

rule: a description of the way a pattern works

Patterns are objects, designs, or numbers that repeat or change in a certain way. The **Find a Pattern** strategy can help you solve problems where the answer can be found by filling in the pattern.

You need to look at the pattern carefully and decide how it was created. This is the **rule** of the pattern, which describes how the pattern works. With numbers, the rule might be "subtract 3" or "divide by 2." With shapes, the rule might describe a repeating pattern of shapes, such as "triangle, square, then circle." To understand the pattern, you must find the rule.

Read: Fill in the missing numbers in the pattern below.

1, 3, 5, _____, 9, _____, _____

What do you know? There are four numbers given in a pattern: 1, 3, 5, and 9.

What do you need to find out? Find the three missing numbers in the pattern.

Plan: Look for a pattern by seeing how the numbers change. Use this pattern to fill in the missing numbers.

Solve: 3 − 1 = 2, 5 − 3 = 2, so the rule is increase by 2. The missing numbers are 7 (which is 5 + 2), 11 (which is 9 + 2), and 13 (which is 11 + 2).

Check: 9 is 2 more than 7, so the numbers fit the pattern. All of these numbers are also odd numbers.

---

1. **Read:** Fill in the missing numbers. Explain what the pattern is.

   98, 88, _____, 68, 58, _____, _____

   What do you know? _____

   What do you need to find out? _____

   Plan: _____

   _____

   Solve: _____

   _____

   Check: _____

   _____

Unit 1, Lesson 3

Problem-Solving Strategy

Make an **X** on the hundreds chart below. Start the first line at 1 and end at 100. Start the second line at 91 and end at 10.

1	2	3	4	5	6	7	8	9	10
11	12	13	14	15	16	17	18	19	20
21	22	23	24	25	26	27	28	29	30
31	32	33	34	35	36	37	38	39	40
41	42	43	44	45	46	47	48	49	50
51	52	53	54	55	56	57	58	59	60
61	62	63	64	65	66	67	68	69	70
71	72	73	74	75	76	77	78	79	80
81	82	83	84	85	86	87	88	89	90
91	92	93	94	95	96	97	98	99	100

2. What is the rule for the line that starts at the top left and moves to the bottom right?
   _____

3. What is the rule for the line that starts at the bottom left and moves to the top right?
   _____

Patterns can also be found in pictures or a series of shapes. For example, the shapes can repeat in a certain order or change the number of sides. You must look carefully to find how the shapes repeat or change.

4. Find the missing shapes. Write the rule below. Then, draw the missing shapes on the lines in the pattern.

   ■ ◆ ● ♥ ■ _____ ● ♥ _____ ◆ _____ _____ ■ ◆ ● ♥

   Rule: _____

5. On a sheet of paper, draw a pattern using numbers or objects. Leave blanks in the pattern. Then exchange with a partner who will find the rule and complete the pattern. What was your partner's rule?
   _____

6. Where might you use the Find a Pattern strategy in your daily life?
   _____
   _____
   _____

Unit 1, Lesson 3

Problem-Solving Strategy

Make a List

VOCABULARY

combination: a group of objects in which order does not matter

tree diagram: a diagram that shows possible combinations branching off each other

When reading, lists are an excellent tool to help you understand the text. In math, the **Make a List** strategy helps you see information in an organized way. For example, lists help you keep track of the possible **combinations** of items. Lists can also help you keep track of possible outcomes. See the example below for one way to use a list.

Read: Luanne has 75 cents. If she only has nickels and dimes, how many different combinations of coins could she have?

What do I know? Luanne has 75 cents.

What do I need to know? How many ways can she make 75 cents from nickels and dimes?

Plan: I can make a list of all the different possible combinations of nickels and dimes that make 75 cents. The list should start with the most possible dimes she could use, and then decrease by one.

Solve: Possible combinations:

1. 7 dimes, 1 nickel
2. 6 dimes, 3 nickels
3. 5 dimes, 5 nickels
4. 4 dimes, 7 nickels
5. 3 dimes, 9 nickels
6. 2 dimes, 11 nickels
7. 1 dime, 13 nickels
8. 0 dimes, 15 nickels

Luanne can make 75 cents in eight different ways.

Check: Make sure each set of nickels and dimes equals 75 cents.

1. **Read:** For breakfast, Selina has a choice of three fruits: bananas, strawberries, or blueberries. How many different combinations can she have if she chooses two fruits? It does not matter what order she chooses the fruits.

   One way to help create a list is to make a **tree diagram**. This diagram shows possible combinations "branching off" like a tree. Here is a tree diagram for this problem. Because order does not matter, you only need to count each combination the first time you see it.

   Bananas — Strawberries, Blueberries
   Strawberries — Blueberries, Bananas
   Blueberries — Strawberries, Bananas

   What do I know? _____
   What do I need to know? _____
   Plan: _____
   Solve: _____
   Check: _____

Problem-Solving Strategy

2. **Read:** Ben has a pair of khaki pants and a pair of black pants. He has a brown jacket and a blue jacket. He has a blue shirt and a white shirt. How many outfits can Ben make?

   What do I know? _____

   _____

   What do I need to know? _____

   _____

   Plan: _____

   _____

   Solve: _____

   _____

   Check: _____

3. In art class, you need to make a design using two different shapes. You can choose from these four shapes. How many possible pairs of shapes can you choose to make your design? The order of the shapes does not matter.

   _____

   _____

4. Sean can choose any combination of three days on which to take guitar lessons. Sunday is the only day he cannot have lessons.

   How many combinations of days can he choose from?

   Show your work.

   _____

   _____

   _____

5. When would you use the Make a List strategy to solve a problem?

   _____

   _____

   _____

6. Write a word problem that you must make a list to solve. Then let a partner solve it.

   _____

   _____

   _____

Unit 1, Lesson 4

Graphic Organizers

Graphic Organizers

Graphic organizers are used to arrange information in a way that makes it easy to understand. You can use a graphic organizer to display information from an article or a word problem.

> **VOCABULARY**
>
> **concept map:** a graphic organizer showing a main topic and related ideas
>
> **flowchart:** a diagram that can be used to show the steps in a process
>
> **three-column chart:** a chart that can be used to take notes or organize ideas
>
> **Venn diagram:** overlapping circles used to compare and contrast ideas

A **Venn diagram** is used to compare and contrast items or ideas. Draw two circles that partly overlap. These circles represent what you want to compare. List the characteristics of one in the left circle. List the characteristics of the other in the right circle. List the characteristics they share in the area where the circles overlap.

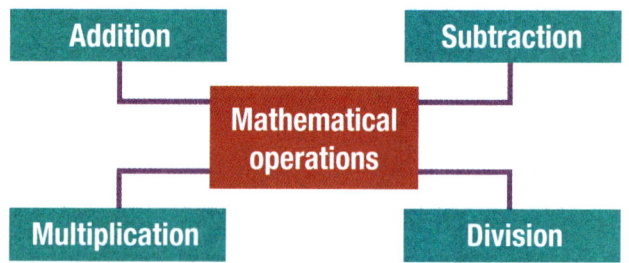

Use a **concept map** when recording supporting details of a main topic. The topic is written in the center box or circle. The supporting details are written in circles or boxes connected to the topic.

For sequencing, writing steps, or creating a timeline, the **flowchart** is an excellent organizer. The arrows show how the boxes "flow" from one to the next.

Step 1: Read — Make sure you understand what the problem is asking.

Step 2: Plan — Decide how you will solve the problem.

Step 3: Solve — Solve the problem using your plan.

Step 4: Check — Check to make sure your answer is correct.

A **three-column chart** is a good way to organize your thoughts about a new topic. In the first column, list what you know about the topic. In the second column, list the things you want to know about the topic. In the third column, list what you learned from the reading.

What I know	What I want to know	What I learned

Unit 1, Lesson 5

Graphic Organizers

Use graphic organizers to answer the following questions.

1. Ask your classmates what kind of music they like: country, pop, or both. On a separate piece of paper, draw a Venn diagram to record the results. How many students liked both?
   _____

2. Read a short article from a newspaper or magazine. What is the main topic of this article?
   _____

   List five supporting details. Then use these details to create a concept map on a separate sheet of paper.
   _____
   _____
   _____
   _____

3. The following steps describe the Make a List strategy. Number the steps in order from one to four. Then, on a separate sheet of paper, write the steps as a flowchart.

   _____ Identify the items to be combined.

   _____ Read the problem.

   _____ Repeat the steps until all the combinations are found. Make sure you do not repeat combinations.

   _____ Choose one item and list all the combinations using that item.

4. Choose a short news article to read. Create a three-column chart below. Title the chart with the topic of the article you have chosen. Then list the things you know about the topic in the first column. In the second column, list the things you want to know about the topic. After you read the article, write what you did learn in the third column.

Unit 1, Lesson 5

Problem-Solving Strategy

Try a Simpler Form of the Problem

What you already know about a topic can help you understand what you read. Math is like that, too. Often in problem solving you are asked a difficult question. It becomes easier to answer when you think about what you already know about part of it. You can solve a simpler form of the problem and use that answer to help you solve the rest.

Read: A factory makes toy trucks. One out of every 20 toy trucks is painted gold. If the factory makes 600 toy trucks in a day, how many of those toy trucks are painted gold?

What do I know? One out of every 20 trucks is painted gold. Every day, the factory makes 600 trucks.

What do I want to know? How many of the 600 trucks are painted gold?

Plan: Solve a simpler form of the problem by finding out how many trucks out of 100 are painted gold. Next, multiply the number by six to find out how many trucks out of 600 are painted gold.

Solve: There are five groups of 20 in 100, so there are five trucks painted gold out of every 100. Out of 600, there are $5 \times 6 = 30$ trucks painted gold.

Check: $600 \div 20 = 30$

1. **Read:** Edward's Vacuum Company sold 40 vacuum cleaners each month for the first three months of the year. For every vacuum cleaner they sold, they also sold four vacuum cleaner bags. How many vacuum cleaner bags did they sell in three months?

What do you know? _____
_____

What do you need to find out? _____

Plan: _____
_____
_____

Solve: _____
_____
_____
_____

Check: _____

Problem-Solving Strategy

2. **Read:** Derek is painting the posts of a fence. He paints the first two posts white. Every third post he paints blue. If Derek continues this pattern, what will be the color of the 22nd post?

   What do you know? _____
   _____

   What do you need to find out? _____

   Plan: _____
   _____

   Solve: _____
   _____

   Check: _____
   _____

3. When is it helpful to use the Try a Simpler Form of the Problem strategy?
   _____
   _____
   _____
   _____

4. Write one question you have about this strategy.
   _____
   _____
   _____
   _____

Problem-Solving Strategy

Make a Table or a Chart

A chart is a way of organizing and displaying information. Different types of charts include flowcharts, graphs, and tables.

A table is made up of information such as words and numbers organized into rows and columns. Rows run across a table and columns run up and down. The heading or label of each column helps explain how the information is organized. The title explains what information is in the table.

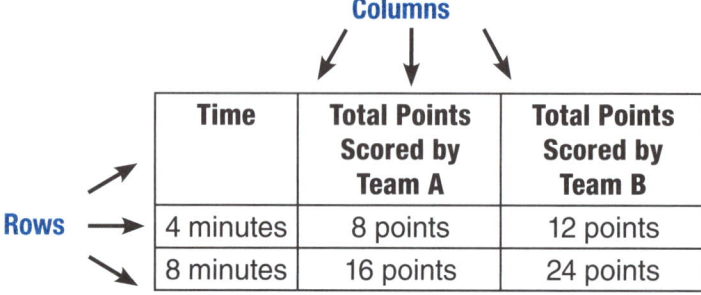

In this table, Team A scores two points every minute, and Team B scores three points every minute. You can make the table larger by adding rows to continue the pattern.

Read: In football, each time a team scores a touchdown, it gets six points. How many points will the team have after scoring four touchdowns? (The team does not make any extra points after a touchdown.)

What do I know? Each touchdown in football is worth six points.

What do I need to know? How many points will the team have after four touchdowns?

Plan: Make a table to display the number of points after each touchdown. Read the table and find the total number of points after four touchdowns.

Solve:
Total Points After Each Touchdown

Number of Touchdowns	Total Points
1	6
2	12
3	18
4	24

The team will have 24 points.

Check: $6 \times 4 = 24$

1. Cherry tomatoes in the community garden are ripe enough to pick. Ling picks 250 cherry tomatoes in an hour. How many does she pick in three hours? Write your table on a separate sheet of paper.

_____
_____

2. Jackie was running for Student Council. Tracy helped her fold fliers to place in lockers. If they folded nine fliers every minute, how many were folded in five minutes? Write your table on a separate sheet of paper.

_____
_____

Problem-Solving Strategy

3. The class fund-raiser last term was to collect glass bottles. If the class collected 20 bottles each day, how many did they collect in 10 days? Write your table in the space below. Then write your answer on the line.

   _____

Tables can also be used to display the information you collect in a survey. Use what you have learned about tables to solve the problem below.

4. Ask your classmates if they have a dog, a cat, both, or neither. Record each classmate's response. Then create a table and find the total number of classmates with each type of pet. Make sure to title your table and label the columns. Write your table on a separate sheet of paper.

   How many classmates have dogs? How many have cats? How many have both types of pets? Neither type?
   _____

5. When is the strategy of making a table useful?
   _____
   _____
   _____

6. Find a table in a newspaper or magazine. Write a question based on the information in the table.
   _____
   _____
   _____

Unit 1, Lesson 7

Problem-Solving Strategy

Guess, Check, and Revise

VOCABULARY

perimeter: the distance around the outside of a shape

When you guess what might happen next in a story, you are predicting. If your prediction is incorrect, you can change it and try a new one until you find one that works. The **Guess, Check, and Revise** problem-solving strategy works the same way. You guess a possible answer. Then you try it to see if it is the correct choice. If it is not the correct choice, you can change it and try again.

Read: The school library has a budget of $300 dollars for this term. Each of the books they wish to buy costs $20. How many books can they buy?

What do I know? The library has $300.

What do I need to know? How many books can the library buy?

Plan: I can guess and check. If my guess is incorrect, I can guess again.

Solve: I can start by guessing that they will buy 10 books. $10 \times 20 = 200$. $200 is less than $300. My first guess showed me that the number of books is greater than 10. I can change my guess by adding 5 extra books. $15 \times 20 = 300$. Now I know the library can buy 15 books.

Check: I can add $20 fifteen times to check my answer.
$20 + $20 + $20 + $20 + $20 + $20 + $20 + $20 + $20 + $20 + $20 + $20 + $20 + $20 + $20 = $300

1. **Read:** The sum of two numbers is 50. The numbers are four apart. What are the two numbers?

What do I know? _____

What do I need to know? _____

Plan: _____

Solve: _____

Check: _____

Problem-Solving Strategy

2. The sum of two numbers is 70. The difference of these numbers is 14. What are the two numbers?
_____

One type of problem that often uses the Guess, Check, and Revise strategy is a **perimeter** problem. Perimeter is the distance around the outside of a shape. The perimeter of a rectangle is the sum of its sides. A rectangle has two sides that are one length and two sides that are another length. A square has four sides that are all the same length.

3. Read: The perimeter of Diane's rectangular garden is 24 feet. What is the length of each side?

What do I know? _____

What do I need to know? _____

Plan: _____

Solve: _____

Check: _____

Are there other possibilities? _____
_____

4. A square has a perimeter of 16 feet. What is the length of each side?
_____

5. What other strategy could you use to help you solve problems 3 and 4?
_____
_____

6. What is one disadvantage of the Guess, Check, and Revise strategy?
_____
_____
_____
_____
_____

Unit 1, Lesson 8

Graphic Organizers

Graphic Organizers

Math graphic organizers can help you compare information.

> **VOCABULARY**
>
> **bar graph:** a way of comparing information using rectangular bars
>
> **circle graph:** a graph shaped like a circle that shows a whole broken into parts
>
> **coordinate grid:** a grid showing ordered pairs
>
> **ordered pair:** a pair of numbers that names one point on a coordinate grid
>
> **plot:** to find and mark the point named by an ordered pair
>
> **scale:** numbers that are the units used on a bar graph

A **bar graph** uses rectangular bars to compare information. The length or height of each bar represents an amount. The **scale** on the side of the graph gives an amount for each height or length.

Circle graphs are used to show parts of a whole. Each piece in a circle graph is a different part of the whole. Think of a pizza that is cut into eight slices. Each piece is one-eighth of the whole pizza. When pieces of a circle graph are different sizes, they show different amounts.

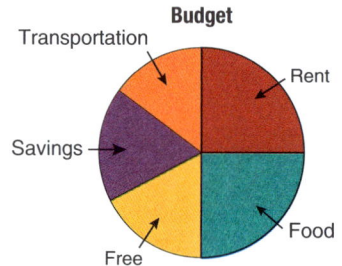

Coordinate grids are used to display pairs of numbers called **ordered pairs.** Each ordered pair names one point on the coordinate grid. Marking a point on a coordinate grid is also known as **plotting** the point. The points you plot can represent lines, shapes, or general information.

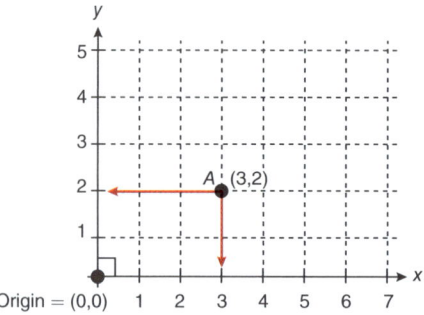

Use graphic organizers to organize information and solve the following problems.

1. Jenny made a bar graph of the change she found in her pockets. How many more pennies did she have than nickels?

   _____

   _____

2. Ramon surveyed his classmates to find out their favorite sports. They could choose only one sport from football, baseball, soccer, and track. He displayed the information in a circle graph.

   Do more students enjoy baseball or track?
   _____
   _____

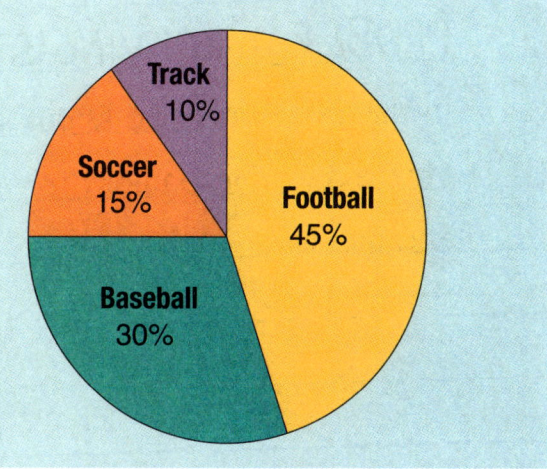

3. Plot these points on a coordinate grid: (1, 1), (1, 3), (3, 3), and (3, 1). Connect the points in order, beginning and ending at (1, 1), and name the shape they make.
   _____
   _____

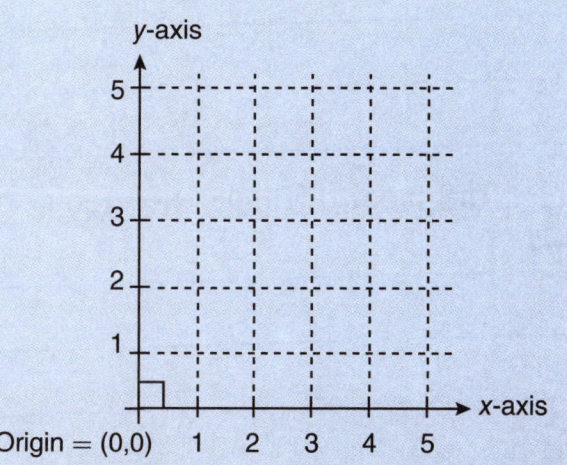

4. When you take a survey, which graph is best to use, a bar graph or a circle graph? Why?
   _____
   _____

5. You want to graph how much you spent on school supplies compared to how much money you started with. Which graph would you use, a bar graph or a circle graph? Why?
   _____
   _____

Unit 1 Reflection

Review and Record What You Learned

PROBLEM-SOLVING STRATEGIES

In this unit, I learned about six problem-solving strategies. The easiest for me to remember and use is

The most difficult strategy is

I do not understand

Unit 1

UNIT 2
Multiplication and Division

MATH SKILLS & STRATEGIES
After you learn the basic **SKILLS**, the real test is knowing when to use each **STRATEGY**.

READING STRATEGY
Learn the steps to good Summarizing.

AMP LINK MAGAZINE
You Do the Math and Math Projects: After you read each magazine article, apply what you know in real-world problems.
Fluency: Make your reading smooth and accurate, one tip at a time.

CONNECTIONS
You own the math when you make your own connections.

VOCABULARY
MATH WORDS:
Know them!
Use them!
Learn all about them!

Reading Comprehension Strategy

Reading Comprehension Strategy: Summarizing

How to Summarize

Step 1:	Step 2:	Step 3:	Step 4:
Identify the **topic**: Ask, *Who or what is this about?*	Identify the **main idea**: Ask, *What is the main thing the writer is saying about the topic?*	Identify the **important details**: Ask, *What details are needed to understand the main idea?*	Use the main idea and important details to **summarize**.

Step 1: Identify the Topic

When you summarize, you identify the most important things in the section you are reading. First, look for the topic. The **topic** is a word or phrase that answers the question, *Who or what is this about?* Good summaries do not include a lot of extra facts. What is the topic of the paragraph below?

Do you have a food allergy? Do you know someone with a food allergy? A food allergy occurs when your body reacts to a food after you touch, smell, or eat it. Nearly 12 million Americans suffer from food allergies.	1. Who or what is this paragraph about? _____

Step 2: Identify the Main Idea

Knowing the topic can help you find the **main idea**, or what the writer wants to tell you about the topic. Any summary should include the author's main idea.

Sometimes, the main idea is in the first or second sentence. Sometimes, it is in the last sentence. Find the main idea in the paragraph below.

Scientists list about eight foods that may cause an allergic reaction. They are milk, eggs, peanuts, other kinds of nuts, seafood, shellfish, soy, and wheat. However, people react differently, so other foods may also cause an allergic reaction.	2. Main idea: _____

Sometimes the main idea is not stated, and you have to figure it out. What is the main idea of this paragraph? How do you know?

Sometimes, after eating a certain food, you may get a rash, or your skin may get itchy. You may cough or sneeze. There are times when more serious things may happen. You might get dizzy or have stomach pains. The way you act might even change.	3. Main idea: _____

Reading Comprehension Strategy

Step 3: Identify Important Details

Once you have identified the topic and the main idea, look for **important details**. Details explain something or add information about the main idea. When you look for important details, ask yourself, *Does this detail help me understand the main idea? Is it important?* Focusing on only the important details will help you understand and remember what you have read.

When you get sick, you see a doctor. When your body reacts to some foods, you may need to see a special doctor called an allergist. The allergist will test you to see if you are allergic to certain foods. A skin prick test or a blood test may be used. Once the allergist has the test results, you can tell which food causes your reaction.	4. What are important details in this paragraph? _____ _____ _____

Step 4: Summarize

When you **summarize,** you briefly state the main idea of a paragraph or passage in your own words. You also include the important details. Think to yourself, *What would I tell a friend about what I just read?*

Below is a passage with two paragraphs. The main idea of the first paragraph is: *There is no cure for food allergies.* A good summary of this paragraph is: *Doctors can tell you what makes you sick, but you have to shop carefully and pay attention to what you eat.*

There is no cure for food allergies, so people with allergies must be careful. When buying food, they must read the labels. This can help people avoid buying foods that could make them sick. Some people cannot even smell or touch the foods they are allergic to. This makes it especially important to pay attention to what they eat. Accidents are always possible. That is why some people carry medicine with them at all times. This lets them treat the allergic reaction when it starts. People with serious allergies may also wear a special kind of jewelry that tells others of their illness. This can help save their lives if they are unable to tell people what is wrong during a reaction.	5. Read the second paragraph of the passage. Write the main idea. _____ _____ 6. Write a summary of the second paragraph. _____ _____ _____ _____

7. Write a brief summary of the whole article (all six paragraphs) by combining the information you have read on these two pages.

   _____

   _____

   _____

8. How might summarizing apply to a math problem?

   _____

   _____

Unit 2

Learn the Skill

Multiplication

Learn the SKILL

Have you ever had to buy food for a class party? Many foods have the number of servings listed on the package. When buying food for a party, what is the fastest way to find out how many people you can feed? For example, if a box of mini muffins feeds four people, how many people will three boxes feed?

> **VOCABULARY**
>
> Watch for the words you are learning about.
>
> **addend:** a number being added
>
> **factor:** a number multiplied by another number
>
> **multiply:** to add a number many times
>
> **product:** the number that results from multiplying two or more numbers together
>
> **sum:** the number that results from adding two or more numbers together

SKILL	EXAMPLE	WRITE AN EXAMPLE
Addition and multiplication are related. To **multiply** a number, you can add the number many times. Learning the basic multiplication facts can make the process of addition much faster.	Addition: $4 + 4 + 4 = 12$ (add 4 three times) The 4s are **addends**. The **sum** is 12. 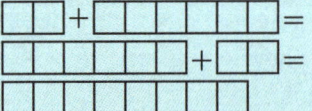 Multiplication: $3 \times 4 = 12$ (add 3 groups of 4) 3 and 4 are **factors**. 12 is the **product**.	Addition: _____ _____ Multiplication: _____ _____
When you add two numbers, the order in which you add them does not change the sum. The order in which you multiply two factors does not change the product.	Addition: $2 + 6 = 6 + 2 = 8$ Multiplication: $6 \times 2 = 2 + 2 + 2 + 2 + 2 + 2 = 12$ $2 \times 6 = 6 + 6 = 12$	Addition: _____ _____ Multiplication: _____ _____
The product of any factor and 0 is 0. The product of any factor and 1 is the factor.	Multiply by 0: $0 \times 3 = 3 \times 0 = 0$ Multiply by 1: $1 \times 8 = 8 \times 1 = 8$	Multiply by 0: _____ Multiply by 1: _____

YOUR TURN

Choose the Right Word

> factors   multiply   product   sum

Fill in each blank with the correct word or phrase from the box.

1. The answer to 2 × 3 is called the _____.

2. When you _____, you add a number repeatedly.

3. In multiplication problems, the numbers you multiply are called _____.

4. The answer to 2 + 3 is called the _____.

Yes or No?

Answer these questions and be ready to explain your answers.

5. Is 3 + 3 + 3 the same thing as 3 × 4? _____

6. Will you get the same answer if you multiply 4 × 2 and 2 × 4? _____

7. If you multiply 1 × 0, will the answer be 1? _____

8. If you multiply 1 × 25, will the answer be 1? _____

9. If you multiply 3 × 0, will the answer be 0? _____

Show That You Know

Write your answer to each exercise in the space provided.

10. 2 + 2 + 2 =

    3 × 2 =

11. 5 × 3 =

    3 + 3 + 3 + 3 + 3 =

12. 4 + 4 + 4 + 4 + 4 + 4 =

    6 × 4 =

13. 8 + 8 + 8 =

    3 × 8 =

    8 × 3 =

    3 + 3 + 3 + 3 + 3 + 3 + 3 + 3 =

14. 2 + 2 + 2 + 2 + 2 + 2 + 2 + 2 =

    8 × 2 =

    2 × 8 =

    8 + 8 =

15. 8 × 1 =

16. 0 × 3 =

17. 1 × 5 =

18. 6 × 0 =

Unit 2, Lesson 1   25

Learn the Skill

SOLVE on Your Own

Skills Practice

Remember, multiplication is repeated addition.

Multiply.

1. 4 × 5 _____
2. 0 × 6 _____
3. 8 × 6 _____
4. 3 × 8 _____
5. 7 × 2 _____
6. 1 × 5 _____

7. 8 × 7 _____
8. 6 × 9 _____
9. 1 × 1 _____
10. 2 × 2 _____
11. 3 × 3 _____
12. 4 × 4 _____

13. 5 × 5 _____
14. 6 × 6 _____
15. 7 × 7 _____
16. 8 × 8 _____
17. 9 × 9 _____

Solve each word problem using multiplication.

18. You buy six packages of pencils. Each package has five pencils. How many pencils did you buy? _____

19. Notebooks come in packages of four. Mrs. Hall buys nine packages for her class. How many notebooks did she buy? _____

20. There are seven desks in each row. If there are six rows in the classroom, how many desks are there? _____

Choose a Strategy

Multiplication
Strategy
Draw a Picture or Use a Model

Step 1: Read Sandra has six radish plants. How many different ways can she plant them in rows and columns? All rows must have the same number of columns.

> **VOCABULARY**
> Watch for the words you are learning about.
> **area model:** a model that uses rectangles to represent multiplication
> **array:** an arrangement of objects in rows and columns
> **represent:** to show an idea using drawings or models

STRATEGY	SOLUTION
Draw a Picture or Use a Model (rectangular arrays) An **array** is an arrangement of objects in rows and columns. It is one way to **represent**, or show, multiplication using drawings or models. In a 1×6 array, the first number, 1, represents the number of rows, and the second number, 6, represents the number of columns. Add the objects in each row.	**Step 2: Plan** Draw rectangular arrays of six radish plants to show all possible arrangements. **Step 3: Solve** 1 row — 6 columns ★★★★★★ This 1×6 array represents: 1 row of $6 = 1 \times 6 = 6$ 2 rows — 3 columns ★★★ / ★★★ This 2×3 array represents: 2 rows of $3 = 3 + 3 = 2 \times 3 = 6$ 3 rows — 2 columns ★★ / ★★ / ★★ This 3×2 array represents: 3 rows of $2 = 2 + 2 + 2 = 3 \times 2 = 6$ 6 rows — 1 column ★/★/★/★/★/★ This 6×1 array represents: 6 rows of $1 = 1 + 1 + 1 + 1 + 1 + 1 = 6 \times 1 = 6$ There are four possible arrangements. **Step 4: Check** Count the radish plants across or up and down. Each array should have a total of six radish plants.
Draw a Picture or Use a Model (area model) An **area model** can also represent multiplication. Each square represents 1. Putting the squares into rectangles is another way to show multiplication.	**Step 2: Plan** Imagine that each radish is planted in a square. Use six squares to make different rectangles. **Step 3: Solve** 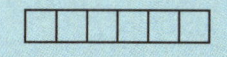 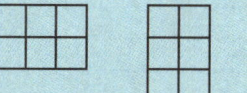 There are four possible rectangles. **Step 4: Check** Count the squares in each area model. Each model should have a total of six squares.

Unit 2, Lesson 2

Choose a Strategy

YOUR TURN

Choose the Right Word

> array   area model   represent

Fill in each blank with the correct word or phrase from the box.

1. An array can be used to _____ the multiplication of two numbers.

2. In a(n) _____, objects are arranged in rows and columns.

3. A(n) _____ uses rectangles to represent multiplication.

Yes or No?

Answer these questions and be ready to explain your answers.

4. Does an array with three rows and six columns represent the same number as an array with six rows and three columns? _____

5. If one array has more columns than another array, will the first array always have more objects than the second? _____

6. Can you make a square area model from nine smaller squares? _____

7. Can you make more than three different area models with nine squares? _____

Show That You Know

Draw each array as indicated. Use a star for each item in the array.

8. Draw a 2 × 7 array.

9. Draw a 5 × 5 array.

10. Draw and label a 2 × 3 array and a 3 × 2 array.

Draw an area model to show each expression.

11. 5 × 5

12. 3 × 6

13. 4 × 9

READ on Your Own

Reading Comprehension Strategy: Summarizing

Food for Thought, *pages 3–5*

Before You Read

How do you know what is good to eat? Think about what you already know about the different types of foods and the nutrients they have.

As You Read

Read "You Are What You Eat," pages 3–5.

Fill in the chart below.

You Are What You Eat

Main Idea:
Eating a variety of foods is important because _____
_____

Important Details:

Food Group	grains	vegetables	fruits	milk	meat & beans
Use in Body					

Summary:
_____
_____

After You Read

How many servings of vegetables should you eat every day? Why?
_____
_____

VOCABULARY

Watch for the words you are learning about.

calories: units that measure the amount of energy in food

carbohydrates: nutrients that give your body energy

diet: a plan for regularly eating certain foods in certain amounts

digestion: how the body breaks down foods to get nutrients

fiber: a substance that helps digestion

nutrients: parts of food that help the body function and grow

nutrition: the study of how the body uses different foods

proteins: nutrients that help build muscles

vitamins: nutrients needed in small amounts for healthy body functions

Fluency Tip

Reread sentences that you have trouble with. Rereading should help you read more smoothly.

Unit 2, Lesson 2   29

Problem Solving

SOLVE on Your Own

Food for Thought, page 5

Organize the Information

Read You Do the Math in the magazine. Complete the table below for one day. On another sheet of paper, complete a table for three more days.

Type of Food	Portions at Breakfast	Portions at Lunch	Portions at Dinner	Total Portions per Day
grains				
vegetables				
fruits				
milk products				
meat and beans				

You Do the Math

Drawing an array or area model will help you answer some of these questions.

Use the information in the table above to answer these questions. Write your answers in the space provided.

1. Which type of food you will eat the most of in four days? Explain how you know.

   _____
   _____

2. Once you have planned your meals, calculate how many ounces of each type of food in total you will eat in four days.

   _____
   _____

After You Solve

How else could you display the information in the table above?

_____
_____

30 Unit 2, Lesson 2

Learn the Skill

Properties of Addition and Multiplication

Learn the SKILL

Apples are on sale at the grocery store. You decide to buy two bags of apples, one weighing 3 pounds and one weighing 5 pounds. How much do the apples cost in total if they are $2 per pound? Can you figure this out without adding the numbers of pounds first?

VOCABULARY

Watch for the words you are learning about.

associative property: the grouping of addends or factors does not affect the sum or product

commutative property: when adding or multiplying numbers, the order does not matter

distributive property: when a sum is multiplied by a factor, you can add first and then multiply, or multiply each addend by the factor and then add

SKILL	EXAMPLE	WRITE AN EXAMPLE
Because addition and multiplication are related, they have similar properties. The **commutative property** states that the order in which you add or multiply does not change the result.	Addition: $2 + 3 = 3 + 2 = 5$ Multiplication: $2 \times 3 = 3 \times 2 = 6$ $2 \times 5 = 5 \times 2 = 10$	Addition: _____ Multiplication: _____
The **associative property** states that the order in which you group addends or factors does not change the final sum or product. Parentheses ( ) can be used to group operations.	Addition: $2 + (4 + 8) = (2 + 4) + 8$ $2 + \;\;12\;\; = \;\;6\;\; + 8 = 14$ Multiplication: $2 \times (3 \times 6) = (2 \times 3) \times 6$ $2 \times \;\;18\;\; = \;\;6\;\; \times 6 = 36$	Addition: _____ Multiplication: _____
If a sum is multiplied by a factor, the **distributive property** of multiplication states you can add first and then multiply or multiply first and then add. Either way, you get the same result.	Add first and then multiply: $2 \times (3 + 5) = 2 \times 8 = 16$ Multiply first and then add: $2 \times (3 + 5) = (2 \times 3) + (2 \times 5)$ $\qquad\qquad = \;\;6\;\; + \;\;10\;\; = 16$	Add first: _____ Multiply first: _____

Unit 2, Lesson 3

Learn the Skill

YOUR TURN

Choose the Right Word

> associative   commutative   distributive

Fill in each blank with the correct word or phrase from the box.

1. The _____ property says that the grouping of addends does not matter when adding.

2. $8 \times (7 + 5) = 56 + 40$ is an example of the _____ property.

3. According to the _____ property, switching the order of two factors does not change the product.

Yes or No?

Answer these questions and be ready to explain your answers.

4. Do addition and multiplication have some of the same properties? _____

5. Will you get the same answer if you add $8 + 2$ and $2 + 8$? _____

6. Will you get the same answer if you multiply 6×2 and 2×6? _____

7. If you multiply first in $10 \times (5 + 2)$, will the answer be different than if you add first? _____

Show That You Know

Write the sum or product in the space provided.

8. $2 + 10 =$

   $10 + 2 =$

9. $3 \times 5 =$

   $5 \times 3 =$

10. $(7 + 6) + 4 =$

    $7 + (6 + 4) =$

11. $(1 \times 5) \times 4 =$

    $1 \times (5 \times 4) =$

12. $(2 \times 4) \times 6 =$

    $2 \times (4 \times 6) =$

13. $5 \times (3 + 2) =$ _____ + _____ = _____

    $5 \times (3 + 2) =$ _____ × _____ = _____

14. $8 \times (1 + 7) =$

15. $9 \times (2 + 3) =$

16. $5 \times (5 + 0) =$

SOLVE on Your Own

According to the commutative property, the order in which you add or multiply does not change the result.

Perform the operations shown. Attempt to first calculate the answer mentally.

Write the name of the property shown on the line.

1. (4 + 5) × 0 = _____

2. 6 × (4 + 3) = _____

3. (4 × 1) × 6 = _____

4. (10 + 4) + 5 = _____

5. 1 × (1 + 1) = _____

6. 8 + (6 + 2) = _____

7. 6 × (6 + 3) = _____

8. (2 × 4) × 7 = _____

9. (1 + 8) + (9 + 2) = _____

10. 5 × (7 + 2) = _____

11. 9 × 0 = 0 × 9 _____

12. 5 + (4 + 3) = (5 + 4) + 3 _____

13. 18 × 10 = 10 × 18 _____

14. 9 × (2 + 2) = 18 + 18 _____

15. 5 + 8 = 8 + 5 _____

16. (5 + 6) + 7 = 5 + (6 + 7) _____

17. 11 × (9 + 9) = 11 × 18 _____

18. 1 + 6 = 6 + 1 _____

19. 1 × (5 + 2) = 5 + 2 _____

20. 2 × (3 × 9) = (2 × 3) × 9 _____

Unit 2, Lesson 3

Choose a Strategy

Properties of Addition and Multiplication

Strategy

Draw a Picture or Use a Model

Step 1: Read A class wants to buy a $30 present for their music teacher. They have not yet decided whether each student will give $3, $4, $5, or $6. All students who donate will give the same amount, but some may not donate. For which numbers of students is it possible to collect exactly the right amount of money?

VOCABULARY

Watch for the words you are learning about.

multiple: the product of a whole number and any other whole number

number line: a line with points representing numbers, increasing from left to right

skip-counting: counting by numbers other than 1

whole number: a number such as 0, 1, 2, 3, 4, and so on

STRATEGY	SOLUTION
Draw a Picture or Use a Model (create equal groups) You can create groups that have the same number of objects in each group. These equal groups can be used to find the factors of a number. They can also be used to model multiplication.	**Step 2: Plan** Find the equal groups that can be made from the number 30 by arranging 30 items into equal groups. One possibility is three groups of $10, as shown below. Repeat this with groups of $3, $4, $5, and $6. Which numbers create equal groups?  **Step 3: Solve** 10 students × $3 = $30 7 students × $4 = $28, 8 students × $4 = $32 6 students × $5 = $30 5 students × $6 = $30 The correct amount can be collected for five, six, or 10 students. **Step 4: Check** According to the commutative property, five students donating $6 is equivalent to six students donating $5, and three students donating $10 is equivalent to 10 students donating $3. These pairs of numbers are all factors of 30.
Draw a Picture or Use a Model (skip-count) You can **skip-count** by "jumping" on a **number line** to show repeated addition. When you multiply, the first number is the number of jumps and the second number is the size of each jump. Each jump lands on a **multiple** of the original number. A multiple is a **whole number** multiplied by any other whole number.	**Step 2: Plan** Use a number line to skip-count, jumping by the different possible dollar amounts. You must land on 30 for the dollar amount to work.  **Step 3: Solve** 10 jumps × $3 = $30 7 jumps × $4 = $28, 8 jumps × $4 = $32 6 jumps × $5 = $30 5 jumps × $6 = $30 The correct amount can be collected for five, six, or 10 students. **Step 4: Check** Use addition to check your answers.

34 Unit 2, Lesson 4

YOUR TURN

Choose the Right Word

> multiple   number line   skip-count

Fill in each blank with the correct word or phrase from the box.

1. A _____ is the product of any two whole numbers.

2. You can _____ to show repeated addition on a number line.

3. A _____ uses points on a line to show numbers.

Choose a Strategy

Yes or No?

Answer these questions and be ready to explain your answers.

4. Are three groups of three objects equal to two groups with five objects? _____

5. If you jump by threes on a number line, do you count by fives to get the answer? _____

6. To represent 2×3, can you make two equal groups of three objects? _____

7. Does counting the number of jumps give you the answer to a multiplication problem? _____

Show That You Know

Draw equal groups to find factors for each number. Write the pair of factors you found.

8. Number: 8   Factors:

9. Number: 15   Factors:

Draw jumps on a number line to represent each expression. Then write the product.

10. $4 \times 4 =$

11. $6 \times 2 =$

Unit 2, Lesson 4

Reading Comprehension

READ on Your Own

Reading Comprehension Strategy: Summarizing

Food for Thought, pages 6–7

VOCABULARY

Watch for the words you are learning about.

bland: without much flavor

salary: the regular pay people get for working

Fluency Tip

Pay attention to punctuation marks. Punctuation marks tell you when to pause and when to raise your voice for a question or an exclamation.

Before You Read

Think back to what you read in "You Are What You Eat." Which of the food groups do you like the most? Which do you like the least?

As You Read

Read "Eat it or Spend It?", page 6.
Fill in the chart below.

Read "White Gold, Black Gold," page 7.
Fill in the chart below.

Eat It or Spend It?	White Gold, Black Gold
Main Idea: Salt and spices used to be costly because _____ _____ _____	**Main Idea:** Salt and pepper were used _____ _____ _____
Important Details: _____ _____ _____	**Important Details:** _____ _____ _____
Summary: Salt and spices were important because _____ _____ _____	**Summary:** Salt and pepper used to be _____ _____ _____

After You Read

Name two spices that you like. Which spice do you think costs more? Why?

_____

36 Unit 2, Lesson 4

SOLVE on Your Own

Food for Thought, page 8

Organize the Information

Read You Do the Math in the magazine. You can use the table below to find how much of each spice would be used in two weeks, three weeks, four weeks, and five weeks.

Spice	Price per 5 Pounds	Pounds per Week	Pounds Used in 2 Weeks	Pounds Used in 3 Weeks	Pounds Used in 4 Weeks	Pounds Used in 5 Weeks
anise seeds	$17	3				
nutmeg	$37	2				
cinnamon	$13	9				
ginger	$16	4				

You Do the Math

Use the information in the table above to answer these questions. Write your answers in the space provided.

You might want to draw the containers of each spice to help you solve these problems.

1. How can you use the table to find an answer to the problem? _____
   _____

2. How many weeks should you buy spices for? _____

3. Which spice do you guess will cost the most? Why? _____
   _____

4. Once you find an answer for the number of weeks, how can you use it find other possible answers?
   _____

After You Solve

What other strategy could you use to solve the problems above?
_____

Unit 2, Lesson 4

Application

Solve It!

The Four-Step Problem-Solving Plan

Step 1: Read	Step 2: Plan	Step 3: Solve	Step 4: Check
Make sure you understand what the problem is asking.	Decide how you will solve the problem.	Solve the problem using your plan.	Check to make sure your answer is correct.

Read the article below. Then answer the questions.

Decisions, Decisions

A school garden takes a lot of planning. Students and teachers must decide what kinds of crops to plant. They must think about things such as climate, soil conditions, and how much time and money they have. Space is also an issue. Certain vegetables such as beets and onions require more space. Corn must be planted in many rows so the plants can grow and reproduce by cross-pollination. These crops are not a good choice if space is limited.

The fresh produce from school gardens may be used in a home economics class. They might be part of social studies and foreign language projects. For example, using anise seed produced in their herb garden, students might learn how to make *pan de muertos*. This special bread is used in celebrations of the Day of the Dead in the Mexican community.

Pan de Muertos	Makes two loaves of bread.
11 cups of flour	1 cup of milk
1 cup of sugar	1 cup of water
2 teaspoons of salt	1 cup of butter
2 teaspoons of anise seed	8 eggs
4 packets of dry yeast	

1. Would it make sense to plant corn in a school garden?

2. A class buys six seed packets of anise. Each packet costs $2 and holds 15 seeds. How much do the six packets cost? How many seeds does the class get?

3. How many packets of yeast would you need to make the recipe three times?

YOUR TURN

Application

Read the article below. Then answer the questions.

Harvest Time

The harvest comes at the end of the growing season. Harvest activities include sorting, cleaning, packing, and preserving. If the harvest is not done quickly, crops may be lost or they will sell for less money. A lot of work must be done in a little time. In some rural areas, schools close during the harvest. That way, children may help their families bring the crops in.

Most vegetables are picked just before they are ripe. This provides the best flavor and texture. It is best to harvest leeks once they have reached an inch in diameter. Lettuce is ready when the plant is 4 inches tall. Asparagus spears are ready when they are 6 to 8 inches tall.

Today, machines play a major role in the harvest. They allow the harvest to be finished more quickly. For example, a tractor can harvest 5 tons of peas every hour.

1. What are some activities that are done during the harvest?
   _____
   _____

2. How many tons of peas can a tractor harvest in an 8-hour day?
   _____

3. How do machines help with the harvest?
   _____
   _____

4. A school garden produces a harvest of 32 asparagus spears. If each spear is 6 inches long, what is the total length of all the spears?
   _____

Fluency Tip
Reread sentences that you have trouble with. Rereading should help you read more smoothly.

Reading Comprehension

READ on Your Own

Reading Comprehension Strategy: Summarizing

Food for Thought, pages 9–11

VOCABULARY

Watch for the words you are learning about.

chemicals: substances used to make or change other substances

edible: able to be eaten safely

greenhouses: structures used for growing plants; mostly made of glass

produce: fresh fruits and vegetables

serfs: farm workers in the Middle Ages who worked on land owned by a lord

Fluency Tip

Be careful to read every word without skipping or substituting words.

Before You Read

Think back to what you read in "Eat It or Spend It?" What spices and other flavorings do you use every day?

As You Read

Read "Planting Seeds," pages 9–10. **Read page 11.**
Complete the first column of the chart below.   Complete the second column of the chart.

Pages 9–10	Page 11
Main Idea: A school garden is _____	**Main Idea:** A school can use a garden for _____
Important Details: To create a school garden, students must _____	**Important Details:** School gardens teach students about _____
Summary: A school garden is _____	**Summary:** A school garden has many benefits, including _____

After You Read

How can cooking help you learn about history?
_____
_____

40   Unit 2, Lesson 5

Problem Solving

SOLVE on Your Own

Food for Thought, page 12

Organize the Information

Read the Math Project in the magazine. Then fill in the number of each type of seed in the table.

Vegetable	1 Packet	2 Packets	3 Packets	4 Packets	5 Packets	6 Packets
zucchini	36					
carrots	27					
lettuce	54					
snap peas	18					

Math Project

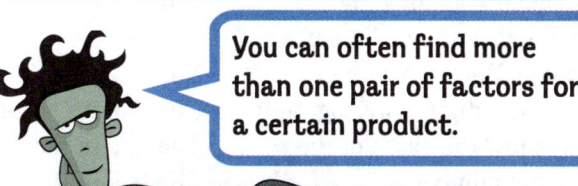

You can often find more than one pair of factors for a certain product.

Use the information in the table above to answer these questions. Write your answers in the space provided.

1. What number can you find in every row of the table above? What is the meaning of this number?
   _____
   _____

2. Draw two possible area models for the garden.

3. Are there other possible numbers of plants that will work? Explain.
   _____

After You Solve

How could you express the same information in the table at the top of the page by drawing pictures?
_____
_____

Unit 2, Lesson 5

Learn the Skill

Place Value and Expanded Notation

Learn the SKILL

Angus is a breed of cattle raised in many places in the United States. The cattle are solid black in color. Angus bulls can grow to more than 2,000 pounds. How could you compare two bulls to find which one is heavier? For example, if one bull weighs 2,135 pounds and the other weighs 2,096 pounds, which bull is heavier?

VOCABULARY

Watch for the words you are learning about.

digit: any numeral between 0 and 9 used to show a number

expanded notation: a number shown as a sum of the number's digits multiplied by their place value

place value: the value assigned to each position in a number

standard notation: a number written as a group of digits

SKILL	EXAMPLE	COMPLETE THE EXAMPLE
A number is made of **digits.** The position of a digit in a number shows its **place value.** Both the place value and the digit work together to show the value of the whole number.	Find the place value of each digit in 2,135. The 5 is in the ones (1) place. The 3 is in the tens (10) place. The 1 is in the hundreds (100) place. The 2 is in the thousands (1,000) place.	Find the place value of each digit in 2,096. _____ _____ _____ _____
The most numbers you see are written in **standard notation.** Writing a number in **expanded notation** shows the value in each place value of the number.	Standard notation: 2,135 Expanded notation: 2,135 = 2 × 1,000 + 1 × 100 + 3 × 10 + 5 × 1	Write the number above in standard notation: _____ Write the number above in expanded notation: _____ _____
Numbers can be compared by looking at the values of each digit in the number from left to right. The larger digit has the greater value. If the first place value has the same digit, compare the place to the right.	2,135 = 2 × 1,000 + 1 × 100 + 3 × 10 + 5 × 1 2,096 = 2 × 1,000 + 0 × 100 + 9 × 10 + 6 × 1 2,135 is greater than 2,096 because the hundreds place value is greater.	Expand two numbers: _____ _____ _____ Compare: _____

YOUR TURN

Learn the Skill

Choose the Right Word

> digits   expanded notation
> place value   standard notation

Fill in each blank with the correct word or phrase from the box.

1. The numerals 0 through 9 are called _____.

2. The _____ of the digits in a number is given by the position of those digits in the number.

3. Writing a number in _____ shows the value of each digit in the number.

4. Normally, numbers you work with are written in _____.

Yes or No?

Answer these questions and be ready to explain your answers.

5. Is the ten thousands place value shown in the number 5,634? _____

6. Is expanded notation longer than standard notation? _____

7. If the number 715 is written in expanded notation, will the result be $7 \times 100 + 1 \times 10 + 5 \times 1$? _____

8. Can expanded notation be used to compare numbers? _____

Show That You Know

Write place of the digit in the space provided.

9. The 3 in 37 is in the _____ place.

10. The 3 in 3,711 is in the _____ place.

11. The 3 in 307 is in the _____ place.

12. The 3 in 8,713 is in the _____ place.

Write the numbers in expanded notation.

16. 88 =

17. 364 =

18. 5,061 =

Write the numbers in standard notation.

13. $7 \times 100 + 9 \times 10 + 2 \times 1 =$

14. $2 \times 1,000 + 5 \times 100 + 0 \times 10 + 2 \times 1 =$

15. $9 \times 1,000 + 0 \times 100 + 7 \times 10 + 0 \times 1 =$

Unit 2, Lesson 6   43

SOLVE on Your Own

Skills Practice

Now you know more about place value and expanded notation. Use what you know to complete the following exercises.

Give the place value of each underlined digit.

1. 1,0<u>3</u>0 _____
2. <u>2</u>8 _____
3. 6,<u>5</u>22 _____
4. <u>9</u>,257 _____
5. 6<u>8</u>5 _____

Write the following numbers in expanded notation.

6. 8,962 _____
7. 341 _____
8. 77 _____
9. 150 _____
10. 2,063 _____

Write the following numbers in standard notation.

11. $9 \times 100 + 8 \times 10 + 2 \times 1$ _____
12. $5 \times 1{,}000 + 7 \times 100 + 0 \times 10 + 9 \times 1$ _____
13. $1 \times 100 + 1 \times 10 + 1 \times 1$ _____
14. $7 \times 1{,}000 + 3 \times 100 + 6 \times 10 + 3 \times 1$ _____
15. $2 \times 1{,}000 + 0 \times 100 + 5 \times 10 + 0 \times 1$ _____

Compare the numbers given and write the one that is greater.

16. 18 and 16 _____
17. 56 and 65 _____
18. 872 and 728 _____
19. 462 and 426 _____
20. 6,584 and 6,499 _____

Place Value and Expanded Notation

Strategies

**Make a Table or a Chart,
Try a Simpler Form of the Problem**

Choose a Strategy

VOCABULARY

Watch for the words you are learning about.

place-value chart: a chart that shows the place value of each digit in a number

Step 1: Read Sheree has 3,801 grains of rice. Curtis will not say how much rice he has, but he does say the digits of his number are 0, 1, 4, 8, and 9. Can you tell who has more grains of rice?

STRATEGY	SOLUTION
Make a Table or a Chart (place-value chart) You can compare two numbers using a **place-value chart**. By comparing the digits in each column, you can decide which number is larger.	**Step 2: Plan** Fill in the place-value chart to show how many grains of rice Sheree has. Fill in two numbers to show the least and greatest number of grains of rice Curtis could have. **Step 3: Solve**	Ten Thousands	Thousands	Hundreds	Tens	Ones	|---|---|---|---|---|		3	8	0	1		1	0	4	8	9		9	8	4	1	0	Curtis must have at least 10,489 grains, so he has more rice. **Step 4: Check** The ten thousands place in Sheree's number is blank, so the value is 0 × 10,000. Curtis's least possible number has a value of 1 × 10,000 in this place value, so Curtis's number is greater.
Try a Simpler Form of the Problem In this problem, you only need to look at the greatest place value in each number. If two numbers do not have the same number of digits, the number that has more digits is greater.	**Step 2: Plan** Look only at the number of digits in Sheree's number and compare it to the number of digits in Curtis's number. **Step 3: Solve** Sheree's number of grains: It is a four-digit number. Curtis's number of grains: It is a five-digit number. A five-digit number is always greater than a four-digit number, so Curtis must have more rice. **Step 4: Check** The first digit of Curtis's number cannot be zero, so he must have at least 10,000 grains, which is greater than 3,801.

Choose a Strategy

YOUR TURN

Choose the Right Word

> digit   expanded notation   place-value chart

Fill in each blank with the correct word or phrase from the box.

1. A number can be written out as a sum of products using _____.

2. Two numbers can be compared using a(n) _____.

3. The value of each _____ in a number is equal to the numeral multiplied by the place value.

Yes or No?

Answer these questions and be ready to explain your answers.

4. Would a four-digit number always be larger than a three-digit number? _____

5. If two numbers have all of the same digits, are they always equal? _____

6. Do you have to include a tens column in a place-value chart if the tens digit is 0? _____

Show That You Know

Create a place-value chart for each of the following numbers.

Write each number in expanded notation.

7. 3,289

Thousands	Hundreds	Tens	Ones

10. 6,222

8. 5,436

Thousands	Hundreds	Tens	Ones

11. 1,648

9. 6,291

Thousands	Hundreds	Tens	Ones

12. 4,130

READ on Your Own

Reading Comprehension Strategy: Summarizing

Food for Thought, *pages 13–14*

Before You Read

Think about what you read in "Planting Seeds." How might an edible garden benefit your school?

VOCABULARY

Watch for the words you are learning about.

harvesting: gathering a crop that is grown and ripe

husk: an outer layer of grains, vegetables, fruits, and nuts

staple: a main food of a daily diet

Fluency Tip

Change your expression as you read.

As You Read

Read "Rice: Food for the World," page 13.
Fill in the chart below.

Read "It Starts with a Plant," page 14.
Fill in the chart below.

Rice: Food for the World	It Starts with a Plant
Main Idea: Rice is a _____	**Main Idea:** Rice can be grown _____
Important Details: Rice is good to eat because _____	**Important Details:** Rice is grown in _____
Summary: Rice is eaten all over the world because _____	**Summary:** Rice is grown _____

After You Read

Think of the many different ways rice is served. What type of food do you most enjoy with rice?

_____
_____

Unit 2, Lesson 7

Problem Solving

SOLVE on Your Own

Food for Thought, page 15

Organize the Information

Read You Do the Math in the magazine. You can use a three-column KWL chart to organize the information you read. Create a similar chart for the remaining columns of numbers.

K	W	L
What I Know	What I Want to Know	What I Learned
These numbers are in column 1 of the table:	Is this number a possible answer?	Are both numbers from this column?
298		
150		
95		

You Do the Math

Use the information in the KWL chart above to answer these questions. Write your answers in the space provided.

1. How could you eliminate some of the numbers in the table on page 15?
   _____
   _____

2. How can you use place value to find possible answers?
   _____
   _____

3. Which months and which grains are the numbers from?
   _____

When you use place-value charts, make sure you do not forget to include zeros.

After You Solve

What other strategy could you use to solve the problem?
_____
_____

The Four-Step Problem-Solving Plan

Step 1: Read	Step 2: Plan	Step 3: Solve	Step 4: Check
Make sure you understand what the problem is asking.	Decide how you will solve the problem.	Solve the problem using your plan.	Check to make sure your answer is correct.

Application

Read the article below. Then answer the questions.

Preservatives

Do you know the story of Passover? The Jewish people had to leave Egypt in a hurry. They did not have time to bake leavened bread. They only took matzoh, which is unleavened bread made from just flour and water.

Leavened bread is made with yeast. Have you ever noticed the holes in bread? These are caused by carbon dioxide gas that yeast gives off. It takes time to bake bread this way because you have to allow the dough to rise. The bread also rises in the oven.

Matzoh lasts much longer than other breads, in part because it is dry and has no oil. Without chemicals or refrigeration, bread will last only a few days. That is because the natural wheat germ oil in the bread spoils, or goes bad. Escaping from Egypt, it is said the Jewish people spent 40 years in the desert. They needed bread that would not spoil.

Other cultures invented different ways to make bread last longer. French toast is one popular solution. To make French toast, you use one egg for each slice of bread. You cook the bread after it soaks in the egg. The French probably did not invent French toast. In fact, one of the early names for it was *pain a la Romaine,* which means "Roman bread."

1. Why does matzoh last longer than leavened bread?

   _____
   _____
   _____

2. If you want to make five slices of French toast, how many eggs do you need?

   _____
   _____

3. If a loaf of bread lasts for three days without refrigeration, how long will four loaves last?

   _____
   _____

Unit 2, Lesson 8   49

Application

YOUR TURN

Read the article below. Then answer the questions.

A Slice of History

Today, you can buy sliced bread in any store. For thousands of years, however, loaves of bread were only available as big solid chunks. You would cut the loaves apart using a knife or tear off bits with your hands. Then, in 1928, Otto Rohwedder's bread-slicing machine hit the market. It could cut a baker's loaf automatically into nice, smooth slices that were all the same thickness. The machine even wrapped the bread to keep it fresh. It was one of those little things that made life easier.

With the arrival of pre-sliced bread, sandwich making became more popular than ever before. Sandwiches were tasty and portable, perfect for workers and students alike. Sandwiches became so popular that, in 1928, there was even a "cookbook" just for sandwiches. The book was *Seven Hundred Sandwiches* by Florence Cowles.

Fluency Tip
To help you read with expression, pretend you are reading aloud to a friend.

1. How did people eat bread before Rohwedder's bread-slicing machine was invented?

   _____
   _____

2. What is useful about having pre-sliced bread?

   _____
   _____
   _____

3. Greg wants to make six peanut butter and jelly sandwiches. How many slices of bread does he need?

   _____

4. Tony is making turkey sandwiches for a family picnic. He will need to make 10 sandwiches. How many slices of bread will he need?

   _____

READ on Your Own

Reading Comprehension

Reading Comprehension Strategy: Summarizing

Food for Thought, *pages 16–18*

Fluency Tip
Identify words that you do not know. Find out how to pronounce them before reading.

Before You Read

Think about what you read in "Rice: Food for the World." What are some of the benefits of eating rice?

As You Read

Read "Between the Slices," pages 16–17. 🛑

What are these pages about? Identify the topic.

_____
_____
_____

Read page 18. 🛑

What is this page about? Identify the topic.

_____
_____
_____

Use your answers above to decide on the main topic for the whole article. Write this topic below.

_____
_____

After You Read

What is your favorite type of sandwich? Why?

_____
_____
_____

Unit 2, Lesson 8

Problem Solving

SOLVE on Your Own

Food for Thought, page 19

Organize the Information

Read the Math Project in the magazine. Use the flowchart to answer the questions below.

Step 1		Step 2		Step 3
Pick type of sandwich and one of its ingredients.		Decide how many of this type of sandwich can be made with this ingredient.		Go through all the ingredients and all the sandwiches. Find the largest number of each sandwich you can make.

Math Project

Use the information in the flowchart to answer these questions. Write your answers in the space provided.

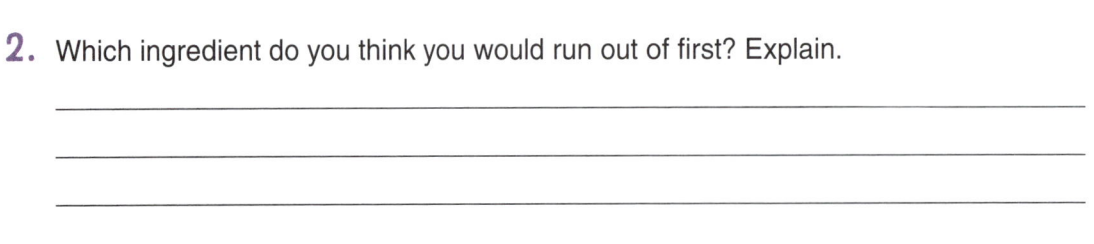

1. How can you simplify this problem?
   _____
   _____

2. Which ingredient do you think you would run out of first? Explain.
   _____
   _____
   _____
   _____

3. What is the largest number of each sandwich you can make? How do you know?
   _____
   _____
   _____

4. How can you use what you have learned about multiplication to solve this problem?
   _____

After You Solve

Do you think that trying a simpler form of the problem was useful? Why or why not?
_____
_____

Put It Together

Connections

Introducing the Breaking-Apart Algorithm

An algorithm is a way to solve a problem. The methods you have learned for adding, subtracting, multiplying, and dividing are all algorithms. You already know that multiplication is repeated addition. However, there are other ways to look at it.

When you multiply two numbers, you can break apart one or both of the factors to make the multiplication simpler. This is called the breaking-apart algorithm.

Multiply 3 × 17.

Break apart a two-digit factor into the ones (7) and the tens (10). Then use the distributive property to multiply.

$3 \times 17 = 3 \times (7 + 10)$
$ = (3 \times 7) + (3 \times 10)$
$ = 21 + 30$
$ = 51$

Look at the simplified area model shown below. This algorithm is the same as breaking apart the rectangle into two smaller rectangles. Multiply to find the number of squares in each and add them together.

	7	10
3	3 × 7 = 21 squares	3 × 10 = 30 squares

Multiply 16 × 23.

Break apart 23 into 3 + 20 and use the distributive property. Then break apart 16 into 6 + 10 and use the distributive property again. Multiply and add the products.

$16 \times 23 = 16 \times (3 + 20)$
$ = (16 \times 3) + (16 \times 20)$
$ = (6 + 10) \times 3 + (6 + 10) \times 20$
$ = (6 \times 3 + 10 \times 3) +$
$ (6 \times 20 + 10 \times 20)$
$ = (18 + 30) + (120 + 200)$
$ = 368$

Look at the simplified area model below. This algorithm is the same as breaking apart the rectangle into four smaller rectangles. Multiply to find the number of squares in each and add them together.

	3	20
6	6 × 3 = 18 squares	6 × 20 = 120 squares
10	10 × 3 = 30 squares	10 × 20 = 200 squares

Practicing the Breaking-Apart Algorithm

Use the breaking-apart algorithm to multiply the following numbers. Show your work.

1. 4 × 19 = _____
2. 11 × 21 = _____

Unit 2, Lesson 9

Connections

YOUR TURN

Thinking About the Breaking-Apart Algorithm

Multiplication is reflexive. This means you can always reverse the order of the numbers that are factors. You have already learned this term as the communicative property of multiplication.

When you use the breaking-apart algorithm, you sometimes end up with the factor on the right and the numbers you want to multiply the factor by on the left. Since you have learned the distributive property with the factor on the left, it may be easier for you to multiply if you reverse the order. For example, consider $(4 + 10) \times 8$. Use a simplified area model to show $(4 + 10) \times 8$ and $8 \times (4 + 10)$.

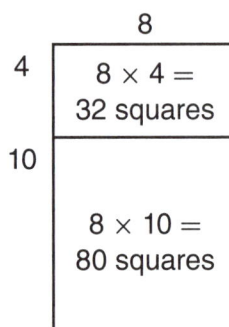

Either way you look at it, the numbers of squares in the area models are the same. The products are equal. Try it both ways. You can choose the way to multiply that works best for you.

Solve the following problems using the breaking-apart algorithm.

1. $18 \times 2 =$
2. $19 \times 5 =$
3. $16 \times 6 =$
4. $31 \times 4 =$

5. Did you ever reverse the order? If so, why? Is there an order that is easier for you?

_____
_____
_____

Tip Use the commutative property of multiplication to simplify multiplication. Remember that you can change the order of the factors without changing the product.

54 Unit 2, Lesson 9

Show That You Know

Read the information below. Use what you have learned about addition and multiplication to answer the questions. Use the space provided to show your work.

> The corner store sells packs of sports trading cards. Each pack has three soccer players, four basketball players, and seven football players. Each pack costs $5.

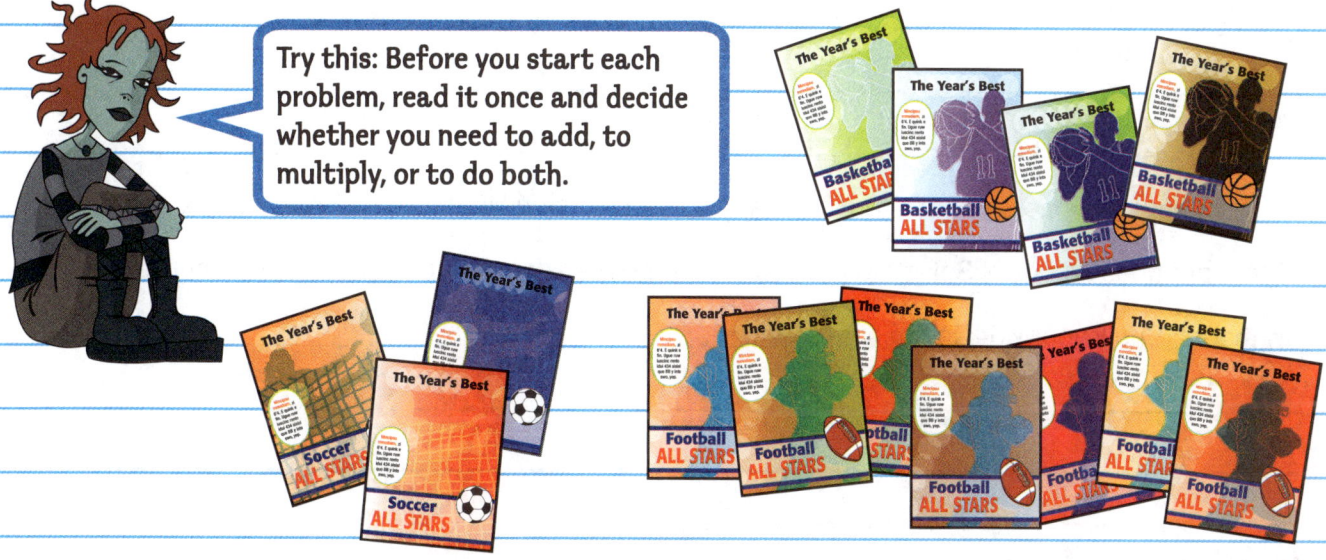

Try this: Before you start each problem, read it once and decide whether you need to add, to multiply, or to do both.

1. How many sports trading cards are in one pack?

2. How many cards of soccer players are in 13 packs?

3. How many cards of basketball players are in 15 packs?

4. How many cards of football players are in 19 packs?

5. How could you use the breaking-apart algorithm to show how many of each card is in 12 packs? Give your totals and how you found them.

Connections

Show That You Know (continued)

6. In the space below, represent the information in problem 5 as one simplified area model. You can use this model to check your answers to problem 5.

7. Elliot buys two packs of cards on Tuesday and six packs on Wednesday. How many of each type of card does he have? Solve the problem using the breaking-apart algorithm or a simplified area model. Show your work in the space below.

Review What You've Learned

8. Describe a situation where you would use the breaking-apart algorithm.
   _____
   _____

9. Which was easier for you to use, the breaking-apart algorithm or the simplified area model? Why?
   _____
   _____

10. How will this algorithm help you as you continue to learn and practice math?
    _____
    _____

Review and Practice

Skills Review

Multiplication and addition

Addition:

5 + 5 + 5 = 15 (add 5 three times)

Multiplication:

3 × 5 = 15 (add 3 groups of 5)

The commutative property

Addition:

5 + 1 = 1 + 5 = 6

Multiplication:

2 × 8 = 8 × 2 = 16

The associative property

Addition:

(1 + 3) + 5 = 1 + (3 + 5) = 9

Multiplication:

(1 × 2) × 3 = 1 × (2 × 3) = 6

The distributive property

Add first:

4 × (4 + 5) = 4 × 9 = 36

Multiply first:

4 × (4 + 5) = 16 + 20 = 36

Find the place values

In 2,135 the 5 is in the ones place, the 3 is in the tens place, the 1 is in the hundreds place, and the 2 is in the thousands place.

Standard notation

2,135

Expanded notation

2,135 = 2 × 1,000 + 1 × 100 + 3 × 10 + 5 × 1

Strategy Review

- Multiplication can be solved by drawing an array or using an area model.
- The factors of a number can be found using drawings of equal-size groups or drawing equal "jumps" on a number line.
- Numbers can be compared by making a place-value chart or by trying a simpler form of the problem. Often, you can compare two numbers by comparing one place value.

Unit 2, Lesson 10 57

Review and Practice

Skills and Strategies Practice

Complete the exercises below.

1. 4 + 4 = _____

2 × 4 = _____

4 × 2 = _____

2 + 2 + 2 + 2 = _____

2. Draw an area model.

3 × 4

3. 6 × (2 + 2) = _____ + _____ = _____

6 × (2 + 2) = _____ × _____ = _____

4. Draw equal groups to find factors of the number.

Number: 9   Factors: _____

5. Complete the place-value chart for 4,327.

Thousands	Hundreds	Tens	Ones

The place value of the 3 in 4,327 is

_____ .

6. Write 3,759 in expanded notation.

_____

_____

TEST-TAKING tip

To prepare for a test, study in short sessions rather than in one long session. During the week before the test, spend time each day reviewing your notes.

Mid-Unit Review

Circle the letter of the correct answer.

1. Find the product of 5 × 4.

   A. 4   C. 9
   B. 5   D. 20

2. Which expression below has the same value as 3 + 3 + 3 + 3?

   A. 3 × 2
   B. 3 × 3
   C. 3 × 4
   D. 3 × 5

3. According to _____, you can choose to add first or multiply first.

   A. the associative property of multiplication
   B. the distributive property of multiplication
   C. the identity property of multiplication
   D. the commutative property of multiplication

4. To find 3 × 5, you make _____ jumps of _____ on a number line.

   A. 3, 3   C. 5, 5
   B. 3, 5   D. 1, 5

5. 4 × 10 is equal to _____.

   A. 4 + 4
   B. 10 + 4
   C. 10 × 4
   D. 4 + 4 + 4 + 4

6. What is the product of 4 × 9?

   A. 9   C. 36
   B. 13   D. 49

7. According to _____, (6 × 7) × 8 = 6 × (7 × 8).

   A. the associative property of multiplication
   B. the distributive property of multiplication
   C. the commutative property of addition
   D. the commutative property of multiplication

8. The place value of 5 in the number 1,235 is _____.

   A. ones   C. hundreds
   B. tens   D. thousands

9. The number 3,000 can also be written as _____.

   A. 3   C. 3 + 1,000
   B. 30   D. 3 × 1,000

10. The area model of 6 × 3 would have _____.

    A. 3 rows, 3 columns
    B. 6 rows, 3 columns
    C. 3 rows, 6 columns
    D. 6 rows, 6 columns

11. According to _____, 4 × 5 = 5 × 4.

    A. the associative property of multiplication
    B. the distributive property of multiplication
    C. the identity property of multiplication
    D. the commutative property of multiplication

Mid-Unit Review

12. According to _____,
    $4 \times (2 + 1) = 4 \times 3$.

    A. the associative property of multiplication
    B. the distributive property of multiplication
    C. the identity property of multiplication
    D. the commutative property of multiplication

13. In which place(s) is the digit 5 found in the number 5,654?

    A. tens
    B. thousands
    C. hundreds
    D. tens and thousands

14. Which digit is found in the thousands place in the number 1,375?

    A. 13   C. 4
    B. 6   D. 1

15. If you draw an array to represent 6×7, how many rows will the array have?

    A. 0   C. 7
    B. 6   D. 10

16. Which expression has the same value as $7 + 7 + 7 + 7$?

    A. 7×1 C. 7×4
    B. 7×3 D. 7×7

17. The number 3,500 can also be written as _____.

    A. $3 \times 1 + 5 \times 1$
    B. $3 \times 10 + 5 \times 10$
    C. $3 \times 1,000 + 5 \times 10 + 0 \times 1$
    D. $3 \times 1,000 + 5 \times 100 + 0 \times 10 + 0 \times 1$

18. $7 + (3 + 4) =$ _____

    A. 7×7 C. $21 + 28$
    B. $7 + 7$ D. 49

19. $4 \times 1 =$ _____

    A. 4   C. $4 + 1$
    B. 5   D. $1 + 4$

20. What is the product of $5 \times (4 + 3)$?

    A. 20   C. 35
    B. 30   D. 40

21. $8 \times (4 + 1) =$ _____

    A. $8 + 4$ C. $8 + 5$
    B. 8×4 D. $32 + 8$

22. What is the sum of $4 + 4$?

    A. 4   C. 16
    B. 8   D. 20

23. What are the factors in 5×5?

    A. 25   C. 5
    B. 10   D. 2

24. The place value of the digit 6 in the number 5,463 is _____.

    A. thousands   C. tens
    B. hundreds   D. ones

25. According to _____,
    $(1 + 2) + 3 = 1 + (2 + 3)$.

    A. the associative property of addition
    B. the distributive property of addition
    C. the commutative property of addition
    D. the identity property of addition

Division

Learn the SKILL

Students often form teams to play games. After lunch, the class needs to divide into teams to play dodge ball. What is a fast way to find out how many people will be on each team? For example, you want to make three teams equal in size from a class of 12 students. How many students are on each team?

VOCABULARY

Watch for the words you are learning about.

difference: the number that results from subtracting one number from another number

divide: to subtract a number many times

dividend: the number being divided

division: repeated subtraction

divisor: the number you divide by

quotient: the number that results from dividing one number by another number

SKILL	EXAMPLE	WRITE AN EXAMPLE
Subtraction and **division** are related. To **divide** a number, you can subtract from the number many times until you reach zero. This repeated subtraction splits the number into equal groups.	Subtraction: $12 - 4 - 4 - 4 = 0$ (Subtract 4 three times.) Division: $12 \div 4 = 3$ (Divide into groups of four. There are three equal groups of four.) 12 is the **dividend.** 4 is the **divisor.** 3 is the **quotient.**	Subtraction: _____ Division: _____
Unlike addition or multiplication, the order in which you subtract or divide two numbers will affect the **difference** or the quotient.	The symbol $\neq$ means "does not equal." Subtraction: $6 - 2 = 4$ $2 - 6 \neq 4$ Division: $6 \div 2 = 3$ $2 \div 6 \neq 3$ Multiplication: $2 \times 6 = 2 + 2 + 2 + 2 + 2 + 2 = 12$ $6 \times 2 = 6 + 6 = 12$	Subtraction: _____ Division: _____
A number divided by 1 is the number itself. Zero divided by a number is 0. Division by 0 is not allowed because you cannot divide a number into groups of zero.	Divide by 1: If you divide 12 people into teams of one, how many teams will there be? $12 \div 1 = 12$ Divide 0 by a number: If you have 0 dodge balls and you try to give four to each team, how many teams get dodge balls? $0 \div 4 = 0$	Divide by 1: _____ Divide 0 by a number: _____

Learn the Skill

YOUR TURN

Choose the Right Word

> divide   division   divisor   quotient

Fill in each blank with the correct word or phrase from the box.

1. The answer to a division problem is called the _____.

2. When you _____, you subtract a number repeatedly.

3. In a division problem, the number you divide by is called the _____.

4. Instead of subtracting a number over and over, you can use _____ to find the number of groups.

Yes or No?

Answer these questions and be ready to explain your answers.

5. Can 12 − 3 − 3 − 3 − 3 be used to find the answer to 12 ÷ 3? _____

6. Will you get the same answer to 8 ÷ 2 and 2 ÷ 8? _____

7. If you divide 0 ÷ 10, will the answer be 0? _____

8. If you divide 10 by 0, will the answer be 10? _____

9. If you divide any number by 1, will the answer always be your original number? _____

Show That You Know

Write your answer to each exercise in the space provided.

10. 6 − 2 − 2 − 2 =

    6 ÷ 2 =

    2 ÷ 6 ≠

11. 10 ÷ 5 =

    5 ÷ 10 ≠

    10 − 5 − 5 =

12. 7 ÷ 21 ≠

    21 − 7 − 7 − 7 =

    21 ÷ 7 =

13. 18 ÷ 0 =

    0 ÷ 18 =

14. 16 ÷ 1 =

    1 ÷ 16 ≠

    16 − 1 − 1 − 1 − 1 − 1 − 1 − 1 − 1 − 1 − 1 − 1 − 1 − 1 − 1 − 1 − 1 =

15. 8 ÷ 1 =

16. 35 ÷ 5 =

17. 9 − 3 − 3 − 3 =

18. 6 ÷ 24 ≠

SOLVE on Your Own

Skills Practice

> Remember, division is repeated subtraction.

Divide.

1. 4 ÷ 2 = _____
2. 6 ÷ 1 = _____
3. 18 ÷ 6 = _____
4. 0 ÷ 6 = _____
5. 48 ÷ 6 = _____
6. 32 ÷ 8 = _____

7. 27 ÷ 3 = _____
8. 1 ÷ 5 ≠ _____
9. 8 ÷ 8 = _____
10. 9 ÷ 0 = _____
11. 54 ÷ 9 = _____
12. 1 ÷ 1 = _____

13. 81 ÷ 9 = _____
14. 36 ÷ 4 = _____
15. 56 ÷ 7 = _____
16. 10 ÷ 5 = _____
17. 42 ÷ 6 = _____

Solve each word problem using division. Write the answer on the line.

18. Mr. Martinez is buying one pad of drawing paper for each student in his art class. Four pads of paper come in one pack. If there are 28 students in his class, how many packs should he buy? _____

19. Coach Ling wants to divide her gym class into basketball teams. If she has 30 students, how many teams of five can she make? _____

20. Twenty people can ride on a roller coaster at the same time. If there are two people in each row, how many rows are there on the ride? _____

Choose a Strategy

Division

Strategy
Draw a Picture or Use a Model

Step 1: Read There are 24 packets of powdered juice on board a space shuttle. There can be anywhere from three to nine astronauts on board. For which numbers of astronauts can the juice packets be divided evenly?

> **VOCABULARY**
> Watch for the words you are learning about.
> **partitioning:** separating a group of objects into smaller equal groups

STRATEGY	SOLUTION
Draw a Picture or Use a Model (number line) To perform repeated subtraction, make equal "jumps" on the number line down from the larger number to zero. If you reach 0, then the number can be divided evenly by that divisor.	**Step 2: Plan** Draw a number line. Select a number to subtract repeatedly from 24. In this way, "jump" down from 24 using equal jumps to see if you can land on zero. Try jumps by 9. Then try the other numbers. **Step 3: Solve** 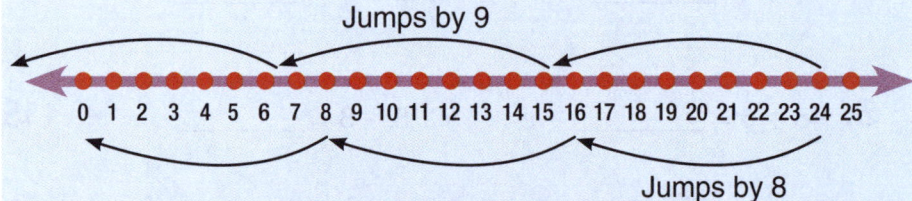 You can jump to zero using jumps of eight, six, four, and three. These numbers of astronauts can share the juice packets equally. **Step 4: Check** Add each number to itself until you get back to 24.
Draw a Picture or Use a Model (partitioning) Draw a set of boxes to represent the dividend. Try to partition the boxes into equal smaller groups through sharing. If you can make the smaller groups equal in size to the divisor, then the larger number can be divided evenly by that divisor.	**Step 2: Plan** Draw 24 boxes. Try to divide the boxes into groups of nine first. Then try other divisors between three and eight. **Step 3: Solve** Color in two groups of nine boxes. This leaves a group of six boxes. You cannot divide the boxes into equal groups of nine. The boxes are not all shared.  Divide by 8. The boxes divide evenly into three groups of eight. 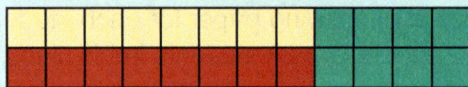 You can divide the boxes into equal groups of eight, six, four, and three. These numbers of astronauts can share the juice packets equally. **Step 4: Check** Multiply to check your answers: $3 \times 8 = 24$, $4 \times 6 = 24$, $6 \times 4 = 24$, and $8 \times 3 = 24$.

YOUR TURN

Choose the Right Word

> partitioning   repeated subtraction

Fill in each blank with the correct word or phrase from the box.

1. To divide, keep on performing _____ _____ until you reach zero.

2. You can separate a number into equal groups through _____.

Choose a Strategy

Yes or No?

Answer these questions and be ready to explain your answers.

3. Can you repeatedly subtract 2 from 5 and end up with 0? _____

4. Can the number 6 be partitioned into three equal groups? _____

5. Can a number be partitioned into one group? _____

6. When you share, can you end up with unequal groups? _____

Show That You Know

Divide. Check using repeated subtraction.

7. $12 \div 3 =$

8. $16 \div 8 =$

9. $9 \div 3 =$

Use partitioning to find each of the following quotients. Draw a model to show your work.

10. $6 \div 3 =$

11. $14 \div 7 =$

12. $15 \div 3 =$

Unit 2, Lesson 12

Reading Comprehension

READ on Your Own

Reading Comprehension Strategy: Summarizing

Food for Thought, pages 20–21

VOCABULARY

Watch for the words you are learning about.

freeze-dried: preserved by removing the water and the air

Fluency Tip

Before reading, look through the sentences for words that you do not know. Find out how to pronounce them.

Before You Read

Think about what you read in "Between the Slices." How many peanut butter and jelly sandwiches do you think you have eaten in your life? Explain how you got that number.

As You Read

Read "Space Food," page 20.

What is this page about? Identify the topic.

_____

_____

Read page 21.

What is this page about? Identify the topic.

_____

_____

_____

After You Read

What space foods have you eaten? Where did you buy them?

_____

_____

_____

Problem Solving

SOLVE on Your Own

Food for Thought, page 22

Organize the Information

Read You Do the Math in the magazine. Use what you learn to fill out the table below.

Food (packets)	Can Be Divided into Groups of					
	3	4	5	6	7	8
soup (90)						
powdered juice (144)						
macaroni and cheese (126)						
strawberries (108)						

You Do the Math

Use the information in the table above to answer these questions. Write your answers in the space provided.

Partitioning a group of objects into smaller, equal groups can help you visualize a problem.

1. Imagine the length of the mission and the number of crew members were not known until the day the shuttle took off. Would there be enough for each astronaut to have at least two packets of each food per day? How do you know?

   _____
   _____
   _____

2. Which combination of number of crew members and mission length will allow the food to be shared equally? Explain why.

   _____
   _____
   _____

After You Solve

Which strategies did you use to solve the problems above?

_____

Unit 2, Lesson 12

Learn the Skill

Multiplication and Division as Inverse Operations

Learn the SKILL

> **VOCABULARY**
>
> Watch for the words you are learning about.
>
> **inverse operations:** operations that undo each other, such as addition and subtraction
>
> **operation:** addition, subtraction, multiplication, or division

You and three friends recycled aluminum cans for the money to go see a movie. After taking the cans to the recycling center, you were given $12. Mentally, you calculated that each person should receive $3. How can you quickly check your answer to make sure your calculation is correct?

SKILL	EXAMPLE	WRITE AN EXAMPLE
Multiplication and division are **inverse operations,** just like addition and subtraction. To undo multiplication, you can divide. To undo division, you can multiply.	Multiply, then divide: $3 \times 4 = 12$; $12 \div 4 = 3$ Also, $4 \times 3 = 12$; $12 \div 3 = 4$ Divide, then multiply: $15 \div 5 = 3$; $3 \times 5 = 15$ Also, $15 \div 3 = 5$; $5 \times 3 = 15$	Multiply, then divide: _____ Divide, then multiply: _____
The repeated addition in multiplication can be undone by the repeated subtraction in division.	Repeated addition: $3 + 3 + 3 = 9$; $3 \times 3 = 9$ Undo with repeated subtraction: $9 - 3 - 3 - 3 = 0$; $9 \div 3 = 3$	Repeated addition: _____ Repeated subtraction: _____
Because multiplication and division are inverse operations, each can be used to check the other. For example, multiplication can be used to check division and division can be used to check multiplication.	Check the division: $36 \div 9 = 3$ Check: $3 \times 9 = 27$ Incorrect. Check the multiplication: $6 \times 6 = 36$ Check: $36 \div 6 = 6$ Correct.	Check: $63 \div 7 = 9$ _____ Check: $4 \times 7 = 35$ _____

YOUR TURN

Choose the Right Word

> operations   inverse operations

Fill in each blank with the correct word or phrase from the box.

1. Addition and multiplication are examples of _____.

2. Operations that cancel each other such as multiplication and division are examples of _____.

Learn the Skill

Yes or No?

Answer these questions and be ready to explain your answers.

3. Will $3 + 3 + 3 + 3$ and 4×3 undo each other? _____

4. Can repeated addition be used to check multiplication? _____

5. Can repeated subtraction be used to undo multiplication? _____

6. If you calculate 6×5 and then divide by 5, will the answer be 5? _____

Show That You Know

Write your answer to each exercise in the space provided.

7. $5 + 5 + 5 =$

   Check:

8. $15 \div 3 =$

   Check:

9. $4 \times 6 =$

   Check:

10. $6 + 6 + 6 + 6 =$

    Check:

11. $32 \div 8 =$

    Check:

12. $7 \times 5 =$

    Check:

13. $1 + 1 + 1 + 1 + 1 + 1 + 1 =$

    Check:

14. $18 - 9 - 9 =$

    Check:

Learn the Skill

SOLVE on Your Own

To undo multiplication, divide. To undo division, multiply.

Write the expression you would use to check each of the following operations. The product or quotient should equal the first number.

1. 10 × 5 _____
2. 4 × 6 _____
3. 6 × 6 _____
4. 8 × 2 _____
5. 0 × 6 _____
6. 11 × 3 _____

7. 81 ÷ 9 _____
8. 12 ÷ 12 _____
9. 42 ÷ 6 _____
10. 18 ÷ 9 _____
11. 12 × 4 _____
12. 5 × 2 _____

13. 30 ÷ 3 _____
14. 45 ÷ 5 _____
15. 5 × 7 _____
16. 48 ÷ 8 _____
17. 72 ÷ 8 _____

Solve each problem below. Write the expression you used to check the math.

18. Wade found five CDs on sale for a total of $35. He guessed that each CD cost $6. Is he correct? _____

19. Valerie put eight library books away on each of seven different shelves. She counted 56 books. Is she correct? _____

20. Mrs. Lee needs to make 54 rolls. Each batch of dough makes six rolls. Can she make 54 rolls with eight batches? _____

Multiplication and Division as Inverse Operations

Strategies

Make a Table or a Chart, Draw a Picture or Use a Model

Step 1: Read A teacher read Scott's lab report. Scott viewed a number of bugs, but he forgot to record how many. The bugs are either all insects or all spiders. Insects have six legs and three body parts each. Spiders have eight legs and two body parts each. Scott counted a total of 24 legs and 12 body parts. Can the teacher tell if Scott viewed insects or spiders? Can she tell how many were viewed?

STRATEGY	SOLUTION
Make a Table or a Chart You can use a table to organize information, especially multiples. Look at the multiples to see if they match the ones given in the problem.	**Step 2: Plan** Start with insects. Use multiples to find the numbers of legs and body parts for two, three, and four insects. Do the same for spiders. **Step 3: Solve** <table><tr><th>Number of Insects</th><th>Number of Legs</th><th>Number of Body Parts</th><th>Number of Spiders</th><th>Number of Legs</th><th>Number of Body Parts</th></tr><tr><td>1</td><td>6 × 1 = 6</td><td>3 × 1 = 3</td><td>1</td><td>8 × 1 = 8</td><td>2 × 1 = 2</td></tr><tr><td>2</td><td>6 × 2 = 12</td><td>3 × 2 = 6</td><td>2</td><td>8 × 2 = 16</td><td>2 × 2 = 4</td></tr><tr><td>3</td><td>6 × 3 = 18</td><td>3 × 3 = 9</td><td>3</td><td>8 × 3 = 24</td><td>2 × 3 = 6</td></tr><tr><td>4</td><td>6 × 4 = 24</td><td>3 × 4 = 12</td><td>4</td><td>8 × 4 = 32</td><td>2 × 4 = 8</td></tr></table> Four insects have 24 legs and 12 body parts. Scott must have viewed four insects. **Step 4: Check** The answer cannot be three spiders. Although three spiders have 24 legs, they only have six body parts.
Draw a Picture or Use a Model (partitioning) You can use partitioning and an area model to divide numbers into equal groups. Dividing both numbers into the same number of equal groups will help you find your answer.	**Step 2: Plan** Try to divide the number of legs (24) and body parts (12) into the same number of equal groups (the same number of bugs). **Step 3: Solve** 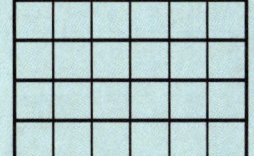 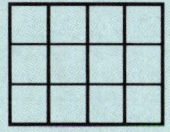 Each number can be divided into four equal groups. The number of legs divides into four equal groups (rows) of six. The number of body parts divides into four equal groups (columns) of three. The bugs must be insects (three body parts, six legs). There were four insects. **Step 4: Check** Use multiplication to check your answer: 4 insects × 6 legs = 24 legs; 4 insects × 3 body parts = 12 body parts

Choose a Strategy

YOUR TURN

Choose the Right Word

> inverse operation   multiples   partitioning

Fill in each blank with the correct word or phrase from the box.

1. To check a division problem with multiplication would be to use the _____.

2. One way to model division is through _____.

3. Multiplying the same number by different factors gives you _____ of that number.

Yes or No?

Answer these questions and be ready to explain your answers.

4. Is subtraction the inverse of addition? _____

5. Is 12 × 4 the inverse operation of 4 × 12? _____

6. Can you check a division problem with multiplication? _____

7. Will dividing by 0 let you check the answer to 1 × 0? _____

Show That You Know

Write your answer to each exercise in the space provided. Check using inverse operations.

8. ____ × 4 = 36

   Check:

9. 5 × ____ = 35

   Check:

10. ____ × 3 = 27

    Check:

11. 7 × ____ = 28

    Check:

12. 48 ÷ ____ = 8

    Check:

13. ____ ÷ 3 = 5

    Check:

14. ____ ÷ 7 = 3

    Check:

15. 24 ÷ ____ = 8

    Check:

Unit 2, Lesson 14

Reading Comprehension

READ on Your Own

Reading Comprehension Strategy: Summarizing

Food for Thought, pages 23–24

Fluency Tip
Be careful to read every word without skipping or substituting words. If a sentence or paragraph does not make sense, reread every word.

Before You Read

Think about what you read in "Space Food." Have you ever seen a video of people eating in zero gravity? What do you think would be the hardest part?

As You Read

Read "Bugs for Breakfast," page 23.
Fill in the chart below.

Read "Bugs Are Big Business," page 24.
Fill in the chart below.

Bugs for Breakfast	Bugs Are Big Business
Summary: People around the world eat bugs because _____ _____ _____ _____ _____	**Summary:** Bugs are big business because _____ _____ _____ _____ _____

After You Read

If you had to eat one kind of bug, which would you want to try? Why?

_____
_____
_____

Unit 2, Lesson 14

Problem Solving

SOLVE on Your Own

Food for Thought, page 25

Organize the Information

Read You Do the Math in the magazine. You can then use the table below to help determine how many crickets Doug's pets will eat over time.

Pet	1 Week	2 Weeks	3 Weeks	4 Weeks	5 Weeks	6 Weeks	7 Weeks
toad	7 small						
tarantula	3 large						

You Do the Math

Use the information in the table above to answer these questions. Write your answers in the space provided.

1. Which bags can Doug buy to use up the small crickets in a multiple of seven days? Explain.
   _____
   _____
   _____

2. Which bags can Doug buy to use up the large crickets in a multiple of seven days? Explain.
   _____
   _____
   _____

   > Drawing an array or area model will help you answer some of these questions.

3. How many bags of small and large crickets should Doug buy so that he uses up all of the crickets in a multiple of seven days?
   _____
   _____
   _____

After You Solve

Is your answer in question 3 the only possible answer? Explain
_____
_____

74 Unit 2, Lesson 14

Application

The Four-Step Problem-Solving Plan

Step 1: Read	Step 2: Plan	Step 3: Solve	Step 4: Check
Make sure you understand what the problem is asking.	Decide how you will solve the problem.	Solve the problem using your plan.	Check to make sure your answer is correct.

Read the article below. Then answer the questions.

Pizza, Pronto!

Pizza is liked by people of all ages. It is simple to make and can have many different shapes, sizes, and flavors. Most pizzas are round like a circle, but some are made in the shape of a square or rectangle. Whatever the shape, pizza usually comes in the following five common sizes: personal (four slices), small (six slices), medium (eight slices), large (12 slices), and extra large (16 slices).

To make a pizza, all you need is flat bread and a topping. Many Americans think of crust, tomato sauce, cheese, and some other topping when they picture a pizza. The toppings can vary from pepperoni and mushrooms to anchovies and pineapple. The crust can also differ from thin to very thick Chicago-style deep dish. Mozzarella is commonly used, but some people prefer special kinds of cheese on their pizzas.

1. If everyone eats one slice, would a small pizza feed a family of eight?

   _____
   _____
   _____

2. How many medium pizzas would it take to feed 64 people at least one slice each?

   _____

3. Would the number change if four people left before you ordered the pizzas?

   _____
   _____
   _____

Unit 2, Lesson 15   75

Application

YOUR TURN

Read the article below. Then answer the questions.

Pizza Around the World

Americans order more than 3 billion pizzas a year. That is about 10 pizzas for every American each year. Americans are not the only ones who enjoy pizza. Some kind of pizza can be found in many countries around the world.

Companies from the United States are helping to spread the love of pizza by building pizzerias overseas. Even people who live in China and India, the two countries with the greatest number of people, are starting to enjoy pizza.

In the United States, pepperoni is the most popular pizza topping. Overseas, the favorite topping varies from place to place. People keep thinking up new pizza toppings.

One thing is certain, people love pizza. Some pizza lovers even go so far as to try and set world records with their pizzas. There are records for eating pizza, cooking pizza, and making different sizes of pizzas.

Fluency Tip

Pay attention to punctuation marks. Punctuation marks tell you when to pause and when to raise your voice for a question or an exclamation.

1. A pizza company decides to start building new pizzerias overseas. The company wants to find a place where pizza sales will likely grow quickly. What country might be a good place to build new stores? Why?
   _____
   _____
   _____
   _____

2. What is the favorite topping in the United States?
   _____

3. If a pizza company grows by eight pizzerias a year, how long will it take to grow by 72 pizzerias?
   _____

4. A restaurant sells 27 pizzas in three hours. On average, how many pizzas did they sell each hour? _____

Reading Comprehension

READ on Your Own

Reading Comprehension Strategy: Summarizing

Food for Thought, pages 26–28

VOCABULARY

Watch for the words you are learning about.

immigrants: people who move to a new country to live

Fluency Tip

If you find yourself reading so quickly that you are missing the meaning, slow down.

Before You Read

Think about the first page you read in "Bugs for Breakfast." Why do people eat different kinds of bugs?

As You Read

Read "The Flip Side of Pizza," pages 26–27.

What are these two pages about? Identify the topic(s).

_____

_____

Read page 28.

What is this page about? Identify the topic(s).

_____

_____

Use your answers above to decide on the main topic for the whole article. Write this topic below.

_____

_____

After You Read

Do you think it is possible for you to try all of the different kinds of pizza? Explain your answer.

_____

_____

Unit 2, Lesson 15

Problem Solving

SOLVE on Your Own

Food for Thought, page 29

Organize the Information

Read the Math Project in the magazine. Use the table below to try out some possible answers.

Number of Pizzas	Total Slices	Is the slices per person a whole number? (4 people)	Is the slices per person a whole number? (6 people)

Math Project

Use the information in the table above to answer these questions. Write your answers in the space provided.

1. What are some possible numbers of pizzas that work if four people come to the party?
   _____
   _____

2. What are some possible numbers of pizzas that work if six people come to the party?
   _____

3. What number of pizzas will work whether there are four people or six people at the party?
   _____

You may need to create more than one table to display all the information.

After You Solve

How could you express the same information in the table by drawing a picture?
_____
_____

Tables, Bar Graphs, and Pictographs

Learn the SKILL

People like to visit natural history museums. Which area in these museums do people like best? If you asked many people, how would you keep track of what they said? How would you use this information? If you asked everyone in your class about their favorite area in a natural history museum, how would you show the information? How could find the most popular area?

VOCABULARY
Watch for the words you are learning about.
data: the information from a survey
key: a chart that explains the parts of a graph
pictograph: a graph that uses pictures to represent data

SKILL	EXAMPLE	WRITE AN EXAMPLE
Tables show **data** in a way that is easy to study. Tables should have a title and labels for the rows and columns. Each piece of data in a table is labeled by its row and its column.	Table: **Favorite Area in a Natural History Museum** | Area | Number of Students | |---|---| | Space | 4 | | Dinosaurs | 8 | | Rocks/gems | 5 | | Mammals | 3 |	Enter your own data in the table. **Favorite Area in a Natural History Museum** | Area | Number of Students | |---|---| | Space | | | Dinosaurs | | | Rocks/gems | | | Mammals | |
A bar graph uses the heights of bars to compare data in different categories. The bars in a bar graph can be horizontal or vertical.	Bar graph: 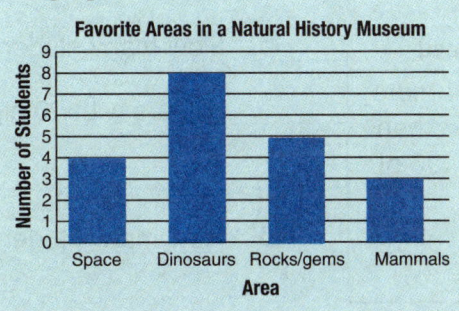	Show your data on a bar graph.
A **pictograph** uses pictures to represent amounts in each category. The **key** shows what each picture represents.	Pictograph: 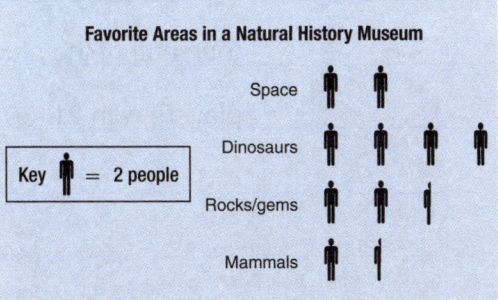	Show your data as a pictograph.

Unit 2, Lesson 16

Learn the Skill

YOUR TURN

Choose the Right Word

bar graph   key   pictograph   table

Fill in each blank with the correct word or phrase from the box.

1. A _____ organizes data into rows and columns.

2. Some graphs use a _____ to help with reading the graph.

3. In a _____, the heights of bars are used to show the data.

4. You could use pictures to show and compare data in a _____.

Yes or No?

Use the table to answer these questions and be ready to explain your answers.

Students' Favorite Sports	
Sport	Number of Students
track	10
softball	3
soccer	6
swimming	5

5. Could a bar graph be used to show the data in the table? _____

6. Was softball chosen as a favorite the least number of times? _____

7. Did four more students choose soccer as a favorite than chose softball? _____

Show That You Know

Make a bar graph from the data and then answer the questions.

Survey of Digital Music Players Owned				
Gigabytes (gB) of Storage Space	0–10 gB	11–20 gB	21–30 gB	more than 30 gB
Number of Students	4	3	8	5

8. How many students have digital music players with 20 gigabytes or less?

9. How many students do the data describe?

10. Do more than half, exactly half, or less than half of the students have digital music players with 21–30 gB of storage?

Unit 2, Lesson 16

SOLVE on Your Own

Tables and graphs show information in a way that is easy to study.

Mrs. Field's class collected data from 30 local soccer clubs. Each club had its own flag. The class recorded data on the color of the flags. Use the data to answer the questions.

Soccer Club Flags

Color	White	Blue	Red	Green	Other
Number of Flags	5	13	7	4	1

1. Make a bar graph in the space below.

2. How many flags include blue? _____

3. How many flags are described by the data? _____

4. Make a pictograph showing the same data in the space below. Make sure to include a key.

5. There are 58 teams in the state soccer league. Each team has its own flag. Based on your data, how many teams would you guess have blue in their flag? Explain.

_____
_____

Learn the Skill

Unit 2, Lesson 16

Choose a Strategy

Tables, Bar Graphs, and Pictographs

Strategy
Make a Table or a Chart

> **VOCABULARY**
> Watch for the words you are learning about.
> **range:** the difference between the greatest data value and the least data value in a set

Step 1: Read A research team studied 28 meals. They calculated the water used to make each meal and displayed the data in the following table. Find the **range** of the number of meals in the different categories.

Gallons of Water Used	Number of Meals
0 to 499	1
500 to 999	8
1,000 to 1,499	13
1,500 to 1,999	6
2,000 to 2,500	2

STRATEGY	SOLUTION
Make a Table or a Chart The range of the data is the greatest value minus the least value in a set. Make sure you use the data to find the range and not the labels for the rows.	**Step 2: Plan** Use a table to find the range of the data. Locate the largest and smallest number of meals and find the difference. **Step 3: Solve** The greatest number of meals in the table above is 13. The least number of meals is 1. The range is 13 − 1 = 12. **Step 4: Check** Use addition to check subtraction: 12 + 1 = 13. The answer checks.
Make a Table or a Chart (bar graph) The highest bar on the bar graph shows the greatest number and the lowest bar shows the least number. The difference in height between the highest and lowest bar is the range.	**Step 2: Plan** Use the bar heights to find the range. **Step 3: Solve** 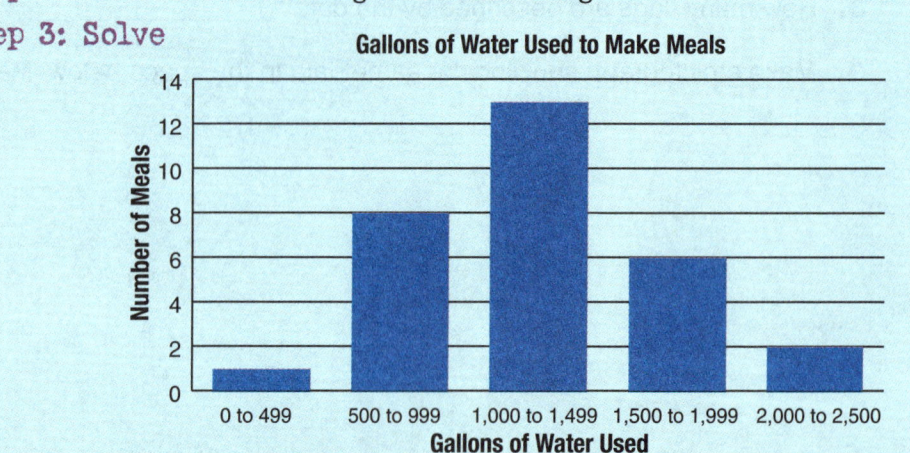 The tallest bar is 13 and the shortest is 1. The range is 13 − 1 = 12. **Step 4: Check** Use addition to check subtraction: 12 + 1 = 13. The answer checks.

YOUR TURN

Choose the Right Word

bar graph   data   range

Fill in each blank with the correct word or phrase from the box.

1. A table shows _____ in rows and columns.

2. To find the _____, you must subtract the lowest value from the highest value.

3. A _____ uses bars to show numerical information.

Choose a Strategy

Yes or No?

Answer these questions and be ready to explain your answers.

4. Can you find the range of a set by subtracting the greatest number from the least number? _____

5. Does the table on page 82 tell you which meals take more than 1,000 gallons of water to make? _____

6. If the tallest bar on a bar graph is 16 and the shortest is 6, is the range of the data 6? _____

Show That You Know

Use the table to answer the questions. Make sure to check your work.

Eating More Than 2,000 Calories per Day	
Group	Number of People
babies	0
men	7
women	5
boys	8
girls	4

Use the bar graph to answer the questions.

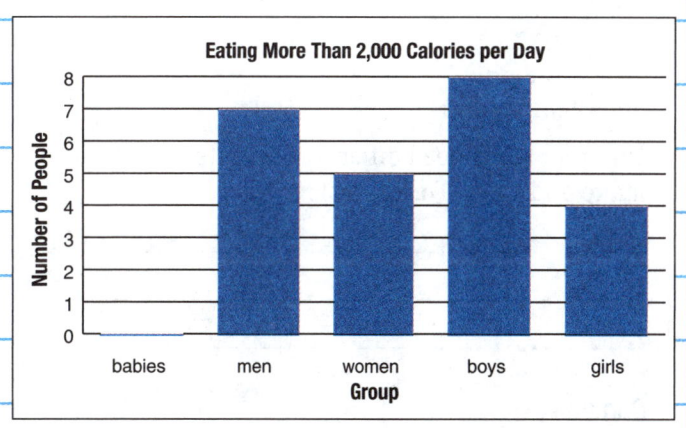

7. How many more boys than men ate more than 2,000 calories per day?

8. How many more women than girls ate more than 2,000 calories per day?

9. How many more men than girls ate more than 2,000 calories per day?

10. What is the range of the data?

Unit 2, Lesson 17   83

Reading Comprehension

READ on Your Own

Reading Comprehension Strategy: Summarizing

Food for Thought, pages 30–31

VOCABULARY
Watch for the words you are learning about.

conserve: to save for later use
irrigated: supplied with water using streams, pipes, or ditches

Fluency Tip
If you find yourself reading so quickly that you are missing the meaning, slow down.

Before You Read

Think about what you read in "The Flip Side of Pizza." How does pizza differ from country to country?

As You Read

Read "How Much Water Did You Just Eat?", page 30. STOP Fill in the chart below.

Read page 31. STOP Fill in the chart below.

You Are What You Eat	
Page 30	**Page 31**
Main Idea: A lot of water is needed to _____	**Main Idea:** You can use less water by _____
Important Details: Different foods need different amounts of water to make and grow. For example, _____	**Important Details:** Water is used in many different ways to grow and make food. For example, _____
Summary: It takes a lot of water to _____	**Summary:** As the world's population grows, _____

After You Read

About how much water do you think it took to make your lunch today? Why? _____

Unit 2, Lesson 17

Problem Solving

SOLVE on Your Own

Food for Thought, page 32

Organize the Information

Read You Do the Math in the magazine. Use the bar graph on page 32 to complete the table below.

Type of Food	Gallons of Water Used
1 serving of lettuce	
1 serving of white bread	
1 serving of whole wheat bread	
1 serving of tomato	
1 serving of carrots	

Make sure to read the labels and the scale of the bar graph carefully.

You Do the Math

Use the information in the table above to answer these questions. Write your answers in the space provided.

1. Which items on the list would you choose first? Why?
   _____

2. List the three snacks you created. What was the most difficult part of making the snacks add up to 40 total gallons of water?
   _____
   _____

After You Solve

Which do you think is easier to use for solving the problems, the bar graph or the table? Explain.
_____
_____

Application

The Four-Step Problem-Solving Plan

Step 1: Read	Step 2: Plan	Step 3: Solve	Step 4: Check
Make sure you understand what the problem is asking.	Decide how you will solve the problem.	Solve the problem using your plan.	Check to make sure your answer is correct.

Read the article below. Then answer the questions.

Food's Place in History

All living things need food to live. So, where you find people, you will also find some sort of food. You can tell a lot about people by what they eat. Their diet mostly depends on what types of plants and animals are found in the area where they live. For example, someone who eats walrus meat probably lives in a cold place where walruses also live. Since people live around the world, they eat everything from fish and octopus to bugs and berries.

Some of the foods people eat today have been enjoyed since ancient times. This means that people have been eating these foods for a long time. For example, people have been eating almonds, dates, honey, fish, eggs, and pork for thousands of years. Other foods have not been eaten until fairly recent times, like muffins and sandwiches. Some foods may surprise you. A form of ice cream was first made in China around 5,000 years ago. However, this ancient ice cream was very different from the treat you enjoy today. Many ancient foods have changed into something totally new through the years.

1. Where would someone who eats fish likely live in the United States?

   _____
   _____
   _____

2. A century is equal to 100 years. About how many centuries has it been since the Chinese first made ice cream? Hint: Skip-count by 100s to 5,000.

   _____
   _____

86 Unit 2, Lesson 18

YOUR TURN

Application

Read the article below. Then answer the questions.

Food to Go

Today, people enjoy many different kinds of food thanks to modern technology. Farm equipment and farming practices make it possible to plant and grow large numbers of crops. Food can be grown or raised in one place and then sold in another. Airplanes, boats, trains, and trucks make it possible to move food great distances. Refrigerators keep food fresh longer by keeping it cold or frozen. This means food can be kept for longer periods of time without it going bad.

You may have noticed at the grocery store that food costs different amounts. The cost can depend on where the food came from and how much there is of it. If a food item is in short supply, it will cost more. For example, milk and bread are common food items that are easy to get, so they do not cost very much. Lobster and fish eggs, called caviar, are not easily gathered. As a result, they can cost a lot.

Fluency Tip
Remember to look up the meanings of unfamiliar words before you read.

1. Strawberries grow in California. They will only stay fresh for a few days. Can someone in Alaska enjoy fresh strawberries from California? Explain.

   _____
   _____
   _____
   _____

2. How can large amounts of fresh vegetables be taken from the United States to Japan?

   _____
   _____

3. Eight people eat dinner. It costs $72 for everyone. How much did dinner cost per person?

   _____

4. A train car can carry 20 crates of strawberries. How many crates can four train cars carry?

   _____

Unit 2, Lesson 18   87

Reading Comprehension

READ on Your Own

Reading Comprehension Strategy: Summarizing

Food for Thought, pages 33–35

VOCABULARY

Watch for the words you are learning about.

region: a geographic area having the same features

Fluency Tip

Everyone reads at a different pace. Practice until you can read at a pace that is comfortable for you.

Before You Read

Think about what you read in "How Much Water Did You Just Eat?" Why is it important to conserve water?

As You Read

Read "Around the World in 80 Meals," page 33.

What is this page about? Identify the topic.

_____

_____

Read pages 34–35.

What are these two pages about? Identify the topic.

_____

_____

Use your answers above to decide on the main topic for the whole article. Write this topic below.

_____

_____

After You Read

Could someone from Ohio have haggis for dinner? Explain your answer.

_____

_____

SOLVE on Your Own

Problem Solving

Food for Thought, *page 36*

Organize the Information

Read the Math Project in the magazine. Use the table below to organize your calculations.

Meal	Price	Cost	Profit per Meal	Number of Meals Sold This Week	Weekly Meal Profit
Harriet's Haggis	$7	$2			
Earl's Escargot	$12	$3			
Bo's Bird's Nest Soup	$5	$2			
Fifi's Fufu	$7	$3			
Izzy's Iguana Burger	$9	$7			
Ena's Grilled Emu	$9	$3			

Math Project

Use the information in the table above to answer these questions. Write your answers in the space provided.

Having all your data in one place makes it easier to study the information.

1. How do you find the profit per meal and the profit for the week?
   _____

2. Which meals had the same profit for the entire week?
   _____
   _____

After You Solve

How could you express the same information in the pictograph by making a bar graph?
_____
_____

Unit 2, Lesson 18

Connections

Put It Together

Introducing the Algorithms

An algorithm is a way to solve a problem. You have learned algorithms for adding, subtracting, multiplying, and dividing. When you add, subtract, and multiply, you work from right to left. However, when you divide, you work from left to right.

1 26 + 15 ――― 41	**Addition:** First, add the ones. Regroup. Then add the tens.	4 14 5̸4̸ − 36 ――― 18	**Subtraction:** Regroup. Subtract the ones. Subtract the tens.	1 37 × 2 ――― 74	**Multiplication:** Multiply 2 by the ones. Regroup. Multiply 2 by the tens and add the regrouped ten.

13 4)52 −4 ――― 12 −12 ――― 0	**Division:** Divide the tens by 4. Place the answer under the tens. Subtract. Carry down the tens and divide by 4 again. Subtract to find a remainder, if any.

Practicing Working Right-to-Left or Left-to-Right

Use these algorithms to solve the following problems. Remember to write the problem in vertical form first.

1. $34 + 29$

2. $59 + 21$

3. $104 + 27$

4. $65 - 47$

5. $114 - 26$

6. $23 - 17$

7. 11×6

8. 30×3

9. 13×5

10. $64 \div 4$

11. $72 \div 3$

12. $125 \div 5$

Connections

Thinking About the Algorithms: Addition and Subtraction

Addition and subtraction are often seen as inverse, or opposite, operations. They "undo" each other.

$1 + 5 = 6 \quad 6 - 5 = 1$
$10 - 3 = 7 \quad 7 + 3 = 10$

When written in vertical form, addition is worked right to left. If these operations are inverses, why is subtraction also worked right to left? Try the following subtraction problems working left to right.

1. 11 − 4	2. 54 − 9	3. 133 − 97	4. 624 − 255

5. Did you run into any problems? If so, what were they?

_____

Thinking About the Algorithms: Multiplication and Division

Multiplication and division also work as inverses.

$5 \times 7 = 35 \quad 35 \div 7 = 5$
$24 \div 6 = 4 \quad 4 \times 6 = 24$

Now try working the following long-division problems right to left. Write them in long-division format first.

6. $54 \div 3$ 7. $56 \div 8$ 8. $60 \div 5$ 9. $100 \div 4$

10. Did you run into any problems? If so, what were they?

_____

_____

 Tip The way an algorithm is set up allows you to solve a problem in the easiest way possible. Now try the long division problems again, this time working from left to right.

Unit 2, Lesson 19

Connections

Show That You Know

Read the information below. Use what you read and the basic operations (addition, subtraction, multiplication, and division) to answer the questions. Remember what you have learned in this lesson about long division. Use the space below the problems to show your work.

> Four classes are making and selling fruit baskets to raise money for charity. Each fruit basket has three oranges, three apples, and a banana. It costs $4 to make each fruit basket. The students are selling them for $10 each.

Now use what you read and the basic operations to answer the questions.

1. How much money is made on each fruit basket?

2. How much money is made on three fruit baskets? (Hint: Use addition to answer this question.)

3. On the first day, students sell eight fruit baskets. How much money do the students make on the first day?

4. The money is split equally between the four classes. How much money does each class earn the first day?

5. On the third day of the fund-raiser, students earn a total of $408 selling fruit baskets. How many fruit baskets do they sell on the third day?

Connections

Show That You Know (continued)

6. How much money does each class make on the third day of selling fruit baskets?

7. How many apples do students need to fill 68 fruit baskets?

8. Which problems did you solve working left to right? Which problems did you solve working right to left?

Review What You've Learned

9. List four situations in which you would use one of these four basic algorithms.

10. What is the most useful thing you learned in this lesson?

Review and Practice

Skills Review

Division is repeated subtraction

$12 - 4 - 4 - 4 = 0$ (subtract 4 three times)

$12 \div 4 = 3$ (divide 12 into three groups of 4)

The order in which you subtract or divide affects the result

Subtraction: Division:

$6 - 2 = 4$ $6 \div 2 = 3$

$2 - 6 \neq 4$ $2 \div 6 \neq 3$

Division rules

Zero divided by a number equals zero: $0 \div 8 = 0$

Any number divided by 1 equals the number: $18 \div 1 = 18$

Multiplication and division are inverse operations

$3 \times 4 = 12$, so $12 \div 4 = 3$

Also, $4 \times 3 = 12$, so $12 \div 3 = 4$

Table

Students' Favorite Types of Movies

Movie Type	Number of Students
Mystery	4
Action	8
Comedy	5
Drama	3

Bar graph

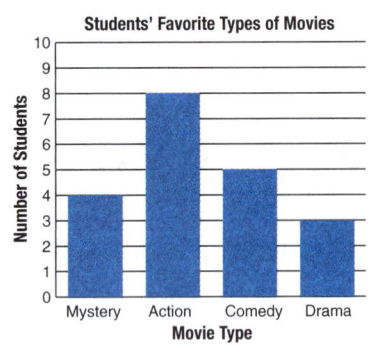

Pictograph

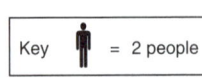

Strategy Review

- Division problems can be solved through jumps on a number line and drawing to show partitioning and sharing.

- Breaking down a large problem into a simpler form of the problem can make it easier to solve.

Review and Practice

Skills and Strategies Practice

Complete the exercises below.

1. $8 - 2 - 2 - 2 - 2 =$ _____
2. $8 \div 2 =$ _____
3. $2 \div 8 =$ _____

4. $1 \div 0 =$ _____
5. $0 \div 4 =$ _____
6. $5 \div 1 =$ _____

7. $6 + 6 + 6 =$ _____
8. $6 \times 3 =$ _____
9. $18 - 6 - 6 - 6 =$ _____
10. $18 \div 3 =$ _____

11. $5 \times 4 =$ _____
12. $20 \div 5 =$ _____
13. $20 \div 4 =$ _____
14. $4 \times 5 =$ _____

15. Look at the bar graph.

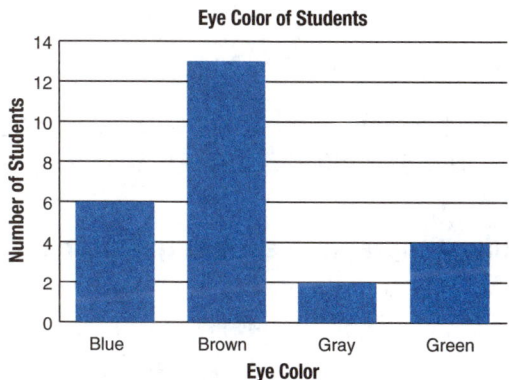

How many more students have brown eyes than blue eyes? _____

Test-Taking tip: Prepare for a test by making a set of flash cards. Write a word or phrase on the front of each card. Write the definition on the back. Use the flash cards in a game to test your knowledge.

Unit 2, Lesson 20

Review and Practice

Unit Review

Circle the letter of the correct answer.

1. Find the quotient of 15 ÷ 3.

    A. 3   B. 5   C. 15   D. 20

2. How many jumps of eight on a number line would get you from 40 to zero?

    A. 2   B. 3   C. 4   D. 5

3. How many equal groups of four are in 16?

    A. 2   B. 3   C. 4   D. 5

4. The inverse of 4 × 5 = 20 is _____.

    A. 4 + 5 = 9   C. 20 ÷ 5 = 4
    B. 20 × 5 = 100   D. 20 − 4 = 16

Use the pictograph to answer questions 5 and 6.

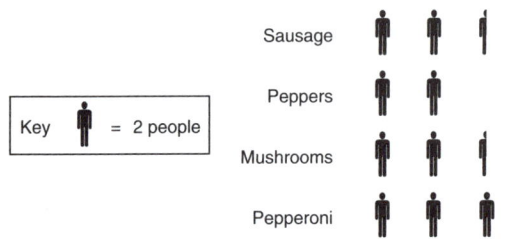

5. Did more men or more women like peppers on their pizza?

    A. men
    B. women
    C. both
    D. cannot tell from the pictograph

6. What is the range of the data?

    A. 2   B. 3   C. 4   D. 5

7. What is the quotient of 6 ÷ 0?

    A. 0   C. 6
    B. 1   D. not possible

8. The inverse of multiplication is _____.

    A. addition   C. multiplication
    B. subtraction   D. division

9. The inverse of addition is _____.

    A. division   C. subtraction
    B. multiplication D. addition

10. What is the inverse of 40 ÷ 10 = 4?

    A. 40 − 4 = 10   C. 40 − 10 = 30
    B. 4 × 10 = 40   D. 10 + 4 = 14

11. A table was made to record students' favorite fruits. If six students liked apples the best, four liked pears, and three liked bananas, how many more students liked apples than bananas?

    A. 3   B. 4   C. 6   D. 9

12. In the table described in question 11, what is the total number of students?

    A. 3   B. 6   C. 9   D. 13

Use this bar graph to answer questions 13–17.

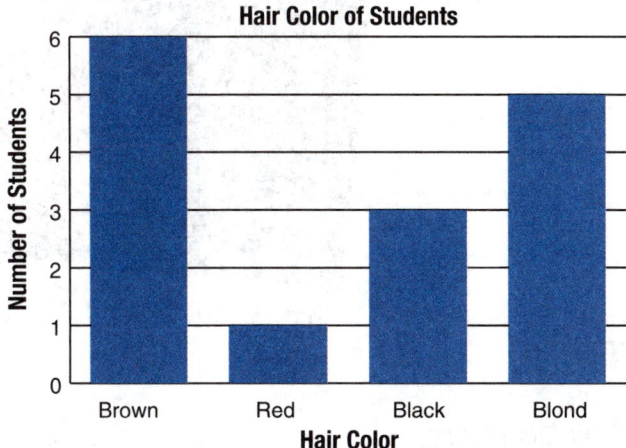

13. How many students have black or brown hair?

    A. 3   C. 9
    B. 6   D. 15

14. What is the total number of students in the class?

    A. 3   C. 12
    B. 9   D. 15

15. How many students have red hair?

    A. 1   C. 5
    B. 3   D. 6

16. How many more students have brown hair than blond hair?

    A. 1   C. 5
    B. 3   D. 6

17. What is the total number of students who do not have blond hair?

    A. 15   C. 4
    B. 10   D. 0

18. Which number sentence is true?

    A. $8 \times 4 = 4 \times 8$
    B. $8 \div 4 = 4 \div 8$
    C. $8 - 4 = 4 - 8$
    D. $8 \times 4 =$ not possible

19. What is $58 \div 1$?

    A. 0   C. 58
    B. 1   D. 85

20. What is $0 \div 58$?

    A. 0   C. 58
    B. 1   D. not possible

21. What is the divisor in $10 \div 2 = 5$?

    A. 10   C. 1
    B. 5   D. 2

22. What is $81 \div 9$?

    A. 81   C. 9
    B. 11   D. 8

23. To model $20 \div 4$, you subtract _____ a total of _____ times to get to 0.

    A. 20, 20   C. 4, 5
    B. 4, 20   D. 5, 5

24. What is the dividend in $24 \div 4 = 6$?

    A. 4   B. 6   C. 24   D. 28

25. What is the inverse of $3 \times 4 = 12$?

    A. $4 \times 3 = 12$ C. $4 + 4 + 4 = 12$
    B. $12 \div 4 = 3$ D. $4 \div 3 = 12$

Unit 2 Reflection

MATH SKILLS

The easiest part about multiplying and dividing is

Multiplication and division are inverse operations because

Food for Thought

MATH STRATEGIES & CONNECTIONS

For me, the math strategies that work the best are

The algorithms are useful because

READING STRATEGIES & COMPREHENSION

The easiest part about summarizing is

One way that summarizing helps me with reading is

The vocabulary words I had trouble with are

INDEPENDENT READING

My favorite part of Food for Thought is

I read most fluently when

UNIT 3
Fractions

MATH SKILLS & STRATEGIES
After you learn the basic **SKILLS**, the real test is knowing when to use each **STRATEGY**.

AMP LINK MAGAZINE
You Do the Math and Math Projects: After you read each magazine article, apply what you know in real-world problems.
Fluency: Make your reading smooth and accurate, one tip at a time.

READING STRATEGY
Learn why Questioning helps you understand what you read.

VOCABULARY
MATH WORDS:
Know them!
Use them!
Learn all about them!

CONNECTIONS
You own the math when you make your own connections.

Reading Comprehension Strategy: Questioning

How to Question

Goal Setting	Question Words	Between the Lines	Beyond the Text
Ask, *What is my reason for reading this text?*	Ask, *What important details can I find in the text?*	Ask, *What decisions can I make about the facts and details in the text?*	Ask, *What connections can I make between the text and my life?*

Asking questions helps you get the most out of what you are reading. Questions such as *What do I think this article is about?* and *What will I learn?* will help you set a goal before you read. Once you have set that goal, you are more likely to remember and understand what you read. Look quickly at the text. Scan for titles, headings, pictures, captions, and boldfaced words. Ask a goal-setting question.

Movie Music

Have you ever watched a scary scene in a movie with the sound turned down? Was it as scary without the music? Even when you are not paying attention to the music during a movie, it can have a big effect on your emotions.

Is this house as scary without the music?

1. What clues will help you ask a good goal-setting question?
_____
_____
_____

Write a goal-setting question below.
_____
_____
_____

Check as you read to make sure the text is answering your question. You may have to change the question.

The earliest movies did not include recorded music or even the actors' voices. These films are sometimes called "silent movies," but this term can be misleading. When theaters showed these films, a musician usually sat in the theater and played an organ or piano along with the movie. They would play upbeat music when the movie's hero was on the screen, and scary or gloomy music for the villain. This helped the audience understand what was happening.

2. Was your goal-setting question answered?
_____
_____

If you need to change your question, write the new question below.
_____
_____
_____

Asking questions about the details helps you remember what you are reading. When reading about people, ask *"Who?"* If something important happened, ask *"What?"*, *"Where?"*, *"When?"*, *"Why?"*, and *"How?"*

Reading Comprehension Strategy

Movie music today is often used in the same way as it was during the silent movie era. A director might ask a composer to create music that sets the mood for a scene or to help the audience understand the plot. If evil-sounding music is playing while a character talks, you can bet he or she is up to no good.

3. What question is answered by details in the passage?
   _____
   _____

While reading, you may think of a question to ask. Using sticky notes can help. Write your question on one and then stick it on the page where you will find the answer. Then you can go back and review all of them after reading the article.

One of the most famous movie composers of all time is John Williams. He composed the music for blockbuster movies like *E.T. The Extra-Terrestrial*, *Jurassic Park*, and all of the Indiana Jones and Star Wars movies. The music for many of these movies is so memorable, you can probably hum or whistle one of them right now.

4. Write two questions you might ask yourself while reading this passage. Then underline the answers in the text.
   _____
   _____
   _____

Sometimes, you may not find the answer to a question in the text. Instead, you have to think about what you are reading. This kind of questioning is called "reading between the lines." How can you decide on good "between the lines" questions? You put together information found in different places in the text. Why did the author include that information? What is the author trying to say? Then put this information together with what you already know about the topic.

Music is such an important part of movies that two Academy Awards® are given out each year for music. The first award is for the best original song. The second award is for the best original film score. The next time you watch a movie, try to pay attention the music. How does it make you feel?

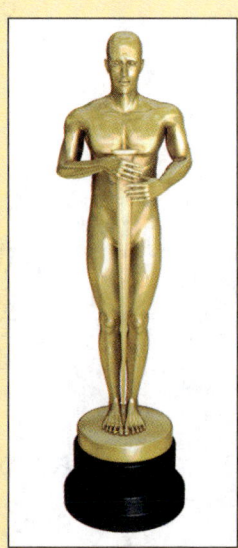

5. Write a "between the lines" question for this paragraph.
   _____

6. What do you already know about movies or music that could help you answer your question?
   _____
   _____

7. Write the answer to your "between the lines" question below.
   _____
   _____

8. How might questioning help you answer a math problem?
   _____

9. What part of using questioning while reading do you have the most difficulty with?
   _____
   _____

Use the Strategies

Use the reading comprehension strategies you have learned to answer questions about the article below.

Buying Locally

When you shop at your local supermarket, stop and think about where all the fruits and vegetables come from. Behind every food item on the shelves is a story about transportation.

Both Florida and California are famous for producing oranges. However, California oranges are often found in Florida supermarkets. This is because 96 percent of Florida oranges are used to make juice. In whatever form, both Florida and California oranges are shipped to every state and travel an average of 2,126 miles.

Not all oranges in your local supermarket are grown in the United States. One leading exporter of oranges is Brazil. The produce on your supermarket shelves may come from all over the world. But how does a Brazilian—or Californian—orange make its way to you?

Oranges are shipped in refrigerators by truck, plane, or train. It takes a lot of fuel to transport the food. Sending food all over the world may make some foods more available. However, the effects on the environment, such as pollution, are a high price to pay.

Some people try to only eat food grown within 200 miles of where they live. They want to support local farmers and save on the energy needed to transport the fruits and vegetables. Buying local also ensures that you are getting the freshest food possible. The next time you shop, try to buy fruits and vegetables that are grown closest to your home. Your taste buds will thank you for it.

1. Read the title and the first sentence of the article. Then write a goal-setting question for this reading.
   _____

2. Write a question about the information in the second paragraph. Then underline the answer.
   _____
   _____

3. Write one or two sentences to summarize where supermarket oranges come from.
   _____
   _____
   _____
   _____

4. What is the main idea of the fourth paragraph?
   _____
   _____

5. Write a "between the lines" question for the last paragraph. Then use what you already know about the topic and the text to write an answer.
   _____
   _____
   _____
   _____

Use the Strategies

Reading Comprehension Strategies: Summarizing, Questioning

Use the reading comprehension strategies you have learned in this and the previous units to answer the questions below.

1. Summarize the reasons why some people are trying to eat only food from near where they live.
   _____
   _____

2. Do you think it is important to eat just the foods that are grown close to home? Why or why not?
   _____
   _____

Problem-Solving Strategies: Draw a Picture or Use a Model, Find a Pattern

Use these problem-solving strategies to answer the questions below.

Imagine you work in a supermarket. You have been asked to make a display of stacked cans. There will always be one can in the top row. The cans will follow the pattern shown to the right.

3. Look at the picture of the cans. Use the Find a Pattern strategy to write a rule for the stacks.
   _____
   _____

4. Draw a picture to continue the pattern. Use your drawing to find the total number of cans needed to stack the cans six rows high.
   _____

5. How many cans will be in the bottom row if the cans are stacked five rows high?
   _____
   _____

6. How many cans high will the display be when there are 10 cans in the bottom row? Explain.
   _____
   _____
   _____

Unit 3   103

Learn the Skill

Proper Fractions

Learn the SKILL

At restaurants, many foods can be divided into equal servings. Caroline's family ordered one pizza. The pizza was served in 10 equal slices. She ate three slices. How can you show how much of the pizza Caroline ate?

VOCABULARY

Watch for the words you are learning about.

denominator: the bottom number in a fraction; shows the number of equal parts the whole is divided into

fraction: a part of a whole

numerator: the top number in a fraction; shows the number of parts in the fraction

proper fraction: a fraction with a numerator that is less than the denominator

SKILL	EXAMPLE	COMPLETE THE EXAMPLE
A **fraction** is used to show a part of a whole. The fraction is written as the number of parts over the total number of equal parts in the whole. A fraction bar separates the part from the whole.	Write the fraction. 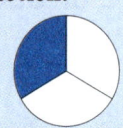 Parts that are blue: 1 Total number of equal parts: 3 The fraction is written as $\frac{1}{3}$.	Write the fraction. 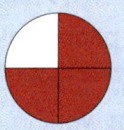 Parts that are red: _____ Total number of equal parts: _____ Fraction: _____
In a fraction, the number on top of the fraction bar is called the **numerator**. The number below the fraction bar is called the **denominator**. To draw a fraction, first use the denominator to determine how many equal parts to divide the whole into. Then use the numerator to determine how many parts to fill in.	Use the numerator and denominator to draw a picture of what the fraction might show. $\frac{1}{2}$ The denominator is 2. The whole is divided into two equal parts. The numerator is 1. One of the parts is shaded green. 	Use the numerator and denominator to draw a picture of what the fraction might show. $\frac{3}{7}$ The numerator is _____. The denominator is _____. Draw and label a picture this fraction might show.
In a **proper fraction,** the numerator is less than the denominator. A proper fraction always represents less than one whole.	Caroline's family ordered a pizza cut into 10 equal slices. Caroline ate three slices. Therefore, Caroline ate $\frac{3}{10}$ of the pizza. Check: 3 is less than 10, so $\frac{3}{10}$ is a proper fraction.	Suppose Caroline's family ordered a pan of lasagna, cut into eight equal pieces. Caroline ate one piece. Write a fraction to show how much of the lasagna she ate. Is your answer a proper fraction? _____ _____

YOUR TURN

Choose the Right Word

> denominator fraction numerator
> proper fraction

Fill in each blank with the correct word or phrase from the box.

1. A _____ shows part of a whole.

2. The _____ is the bottom part of the fraction.

3. In a _____, the numerator is less than the denominator.

4. The _____ is the top part of the fraction.

Learn the Skill

Yes or No?

Answer these questions and be ready to explain your answers.

5. In the fraction $\frac{3}{5}$, is 5 the denominator? _____

6. Does the numerator show how many parts something is divided into? _____

7. Is the numerator ever greater than the denominator in a proper fraction? _____

8. Is $\frac{1}{10}$ a proper fraction? _____

Show That You Know

State whether the fraction is a proper fraction or not a proper fraction.

9. $\frac{5}{7}$

10. $\frac{7}{5}$

11. $\frac{5}{5}$

12. $\frac{3}{2}$

Draw a picture to show each fraction.

13. $\frac{7}{9}$

14. $\frac{3}{5}$

15. $\frac{3}{8}$

Unit 3, Lesson 1   105

Learn the Skill

SOLVE on Your Own

Skills Practice

Okay, now you know all about fractions. Show it by completing these exercises.

Identify the numerator and denominator of each fraction. Fill in each blank with "numerator" or "denominator."

1. $\frac{7}{11}$ Seven is the _____, and 11 is the _____.

2. $\frac{2}{5}$ Five is the _____, and two is the _____.

3. $\frac{1}{18}$ Eighteen is the _____, and one is the _____.

4. $\frac{5}{6}$ Five is the _____, and six is the _____.

5. $\frac{3}{4}$ Four is the _____, and three is the _____.

Draw a picture showing each fraction.

6. $\frac{7}{11}$

7. $\frac{5}{8}$

8. $\frac{1}{3}$

9. $\frac{1}{2}$

10. $\frac{3}{4}$

Are the fractions proper fractions? Write yes or no.

11. $\frac{7}{5}$ _____

12. $\frac{5}{18}$ _____

13. $\frac{1}{79}$ _____

14. $\frac{3}{3}$ _____

15. $\frac{1}{2}$ _____

Proper Fractions

Strategy

Draw a Picture or Use a Model

Step 1: Read Mariah bought four new shirts. Three of the shirts are blue. What fraction of Mariah's new shirts are blue? What fraction of these shirts are not blue?

STRATEGY	SOLUTION
Draw a Picture or Use a Model Fractions are sometimes used to describe part of a set of objects. You can model this type of fraction by drawing a rectangle or circle to represent the whole set. Divide the shape into equal parts to show the total number of objects in the set. Then shade or color the number of parts the fraction describes.	**Step 2: Plan** Draw a rectangle and then divide it into equal parts to represent the total number of shirts. Shade or color some of the parts to show the number of blue shirts. Then use the model to find the fraction of the shirts that are blue and the fraction of the shirts that are not blue. **Step 3: Solve** Mariah bought four shirts in all. So, draw a rectangle and divide it into four equal parts. 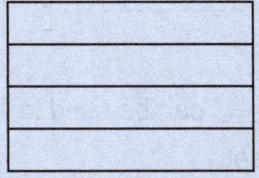 Shade or color three of the parts to show the number of shirts that are blue. 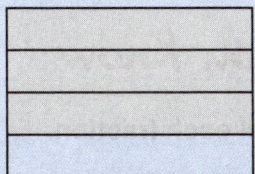 The numerator = the number of shaded parts = 3. The denominator = the total number of equal parts = 4. Therefore, $\frac{3}{4}$ of the shirts are blue. One out of the four parts is not shaded. Therefore, $\frac{1}{4}$ of the shirts are not blue. **Step 4: Check** Use subtraction to check your answer. 4 shirts − 3 blue shirts = 1 shirt that is not blue So, one out of four shirts, or $\frac{1}{4}$ of the shirts, are not blue.

Choose a Strategy

Choose a Strategy

YOUR TURN

Choose the Right Word

> denominator   fraction
> numerator   proper fraction

Fill in each blank with the correct word or phrase from the box.

1. $\frac{3}{7}$ is a _____, but $\frac{7}{3}$ is not.

2. The total number of equal parts is the _____ of the fraction.

3. The number of parts shaded in a model can show the _____ of the fraction.

4. A _____ can be used to describe part of a set.

Yes or No?

Answer these questions and be ready to explain your answers.

5. In a model of a fraction, do all the parts need to be drawn the same size? _____

6. Does the numerator of a proper fraction tell you how many equal parts there are in a shape? _____

7. Does the denominator stay the same, no matter how many of the parts you shade? _____

8. If all of the parts of a model are shaded, does the model show a proper fraction? _____

Show That You Know

Draw a picture to model each fraction.

9. $\frac{2}{3}$

10. $\frac{5}{8}$

11. $\frac{3}{5}$

Solve each problem. Use the Draw a Picture or Use a Model strategy to help.

12. Roberto has read five of the seven books on his summer reading list. What fraction of the books list has Roberto read?

13. Trisha answered seven questions correctly on a quiz. If the quiz had eight questions in all, what fraction of the questions did she answer correctly?

READ on Your Own

Reading Comprehension

Reading Comprehension Strategy: Questioning

Sound Bites, pages 3–4

VOCABULARY

Watch for the words you are learning about.

pitch: the highness or lowness of a sound

Fluency Tip

Keep a list of the fluency tips that work best for you. As you improve your fluency, you will also improve your understanding of what you read.

Before You Read

What do you know about how sounds are made? What different ways can musicians make music with their instruments?

As You Read

To preview, look at headings, pictures, captions, and boldfaced words.

Preview "Sources of Sound," pages 3–4. **Read "Sources of Sound," pages 3–4.**

Write a goal-setting question in the chart below.   Answer your question in the chart below.

Sources of Sound	
Goal-setting question	Answer
_____	_____
_____	_____
_____	_____

After You Read

Think about a musical instrument that you have played. How did you make the sound?

_____
_____
_____

Unit 3, Lesson 2   109

Problem Solving

SOLVE on Your Own

Sound Bites, page 5

Organize the Information

Read You Do the Math in the magazine. Then find a picture of a piano keyboard. Shade in the number of black keys in each group of 12 keys.

You Do the Math

Drawing a picture or using a model may help you answer the magazine questions.

Use the information in the drawing above to answer these questions. Write your answers in the space provided.

1. What do the shaded and total number of sections on the fraction model above represent?

   _____
   _____

2. How many keys would you expect to be black on a keyboard with 88 keys? Explain your answer.

   _____
   _____
   _____

3. How would you determine exactly what fraction of the keys are black?

   _____
   _____

After You Solve

Think of another instrument you can describe using a fraction. Write the fraction and what it represents.

_____
_____

Improper Fractions and Mixed Numbers

Learn the SKILL

Andre bought a bag full of oranges to share with his friends. He sliced each orange into four equal pieces. If Andre ate seven pieces, how many oranges did he eat?

VOCABULARY

Watch for the words you are learning about.

improper fraction: a fraction with a numerator that is greater than or equal to its denominator

mixed number: a whole number and a proper fraction together

SKILL	EXAMPLE	COMPLETE THE EXAMPLE
An **improper fraction** is a fraction with a numerator that is greater than or equal to the denominator. Improper fractions describe amounts equal to or greater than one whole.	Each orange has four equal parts. So four pieces, or $\frac{4}{4}$, equals one whole orange. Andre ate seven pieces, which is greater than one whole orange. 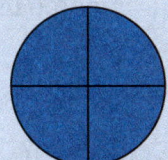 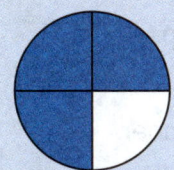 Write the number of parts for the numerator and the number of parts for the denominator: Andre ate $\frac{7}{4}$ oranges.	Suppose five laps around your school track is one mile. If you ran eight laps around the track, how could you write the number of miles you ran as an improper fraction? _____
A **mixed number** is a whole number and a proper fraction together. You can change an improper fraction into a mixed number by finding how many whole sets are in each improper fraction. The part left over is the fractional part.	Look at the model of $\frac{7}{4}$ above. The first four slices equal one whole orange. This leaves three slices left over because $7 - 4 = 3$. Write the whole number and then the part left over as a fraction: Andre ate $1\frac{3}{4}$ oranges.	Change $\frac{7}{3}$ into a mixed number. _____
Change a mixed number into an improper fraction by multiplying the denominator by the whole number. Add the product to the original numerator, and then put the total over the denominator.	Multiply the whole number by the denominator: $1 \times 4 = 4$. Add this product to the original numerator: $3 + 4 = 7$. Use this number for the numerator, along with the original denominator, to write the improper fraction: $\frac{7}{4} = 1\frac{3}{4}$.	Change $2\frac{1}{5}$ into an improper fraction. _____

Unit 3, Lesson 3

Learn the Skill

YOUR TURN

Choose the Right Word

> denominator   improper fraction
> numerator   proper fraction

Fill in each blank with the correct word or phrase from the box.

1. In an improper fraction, the _____ is equal to or greater than the denominator.

2. The denominator is greater than the numerator in a(n) _____.

3. To turn a mixed number into an improper fraction, first multiply the _____ by the whole number.

4. The denominator is less than or equal to the numerator in a(n) _____.

Yes or No?

Answer these questions and be ready to explain your answers.

5. Does the fraction $\frac{5}{5}$ equal one whole? _____

6. Can a proper fraction be expressed as a mixed number? _____

7. Can the numerator be greater than the denominator in the fractional part of a mixed number? _____

8. A game uses eight pieces and Marcy has 10 game pieces. Can the number of sets she has be expressed as an improper fraction? _____

Show That You Know

Write each improper fraction as a mixed number.

9. $\frac{3}{2}$

10. $\frac{9}{4}$

11. $\frac{8}{5}$

Write each mixed number as an improper fraction.

12. $3\frac{1}{2}$

13. $1\frac{3}{4}$

14. $10\frac{2}{3}$

SOLVE on Your Own

Skills Practice

Write an improper fraction to answer each problem.

1. Randy buys stamps in books of 10. If he uses 17 stamps, what fraction shows the number of books of stamps he used? _____

2. Each carton has 12 eggs. Mindy has 17 eggs. What fraction shows the number of cartons of eggs she has? _____

3. Luis's vacation lasted for 12 days. What fraction shows the number of weeks he was on vacation? _____

Write each improper fraction as a mixed number or whole number. Show your work.

4. $\frac{5}{2}$ _____

5. $\frac{11}{7}$ _____

6. $\frac{19}{9}$ _____

7. $\frac{12}{4}$ _____

> Remember, in an improper fraction the numerator is equal to or greater than the denominator.

Write each mixed number as an improper fraction. Show your work.

8. $3\frac{1}{4}$ _____

9. $5\frac{2}{5}$ _____

10. $3\frac{6}{7}$ _____

11. $2\frac{11}{12}$ _____

12. $4\frac{2}{11}$ _____

13. $1\frac{99}{100}$ _____

14. $3\frac{4}{15}$ _____

Choose a Strategy

Improper Fractions and Mixed Numbers

Strategies
Make a Table or a Chart, Draw a Picture or Use a Model

Step 1: Read The guests at Teresa's birthday party ate 35 pieces of lasagna in all. The pans of lasagna were all the same size. Each whole pan of lasagna was cut into eight equal pieces. What mixed number shows the number of pans of lasagna the guests ate?

STRATEGY	SOLUTION

Make a Table or a Chart

You can use a table to help you change an improper fraction into a mixed number. Make a table to display the number of parts equal to each whole number. Then use the table to find the number of whole sets in the improper fraction. Subtract the number of pieces in the whole sets to find the fractional part of the mixed number.

Step 2: Plan Write the number of pans the guests ate as an improper fraction. Use a table to find how many whole pans are in the fraction.

Step 3: Solve Make the table by increasing the number of pieces by eight for each whole pan.

Number of Pans of Lasagna	1	2	3	4	5	6
Number of Pieces	8	16	24	32	40	48

Use the table to find the number of whole pans in $\frac{35}{8}$. $32 < 35 < 40$, so there are four whole pans. 35 is three more pieces than four pans (35 pieces − 32 pieces = 3 pieces).

Therefore, $\frac{35}{8}$ pans = 4 whole pans + 3 pieces = $4\frac{3}{8}$ pans.

Step 4: Check Change $4\frac{3}{8}$ to an improper fraction: $4 \times 8 = 32$; $32 + 3 = 35$. $4\frac{3}{8}$ pans of lasagna = $\frac{35}{8}$ pans of lasagna

Draw a Picture or Use a Model

You can solve many fraction problems by drawing pictures to model the fractions.

Step 2: Plan Draw pictures of pans of lasagna divided into eight equal pieces. Shade the pieces, counting up until you reach 35 pieces.

Step 3: Solve

There were $4\frac{3}{8}$ pans of lasagna eaten.

Step 4: Check Write an addition expression to show your model: $8 + 8 + 8 + 8 + 3 = 35$. Four whole pans, plus three additional pieces, equals 35 total pieces.

YOUR TURN

Choose the Right Word

> denominator   improper fraction
> mixed number   numerator

Fill in each blank with the correct word or phrase from the box.

1. A number that has a whole number part and a fractional part is a(n) _____.

2. In the fraction $\frac{8}{3}$, the _____ is 8.

3. A fraction with a numerator greater than the denominator is a(n) _____.

4. The _____ shows the total number of parts equal to one whole.

Yes or No?

Answer these questions and be ready to explain your answers.

5. Can a mixed number be less than one whole? _____

6. If you changed $\frac{7}{3}$ into a mixed number, would the fractional part be $\frac{2}{3}$? _____

7. Can a proper fraction be changed to a mixed number? _____

8. Is the mixed number $3\frac{2}{5}$ equal to the improper fraction $\frac{17}{5}$? _____

Show That You Know

Lien needs 29 batteries. The store sells batteries in packs of six.

9. Write the number of packs Lien needs as an improper fraction.

10. Complete the table to show the total batteries for each whole pack.

Packs	1	2		4	5	
Batteries	6		18			

11. Write the number of packs Lien needs as a mixed number.

Solve each problem below. Write your answer as an improper fraction and as a mixed number.

12. A gym class with 41 students was divided into teams. How many teams of 12 people could be made?

13. There were 37 people in the audience at the school orchestra's concert. Each row of the theater had 10 seats. How many rows of people were there in the concert audience?

Unit 3, Lesson 4   115

Reading Comprehension

READ on Your Own

Reading Comprehension Strategy: Questioning

Sound Bites, *pages 6–7*

Before You Read

Think back to what you read in "Sources of Sound." How do musical instruments produce sound?

As You Read

As you read "Hundreds of Times a Second," think about what the author is saying and the words the author uses. Ask yourself questions like "Why is the author providing this information?" and "Why did the author choose to use these words?"

Read "Hundreds of Times a Second," pages 6–7. 🛑

Write a "between the lines" question below. Then write the answer.

Hundreds of Times a Second
"Between the lines" question:
_____
_____
Answer:
_____
_____

After You Read

Which would you rather learn to play, a string instrument such as a violin or a wind instrument such as a flute? Why?

_____

_____

VOCABULARY

Watch for the words you are learning about.

frequency: the number of vibrations per second

hertz (Hz): one vibration or cycle per second

overtones: frequencies produced along with the main note

Fluency Tip

Be careful to read every word without skipping or substituting words. If a sentence or paragraph does not make sense, reread every word.

Problem Solving

SOLVE on Your Own

Sound Bites, page 8

Organize the Information

Read You Do the Math in the magazine. Then complete the following table using what you learn.

Frequency	Cycles per Second (Hz)	Length of Time for One Cycle
1 Hz	1	1 second
	16	
32 Hz		
		$\frac{1}{512}$ second
	2,048	
8,192 Hz		
	16,000	

Organizing frequency information will help you answer the magazine questions.

You Do the Math

Use the information in the table above to answer these questions. Write your answers in the space provided.

1. List your sounds in order from lowest pitch to highest pitch. What did you base this order on?

   _____
   _____

2. Do the low-pitched sounds or high-pitched sounds on your list take longer to complete one cycle? Explain your answer.

   _____
   _____

After You Solve

Have you ever heard high-pitched or low-pitched sounds that other people could not hear? Explain.

_____
_____

Application

The Four-Step Problem-Solving Plan

Step 1: Read	Step 2: Plan	Step 3: Solve	Step 4: Check
Make sure you understand what the problem is asking.	Decide how you will solve the problem.	Solve the problem using your plan.	Check to make sure your answer is correct.

Read the article below. Then answer the questions.

Length of a Note

Most people know that the symbols written on sheet music tell the musician which notes to play. Did you know that they also tell the musician how long to play, or sustain, each note?

Each type of note shown should be played for a specific amount of time compared to the other notes. A half note should be played for half ($\frac{1}{2}$) the time that the whole note is played. This means that you can play two half notes in the same time it takes you to play one whole note. A quarter note should be played for a quarter ($\frac{1}{4}$) of the time that the whole note is played. This means that the time it takes to play four quarter notes is equal to the time it takes to play one whole note.

1. What are two things reading music can tell a musician?

   _____

   _____

   _____

2. How can you write the time it takes to play three quarter notes as a fraction of the time it takes to play one whole note?

   _____

   _____

3. Natalie and Eric are playing their violins together. If Natalie plays nine half notes, how many whole notes can Eric play in the same time? Write your answer as an improper fraction.

   _____

118   Unit 3, Lesson 5

YOUR TURN

Application

Read the article below. Then answer the questions.

Metronomes

If you play the piano, you probably have a metronome. A metronome is a small device that makes a constant ticking noise. You can set a metronome so that the time between ticks is long or short. These ticks keep musicians from speeding up or slowing down as they play. This is called keeping a steady beat or tempo.

When using a metronome, musicians need to know what time signature the music is written in. This is because the time signature tells the musician how many ticks of the metronome, or beats, each type of note should be played for. For example, in the common time signature, each whole note should be played for four beats. Remember that a half note lasts half as long as a whole note. This means that a half note should only last two beats. You can see how using a metronome can help a musician play each note for exactly the right length of time.

Fluency Tip
Reread difficult paragraphs as if you were telling the information to a friend.

1. What is a metronome? What is it used for?

   _____
   _____
   _____
   _____

2. Why must musicians know the time signature of the music they are playing?

   _____
   _____
   _____

3. In the common time signature, how many whole notes can be played in 15 ticks or beats? Write the answer as a mixed number.

   _____

Unit 3, Lesson 5

Reading Comprehension

READ on Your Own

Reading Comprehension Strategy: Questioning

Sound Bites, pages 9–11

VOCABULARY

Watch for the words you are learning about.

chord: three or more notes that are played together

consonance: an agreeable combination of sounds

dissonance: a disagreeable combination of sounds

octave: the interval between two musical notes, where one note has half or twice the frequency of the other

Fluency Tip

Pay attention to punctuation marks. Punctuation marks tell you when to pause and when to raise your voice for a question or an exclamation.

Before You Read

Think back to what you read in "Hundreds of Times a Second." Can you imagine something vibrating hundreds of times each second? What might make this easier to imagine?

As You Read

Preview pages 9–11 of "Consonance and Dissonance."

In the first column of the chart, write a question that comes to mind as you read the page.

Carefully read pages 9–11 of "Consonance and Dissonance."

In the second column of the chart, write the answers you found in the reading. Some questions may not have an answer in the reading.

What Will I Learn?	Answers I Found in the Reading
_____	_____
_____	_____
_____	_____
_____	_____

After You Read

How does dissonance in music make you feel? Explain your answer.

_____
_____
_____

SOLVE on Your Own

Sound Bites, page 12

Organize the Information

Read the Math Project in the magazine. Then complete the table below.

Frequency	Divide by 2	Divide by 3	Divide by 4	Divide by 5	Divide by 6	Divide by 8	Divide by 9	Divide by 15
D—294	147	98	X	X	49	X	X	X
D♯/E♭—311								
E—330								
F—349								
F♯/G♭—370								
G—392								
G♯/A♭—415								
A—440								
A♯/B♭—466								
B—495								

Math Project

Use the information in the table above to answer these questions. Write your answers in the space provided.

1. What consonant pairs did you find? List each pair with the improper fractions you used to find them.

If the frequency does not divide evenly, put an X in the box.

2. What dissonant pair did you find? List the improper fraction you used to find it.

After You Solve

If you checked your work using a piano, how did what you hear compare to your calculations?

Learn the Skill

Comparing Fractions

Learn the SKILL

Anton and Beth both brought their digital cameras to camp. Each camera uses the same type of memory card. Each memory card can hold the same number of pictures. On the first day of camp, Anton filled $\frac{3}{5}$ of a memory card and Beth filled $\frac{2}{5}$ of a memory card. On the second day, Anton filled $2\frac{3}{4}$ memory cards and Beth filled $5\frac{1}{4}$. On the last day, Anton filled $1\frac{2}{3}$ memory cards and Beth filled $1\frac{1}{3}$ memory cards. Who took the greater number of pictures on each of the three days?

SKILL	EXAMPLE	WRITE AN EXAMPLE
When comparing fractions with the same denominator, the fraction with the greater numerator is greater.	To compare $\frac{3}{5}$ and $\frac{2}{5}$, first check that the denominators are the same: the denominator for both fractions is five. Then compare the numerators: three is greater than two, so $\frac{3}{5}$ is greater than $\frac{2}{5}$. $\frac{3}{5} > \frac{2}{5}$	Write two fractions with the same denominator and compare them using the greater than (>) or less than (<) symbols. _____
When comparing mixed numbers, first compare the whole numbers. If one whole number is greater than the other, then that mixed number is greater than the other.	To compare $2\frac{3}{4}$ and $5\frac{1}{4}$, first compare the whole numbers. Two is less than five, so $2\frac{3}{4}$ is less than $5\frac{1}{4}$. $2\frac{3}{4} < 5\frac{1}{4}$	Compare two mixed numbers using the greater than (>) or less than (<) symbols. _____
If the whole numbers are the same in both mixed numbers, compare the fractional part. Remember, if two fractions have the same denominator, compare the numerators to find which fraction is greater.	The mixed numbers $1\frac{1}{3}$ and $1\frac{2}{3}$ both have the same whole number, 1. To compare the fractional parts, first check that the denominators are the same: the denominator for both fractional parts is 3. Then compare the numerators: 2 is greater than 1, so $\frac{2}{3}$ is greater than $\frac{1}{3}$. $\frac{2}{3} > \frac{1}{3}$ Therefore, $1\frac{2}{3}$ is greater than $1\frac{1}{3}$.	Write two mixed numbers with the same whole number part and the same denominators in their fractional parts. Compare the numbers using the greater than (>) or less than (<) symbols. _____

YOUR TURN

Learn the Skill

Choose the Right Word

fraction   mixed number   whole number

Fill in each blank with the correct word or phrase from the box.

1. The _____ in $4\frac{2}{7}$ is 4.
2. A _____ describes part of a whole.
3. Three and a half sandwiches can be written as a _____.

Yes or No?

Answer these questions and be ready to explain your answers.

4. When comparing mixed numbers, if the whole numbers are the same, do the fractions have to be compared? _____
5. If the denominators are equal, can you compare two fractions by finding the one with the greater numerator? _____
6. If a mixed number has a greater fractional part than another mixed number, is it always the greater of the two numbers? _____
7. Do the fractional parts have to be compared if the whole numbers are different? _____

Show That You Know

Compare. Write > or <.

8. $\frac{5}{6}$ ___ $\frac{1}{6}$

9. $\frac{13}{18}$ ___ $\frac{17}{18}$

10. $5\frac{1}{4}$ ___ $9\frac{3}{4}$

11. $6\frac{5}{6}$ ___ $6\frac{1}{6}$

12. $7\frac{1}{3}$ ___ $\frac{4}{3}$

13. $4\frac{2}{7}$ ___ $4\frac{3}{7}$

14. $12\frac{1}{12}$ ___ $11\frac{11}{12}$

15. $4\frac{3}{10}$ ___ $4\frac{9}{10}$

16. $2\frac{1}{3}$ ___ $3\frac{2}{3}$

17. $21\frac{1}{2}$ ___ $12\frac{1}{2}$

Unit 3, Lesson 6

Learn the Skill

SOLVE on Your Own

Skills Practice

When comparing mixed numbers, if the whole number parts are the same, you need to compare the fraction parts.

Compare. Write > or <.

1. $\dfrac{4}{5}$ ___ $\dfrac{2}{5}$

2. $\dfrac{7}{8}$ ___ $\dfrac{9}{8}$

3. $\dfrac{3}{7}$ ___ $\dfrac{5}{7}$

4. $\dfrac{7}{7}$ ___ $\dfrac{6}{7}$

5. $\dfrac{11}{15}$ ___ $\dfrac{8}{15}$

6. $4\dfrac{1}{3}$ ___ $4\dfrac{2}{3}$

7. $6\dfrac{1}{10}$ ___ $6\dfrac{7}{10}$

8. $1\dfrac{3}{7}$ ___ $1\dfrac{5}{7}$

9. $7\dfrac{8}{9}$ ___ $7\dfrac{4}{9}$

10. $8\dfrac{7}{8}$ ___ $8\dfrac{3}{8}$

11. $4\dfrac{3}{4}$ ___ $5\dfrac{3}{4}$

12. $9\dfrac{3}{10}$ ___ 10

13. $1\dfrac{3}{4}$ ___ $3\dfrac{1}{4}$

14. $6\dfrac{2}{5}$ ___ $3\dfrac{4}{5}$

15. $\dfrac{2}{6}$ ___ $2\dfrac{5}{6}$

124   Unit 3, Lesson 6

Comparing Fractions

Strategy
Draw a Picture or Use a Model

Step 1: Read Jesse and Danielle decided to repaint their bedroom walls yellow and the trim around the doors and windows brown. Jesse used $\frac{4}{5}$ of a can of brown paint and $1\frac{3}{8}$ cans of yellow paint. Danielle used $\frac{2}{5}$ of a can of brown paint and $1\frac{5}{8}$ cans of yellow paint. Who used a greater amount of brown paint? Who used a greater amount of yellow paint?

STRATEGY

Draw a Picture or Use a Model (number line)

You can draw a number line to help you compare fractions and mixed numbers with the same denominators.

On a number line, proper fractions are found at points between zero and one. To find a fraction, divide the distance between zero and one into the number of equal parts shown by the denominator. Then use the numerator to determine where the fraction is located.

Mixed numbers are found between whole numbers. To find a mixed number, first determine which two whole numbers it is between. Then use the fractional part to divide the distance between the two whole numbers and find the location.

Remember that, on a number line, the number to the right is the greater of the two numbers.

SOLUTION

Step 2: Plan Draw a number line to compare the amount of brown paint Jesse and Danielle used. Draw another number line to compare the amount of yellow paint Jesse and Danielle used.

Step 3: Solve To compare the proper fractions, draw a number line from 0 to 1. The denominator for both fractions is 5, so divide the distance between 0 and 1 into five equal parts.

Use the numerators to find the distance from zero for each number: four out of the five parts for $\frac{4}{5}$ and two out of the five parts $\frac{2}{5}$.

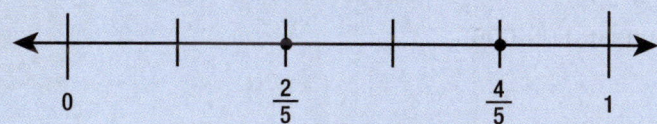

$\frac{4}{5}$ is to the right of $\frac{2}{5}$, so Jesse used a greater amount of brown paint ($\frac{4}{5}$ of a can > $\frac{2}{5}$ of a can).

Both mixed numbers have a whole number part of 1, so they are located between 1 and 2. The denominator for both fractional parts is 8, so divide the distance between 1 and 2 into eight equal parts and use the numerators in the fractional parts to locate each number.

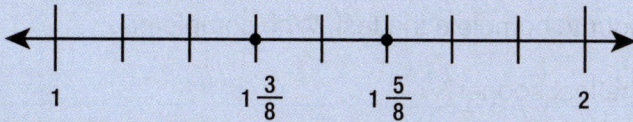

$1\frac{5}{8}$ is to the right of $1\frac{3}{8}$, so Danielle used a greater amount of yellow paint ($1\frac{5}{8}$ cans > $1\frac{3}{8}$ cans).

Step 4: Check $\frac{2}{5}$ and $\frac{4}{5}$ both have the same denominator, so compare the numerators: $4 > 2$, so $\frac{4}{5} > \frac{2}{5}$. $1\frac{3}{8}$ and $1\frac{5}{8}$ have the same whole number part and the same denominator in the fractional part, so compare the numerators: $5 > 3$, so $1\frac{5}{8} > 1\frac{3}{8}$.

Choose a Strategy

YOUR TURN

Choose the Right Word

> denominator   greater than   less than
> number line   numerator

Fill in each blank with the correct word or phrase from the box.

1. Every point on a _____ represents a different number.

2. In a fraction, the _____ is located above the _____.

3. A number to the right of another number on a number line is _____ the other number.

4. A proper fraction is _____ a mixed number.

Yes or No?

Answer these questions and be ready to explain your answers.

5. Can you compare a fraction and a whole number using a number line? _____

6. Do the numbers become less as you move right on a number line? _____

7. Can any fraction be shown on a number line? _____

8. Is the number $4\frac{5}{6}$ located between the whole numbers 5 and 6 on the number line? _____

9. Is a fraction greater than another fraction as long as its numerator is greater? _____

Show That You Know

Draw a number line to model each problem. Use each number line to solve the problem.

10. For the final exam, Maya took $\frac{1}{4}$ of an hour to complete the test and Diana took $\frac{3}{4}$ of an hour to complete the test. Who completed the test sooner?

11. On Sunday, Terence rode his bike for $3\frac{5}{6}$ miles. Rey rode his bike for $3\frac{1}{6}$ miles. Who rode the greater distance?

READ on Your Own

Reading Comprehension Strategy: Questioning

Sound Bites, pages 13–14

Before You Read

Think about what you read about combinations of notes in "Consonance and Dissonance." How might consonant and dissonant combinations of notes be used in a piece of music?

As You Read

Think about "question word" questions that ask *Who?*, *What?*, *When?*, *Where?*, *Why?*, and *How?* as you read. Place stick-on notes next to the answers.

Read "String Instruments," pages 13–14. STOP

Write down a "question word" question in the chart below. Then write the answer when you find it.

String Instruments
"Question word" question
_____
_____
Answer
_____
_____

After You Read

What other characteristics of string instruments add to or change the way they sound?

_____

_____

VOCABULARY

Watch for the words you are learning about.

antinode: the part of a standing wave that moves the greatest distance

node: a point on a vibrating object where there is no movement

pulse: a movement that travels up and down the string

standing wave: a wave that appears to be frozen in place

Fluency Tip

Let your voice rise at the end of a question.

Problem Solving

SOLVE on Your Own

Sound Bites, page 15

Organize the Information

Read You Do the Math in the magazine. Then fill out the following table to show how the frequency changes. The fraction represents the distance from the end of the string. A fraction of $\frac{1}{5}$ means the string is now $\frac{1}{5}$ of its original length.

When the string is held at a fraction of _____,	the frequency is _____ times higher.
$\frac{1}{5}$	
	3
$\frac{1}{2}$	2
$\frac{2}{3}$	
	$\frac{4}{3}$

Listing possible answers may help you answer the magazine questions.

You Do the Math

Use the information in the table above to answer these questions. Write your answers in the space provided.

1. If you hold down the string to make it $\frac{3}{5}$ of its length, will the frequency be higher or lower than when you hold it down at $\frac{3}{4}$ the length? Use what you know about comparing fractions.

   _____
   _____

2. You can find consonant chords by comparing the numerators in the fractions in the second column when the denominators are equal. Give one set of fractions that create a consonant chord. Explain how you know.

   _____
   _____

After You Solve

Without playing it, how could you tell whether a musical instrument plays a high or low frequency sound?
_____

Solve It!

The Four-Step Problem-Solving Plan

Step 1: Read	Step 2: Plan	Step 3: Solve	Step 4: Check
Make sure you understand what the problem is asking.	Decide how you will solve the problem.	Solve the problem using your plan.	Check to make sure your answer is correct.

Application

Read the article below. Then answer the questions.

The Pan Flute

Pan flutes, or pan pipes, are one of the most ancient types of musical instrument still in use today. To make a pan flute, hollow tubes, or pipes, of different lengths are tied together. Often, bamboo or hollow reeds are used, but the pipes can be made out of other materials, too. To play the instrument, the musician blows across the tops of the pipes.

The pan flute is named after the Greek god Pan. In Greek mythology, Pan is said to have chased a beautiful nature spirit named Syrinx to a river. To escape Pan, she was turned into hollow reeds. When Pan sighed in disappointment, his breath made the reeds moan. He cut the reeds down and tied them together to make a flute.

Although the story of Pan is a myth, it is likely that the first pan pipes were created in a similar way. Early humans probably noticed that broken reeds by a river or lake made noise when the wind blew across them. If they cut the reeds and blew across the top, they would have discovered that they could recreate the sound.

1. How did early humans likely invent the pan flute?

   _____
   _____
   _____
   _____

2. Suppose you had 31 pipes of different sizes. How many 12-pipe pan flutes could you make? Write your answer as an improper fraction and a mixed number.

   _____
   _____

Unit 3, Lesson 8   129

Application

YOUR TURN

Read the article below. Then answer the questions.

Pitch and the Pan Flute

Each pipe on a pan flute creates a different musical note, or pitch. In general, the longer the pipe, the lower the sound it creates when the musician blows over it. The width of the pipe also affects the pitch the pipe produces. Two pipes with the same length but different widths will play different notes. The pipe with the greater width will have the lower pitch.

The pipes in a pan flute are usually arranged in order of length. This way, the pitch of the pipes increases or decreases as the musician moves from one side of the flute to the other. In this way, the pipes on a pan flute are similar to the keys on a piano.

To get a better sense of how a pan flute works, find an empty glass bottle. Place your lips just above the bottle and blow so that the air moves across the opening. Try changing the shape of your lips and the try tilting the bottle back and forth until you get the best sound. Does the pitch sound high or low? Try bottles with different lengths and sizes. Can you guess what the bottle will sound like before you try to play it?

1. What are two things that affect the pitch of a pan flute pipe?

   _____

2. Suppose there are two pipes with the same length. The width of the first pipe is $\frac{11}{16}$ of an inch and the width of the second is $\frac{13}{16}$ of an inch. Which pipe will produce a lower pitch? Why?

   _____
   _____

3. Ms. Fan cut a piece of bamboo into two pipes. One pipe is $3\frac{7}{8}$ inches long and the other is $3\frac{5}{8}$ inches long. Which pipe should produce a higher pitch? Why?

   _____
   _____

Fluency Tip

Use periods, commas, question marks, and exclamation points to tell you when to pause.

Reading Comprehension

READ on Your Own

Reading Comprehension Strategy: Questioning

Sound Bites, pages 16–18

VOCABULARY

Watch for the words you are learning about.

reed: a thin piece of wood or plastic in a musical instrument that vibrates to create sound

Fluency Tip

Remember to read smoothly. Try to read phrases instead of individual words.

Before You Read

Think about the way music is made with the stringed instruments you read about in "String Instruments." How do you imagine music is made with wind instruments?

As You Read

Read "Wind Instruments," pages 16–18.

Fill in the concept map below.

- What is their history?
- How is sound made?
- What materials are used to make them?
- What are wind instruments?
- What are some examples?
- How is the pitch changed?

After You Read

What wind instruments have you heard or played? Which instruments sound most pleasant or unpleasant to you? Explain your answer.

_____
_____
_____

Unit 3, Lesson 8   131

Problem Solving

SOLVE on Your Own

Sound Bites, page 19

Organize the Information

Read the Math Project in the magazine. Then use the number lines below and the location chart in the magazine to find the positions of the flute's holes.

|—————————————————|
0   1

|—————————————————|
0   1

|—————————————————|
0   1

|—————————————————|
0   1

|—————————————————|
0   1

Remember to divide each number line into equal parts.

Math Project

Use the information on the number lines above to answer these questions.
Write your answers in the space provided.

1. Do any of the divisions on your number lines line up? Why do you think this happens?

   _____
   _____

2. On a separate sheet of paper, draw the flute with all of its holes in their proper positions. What might you do if you wanted to make a flute that had a lower pitch?

   _____
   _____

After You Solve

Compare your drawing to a flute or other woodwind instrument, such as a clarinet or saxophone. How do they compare?

_____

Put It Together

Connections

Introducing Fractions in Measurements

You have learned that a fraction is a number that shows part of a whole. Common units of length are excellent examples of where you use fractions every day. For example, a yard is equal to 3 feet, so each foot is $\frac{1}{3}$ of a yard.

1 yd = 3 ft

How would you write 2 feet as a fraction of a yard? Since there are 3 feet in a yard, 2 feet is equal to $\frac{2}{3}$ of a yard.

A foot is equal to 12 inches, so each inch is $\frac{1}{12}$ of a foot.

1 ft = 12 in.

How would you write 5 inches as a fraction of a foot? Since there are 12 inches in a foot, 5 inches are equal to $\frac{5}{12}$ of a foot.

An inch can be divided into equal parts as well. Most commonly, an inch is divided into four, eight, or 16 parts.

1 inch divided into fourths, eighths, and sixteenths

If an inch is divided into eight parts, how would you write three of these parts as a fraction of an inch? Since the inch is divided into eight parts, the fraction representing three out of eight parts is $\frac{3}{8}$.

Practicing Fractions in Measurements

Show what you have learned about fractions in measurements by answering the questions below.

1. What fraction of a yard is 1 foot? _____

2. What fraction of a foot is 1 inch? _____

3. What fraction of a foot is 7 inches? _____

4. How many whole inches are in $\frac{24}{8}$ inches? _____

5. How many whole inches are in $\frac{34}{4}$ inches? _____

Connections

YOUR TURN

Thinking About Fractions in Measurements

How would you write 23 inches as a fraction of a yard?

> Since there are 3 feet in a yard, and 12 inches in each foot, there are 36 inches in a yard ($12 \times 3 = 36$).
>
> Therefore, 23 inches can be written as $\frac{23}{36}$ of a yard.

How can you write 13 inches as part of a foot? One way is to write the fraction $\frac{13}{12}$. Notice the numerator is greater than the denominator. This is an improper fraction, so 13 inches must be greater than 1 foot. Remember that improper fractions can be changed to mixed numbers: $\frac{13}{12}$ inch = $1\frac{1}{12}$ inches.

1. When you change 33 inches to feet, how can you easily tell if your answer will be an improper fraction?

   _____
   _____

2. How do you know that $\frac{31}{36}$ yard is less than one whole yard?

   _____

3. How does your understanding of mixed numbers and improper fractions help you express $2\frac{4}{12}$ feet in inches?

   _____
   _____

4. How would you express 41 inches as a mixed number of yards?

   _____
   _____

Show That You Know

Read the information in the box below. Use what you have learned about fractions in measurements to solve the problems that follow. Use the space provided to show your work.

> Mr. Small bought three new trees to plant in his yard. The maple tree measured 4 feet, the dogwood tree measured 41 inches, and the apple tree measured 1 yard. He would like to compare the heights of the three trees.

Remember what you have learned about how different measurements are related.

1. What is the height of the dogwood tree in feet? Write your answer as an improper fraction.

2. How can you rewrite the height of the dogwood tree as a mixed number?

3. Compare the height of the dogwood tree in feet to the height of the apple tree in feet. Which tree is taller? Why?

Unit 3, Lesson 9

Connections

Show That You Know (continued)

4. What is the height of the maple tree in yards? Write your answer as a mixed number.

5. Compare the height of the apple tree in yards to the maple tree in yards. Which tree is taller? Why?

6. Which tree is taller, the dogwood tree or the maple tree? Why? (Hint: Convert the height of both trees to yards.)

Review What You've Learned

7. What have you learned in this Connections lesson about expressing units of length as proper and improper fractions?

8. How can fractions help you measure something very small?

9. How do fractions help you compare measurements made using different units?

Review and Practice

Skills Review

Fractions

A fraction shows a part of a whole or a part of a set. $\frac{4}{21}$ is an example of a fraction.

4 is the numerator, which shows the number of parts.

21 is the denominator, which shows the total number of equal parts in the whole.

Proper fractions

The denominator is greater than the numerator in a proper fraction.

$\frac{1}{10}$, $\frac{7}{34}$, $\frac{2}{15}$, and $\frac{3}{17}$ are all examples of proper fractions.

Improper fractions

The numerator is greater than or equal to the denominator in an improper fraction.

$\frac{10}{6}$, $\frac{3}{3}$, $\frac{15}{4}$ and $\frac{19}{2}$ are examples of improper fractions.

To change an improper fraction into a mixed number, find how many times the denominator fits into the numerator. The number that is left over is the numerator of the fractional part of the mixed number.

Mixed numbers

A mixed number has a fractional part and a whole number part. Examples of mixed numbers include $1\frac{3}{4}$, $2\frac{7}{8}$, and $3\frac{1}{3}$ are examples of mixed numbers.

To change a mixed number into an improper fraction, multiply the whole number by the denominator and then add the numerator. Write this number over the denominator.

Comparing fractions with the same denominator

When two fractions have the same denominator, the fraction with the greater numerator is greater.

$\frac{1}{4} < \frac{3}{4}$

$\frac{13}{3} > \frac{10}{3}$

Comparing mixed numbers

To compare mixed numbers, first compare the whole numbers, and then compare the fractions.

$12\frac{2}{7} > 11\frac{2}{7}$

$12\frac{2}{7} > 12\frac{1}{7}$

$12\frac{2}{7} < 12\frac{5}{7}$

Strategy Review

- Making a model can help solve problems involving fractions. Draw a shape to represent the whole and divide it into equal parts (the denominator). Then shade the number of parts the fraction describes (the numerator).
- Making a table or chart can help you keep track of the number of parts in several wholes.
- You can use a number line to compare fractions or mixed numbers with the same denominators. First, determine which whole numbers the fractions or mixed numbers are between. Then divide the distance between the whole numbers into the number of equal parts given in the denominators. Locate the numbers using their numerators. The numbers to the right are greater than those to the left.

Review and Practice

Skills and Strategies Practice

Complete the exercises below.

1. Draw a picture that represents $\frac{4}{7}$.

2. The numerator of a proper fraction is 6. What number must the denominator be greater than?

3. Rosa had three goals in one soccer game. Her team scored five goals in all. What fraction of her team's goals did Rosa kick?

4. Change $\frac{14}{3}$ into a mixed number.

5. Change $3\frac{1}{5}$ into an improper fraction.

6. Which of the following numbers is greater?
   $3\frac{2}{7}$ or $3\frac{5}{7}$

7. List the following fractions in order from least to greatest:
   $\frac{2}{5}, \frac{1}{5}, \frac{3}{5}, \frac{4}{5}$

8. Which of the following numbers is greater? (Hint: Change both numbers into improper fractions or mixed numbers before comparing.)
   $2\frac{2}{9}$ or $\frac{22}{9}$

Prepare for a test by making a set of flash cards to help you remember vocabulary terms. On one side of the card, write the vocabulary word. On the other side, write the definition for the word. Have a friend or classmate work through the cards with you. If they show you the definition, try to remember which word it matches. If they show you the word, try to recall the definition.

Mid-Unit Review

Circle the letter of the correct answer.

1. Which of the following is a proper fraction?
   A. $\frac{4}{4}$　　C. $\frac{8}{7}$
   B. $\frac{5}{3}$　　D. $\frac{3}{4}$

2. In the fraction $\frac{7}{3}$, what is the 7?
   A. the denominator
   B. the fractional part
   C. the numerator
   D. the whole number part

3. Which of the following is an improper fraction?
   A. $\frac{2}{13}$　　C. $\frac{7}{2}$
   B. $\frac{2}{7}$　　D. $\frac{7}{13}$

4. What fraction is greater than $\frac{3}{5}$?
   A. $\frac{1}{5}$　　C. $\frac{3}{5}$
   B. $\frac{2}{5}$　　D. $\frac{4}{5}$

5. One pot roast can serve six people. Which of the following shows how many pot roasts are needed to serve 17 people?
   A. $6\frac{11}{17}$　　C. $2\frac{5}{6}$
   B. $2\frac{17}{6}$　　D. $1\frac{6}{7}$

6. Which of the following is true?
   A. $1\frac{4}{7} > 2\frac{1}{7}$　　C. $\frac{5}{3} < \frac{2}{3}$
   B. $3\frac{1}{6} < 3\frac{5}{6}$　　D. $7\frac{2}{9} > 7\frac{4}{9}$

7. $\frac{13}{9}$ written as a mixed number is _____.
   A. $1\frac{4}{9}$　　C. $1\frac{9}{13}$
   B. $1\frac{3}{9}$　　D. $1\frac{4}{13}$

8. Which of the following is not a proper fraction?
   A. $\frac{29}{30}$　　C. $\frac{30}{29}$
   B. $\frac{2}{3}$　　D. $\frac{9}{16}$

9. If you draw a picture to model a fraction, which part of the model shows the numerator?
   A. the total number of equal parts
   B. the total number of unequal parts
   C. the number of shaded parts
   D. the number of unshaded parts

10. Which of the following is greater than $\frac{3}{8}$?
    A. $\frac{1}{8}$　　C. $\frac{3}{8}$
    B. $\frac{2}{8}$　　D. $\frac{5}{8}$

11. Which of the following is less than $\frac{2}{3}$?
    A. $\frac{1}{3}$　　C. $\frac{3}{3}$
    B. $\frac{2}{3}$　　D. $1\frac{1}{3}$

12. Which number has the least value?
    A. $6\frac{11}{67}$　　C. $5\frac{1}{67}$
    B. $3\frac{2}{67}$　　D. $3\frac{11}{67}$

Review and Practice

Mid-Unit Review

13. There are 12 bagels in a dozen. A man buys 13 bagels. How many dozens does he buy?

    A. $1\frac{1}{12}$ C. $1\frac{1}{13}$

    B. $1\frac{12}{13}$ D. $1\frac{13}{12}$

14. Which mixed number has the greatest value?

    A. $4\frac{2}{3}$ C. $3\frac{1}{3}$

    B. $1\frac{3}{3}$ D. $3\frac{3}{3}$

15. There are seven apples in a bag. If Mona has 12 apples, how many bags of apples does she have?

    A. $\frac{5}{12}$ C. $\frac{12}{7}$

    B. $\frac{7}{12}$ D. $\frac{12}{5}$

16. $\frac{16}{15}$ written as a mixed number is _____.

    A. $\frac{15}{16}$ C. $1\frac{1}{15}$

    B. $1\frac{15}{16}$ D. $1\frac{1}{16}$

17. On the number line, between which two whole numbers is $\frac{23}{5}$ located?

    A. 0 and 1   C. 5 and 6

    B. 4 and 5   D. 22 and 23

18. Which mixed number has the least value?

    A. $7\frac{7}{48}$ C. $7\frac{47}{48}$

    B. $6\frac{7}{48}$ D. $6\frac{47}{48}$

19. The numerator is greater than 4 in _____.

    A. $\frac{5}{4}$ C. $\frac{2}{3}$

    B. $\frac{1}{7}$ D. $\frac{3}{5}$

20. Which of the following is a proper fraction?

    A. $\frac{3}{3}$ C. $\frac{101}{110}$

    B. $\frac{3}{2}$ D. $\frac{110}{101}$

21. A classroom has 37 seats. Students sit in 33 of those seats. What fraction of the seats are students sitting in?

    A. $\frac{4}{37}$ C. $1\frac{4}{37}$

    B. $\frac{37}{33}$ D. $\frac{33}{37}$

22. Which mixed number is greater than $41\frac{7}{8}$?

    A. $41\frac{5}{8}$ C. $40\frac{7}{8}$

    B. $40\frac{5}{8}$ D. $42\frac{7}{8}$

23. Which number is equal to $\frac{3}{3}$?

    A. 1   C. 3

    B. $1\frac{1}{3}$ D. 6

24. A store has nine hats for sale. Mrs. Grey buys two hats. What fraction of the store's hats did she buy?

    A. $\frac{9}{2}$ C. $\frac{2}{11}$

    B. $\frac{2}{9}$ D. $\frac{9}{11}$

25. $\frac{51}{50}$ written as a mixed number is _____.

    A. $1\frac{1}{51}$ C. $\frac{1}{55}$

    B. $1\frac{1}{50}$ D. $1\frac{50}{51}$

Benchmark Fractions and Common Numerators or Denominators

Learn the SKILL

Laila, Julie, and Tom each have an orange. Laila eats $\frac{3}{4}$ of her orange, Julie eats $\frac{1}{4}$ of her orange, and Tom eats $\frac{1}{9}$ of his. How can you compare how much each person ate?

VOCABULARY
Watch for the words you are learning about.

benchmark fraction: a common fraction that can be used to estimate the value of other fractions

common denominator: a denominator shared by two fractions

common numerator: a numerator shared by two fractions

SKILL	EXAMPLE	COMPLETE THE EXAMPLE
You already know that, if two fractions have a **common denominator**, the one with the greater numerator is the greater of the two fractions.	$\frac{1}{4}$ and $\frac{3}{4}$ have a common denominator. 1 is less than 3. So $\frac{1}{4} < \frac{3}{4}$.	Compare: $\frac{8}{9}$ ——— $\frac{5}{9}$
If two fractions have a **common numerator**, then the one with the greater denominator is the lesser of the two fractions. This is because the more equal parts the whole is divided into, the less each part represents.	$\frac{1}{4}$ and $\frac{1}{9}$ have a common numerator. 4 is less than 9. So $\frac{1}{4} > \frac{1}{9}$. 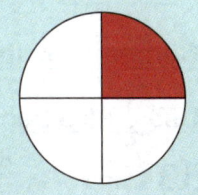 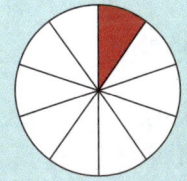	Compare: $\frac{5}{8}$ ——— $\frac{5}{10}$
If two fractions have different numerators and denominators, you can sometimes compare them by using a **benchmark fraction** to estimate their size. For example, both fractions can be compared to the benchmark fraction $\frac{1}{2}$ to see if one fraction is clearly greater than the other.	$\frac{3}{4}$ and $\frac{1}{9}$ do not have a common denominator or numerator. Compare $\frac{3}{4}$ to benchmark fraction $\frac{1}{2}$. $\frac{3}{4}$ is three out of four parts. Half of four parts is two parts, so $\frac{3}{4} > \frac{1}{2}$ of the whole. Compare $\frac{1}{9}$ to benchmark fraction $\frac{1}{2}$. One out of nine parts is less than half of the parts, so $\frac{1}{9} < \frac{1}{2}$ of the whole. If $\frac{3}{4} > \frac{1}{2}$ and $\frac{1}{9} < \frac{1}{2}$, then $\frac{3}{4} > \frac{1}{9}$.	Compare: $\frac{1}{5}$ ——— $\frac{1}{2}$ $\frac{5}{8}$ ——— $\frac{1}{2}$ Therefore, $\frac{1}{5}$ ——— $\frac{5}{8}$.

Unit 3, Lesson 11

Learn the Skill

YOUR TURN

Choose the Right Word

> benchmark fraction   common denominator
> common numerator

Fill in each blank with the correct word or phrase from the box.

1. The fractions $\frac{3}{7}$ and $\frac{6}{7}$ share a _____.

2. A _____ can be used to estimate the value of a fraction.

3. Two fractions with the same number above the fraction bar have a _____.

Yes or No?

Answer these questions and be ready to explain your answers.

4. If two fractions have common numerators, do you compare them by comparing their numerators? _____

5. If a fraction is less than a benchmark fraction, can it be greater than a fraction that is greater than the same benchmark fraction? _____

6. Can you compare the numerators if two fractions have common denominators? _____

7. Do $\frac{4}{7}$ and $\frac{4}{17}$ have common numerators? _____

Show That You Know

Compare the fractions. Then name the common numerator or denominator.

8. $\frac{5}{6}$ $\frac{1}{6}$
   Common _____ is ____.

9. $\frac{4}{9}$ $\frac{4}{3}$
   Common _____ is ____.

10. $\frac{5}{8}$ $\frac{5}{7}$
    Common _____ is ____.

Compare. Write > or <. Use $\frac{1}{2}$ as a benchmark fraction.

11. $\frac{2}{9}$ $\frac{3}{5}$

12. $\frac{2}{3}$ $\frac{1}{4}$

13. $\frac{5}{8}$ $\frac{2}{5}$

SOLVE on Your Own

Learn the Skill

Skills Practice

Compare. Name the common denominator.

When comparing two fractions with a common numerator, the fraction with the lesser denominator is greater.

1. $\dfrac{3}{4}$ _____ $\dfrac{5}{4}$
Common denominator: _____

2. $\dfrac{7}{8}$ _____ $\dfrac{3}{8}$
Common denominator: _____

3. $\dfrac{1}{10}$ _____ $\dfrac{3}{10}$
Common denominator: _____

4. $\dfrac{23}{25}$ _____ $\dfrac{14}{25}$
Common denominator: _____

5. $\dfrac{17}{32}$ _____ $\dfrac{21}{32}$
Common denominator: _____

Compare. Name the common numerator.

6. $\dfrac{1}{3}$ _____ $\dfrac{1}{8}$
Common numerator: _____

7. $\dfrac{7}{9}$ _____ $\dfrac{7}{10}$
Common numerator: _____

8. $\dfrac{6}{7}$ _____ $\dfrac{6}{3}$
Common numerator: _____

9. $\dfrac{4}{11}$ _____ $\dfrac{4}{17}$
Common numerator: _____

10. $\dfrac{10}{9}$ _____ $\dfrac{10}{11}$
Common numerator: _____

Compare. Use $\dfrac{1}{2}$ as a benchmark fraction.

11. $\dfrac{5}{8}$ _____ $\dfrac{2}{5}$

12. $\dfrac{2}{3}$ _____ $\dfrac{3}{8}$

13. $\dfrac{6}{7}$ _____ $\dfrac{8}{21}$

14. $\dfrac{1}{4}$ _____ $\dfrac{4}{5}$

15. $\dfrac{1}{24}$ _____ $\dfrac{7}{10}$

Unit 3, Lesson 11

Choose a Strategy

Benchmark Fractions and Common Numerators or Denominators

Strategy

Draw a Picture or Use a Model

Step 1: Read Nate has two identical computer disks. He has filled $\frac{3}{8}$ of the first disk and $\frac{4}{5}$ of the second disk. If Nate wants to save a new file onto the disk that is filled the least, which one should he use?

STRATEGY	SOLUTION
Draw a Picture or Use a Model Drawing models of fractions can help you compare them to benchmark fractions. Remember that you can model a fraction by dividing a shape into the number of equal parts shown in the denominator. Then shade or color the number of parts equal to the numerator.	Step 2: Plan Draw models to show $\frac{3}{8}$ and $\frac{4}{5}$ and compare them using the benchmark fraction $\frac{1}{2}$. Step 3: Solve Model $\frac{3}{8}$ by dividing a shape into eight equal parts and shading three red. Compare the model to the benchmark fraction $\frac{1}{2}$. Less than $\frac{1}{2}$ of the circle is shaded, so $\frac{3}{8}$ is less than $\frac{1}{2}$. 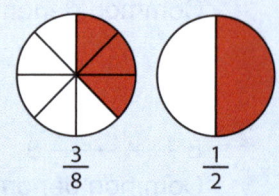 Model $\frac{4}{5}$ and compare the model to $\frac{1}{2}$. Greater than $\frac{1}{2}$ of the circle is shaded blue, so $\frac{4}{5}$ is greater than $\frac{1}{2}$. $\frac{3}{8} < \frac{1}{2}$ and $\frac{4}{5} > \frac{1}{2}$, so $\frac{3}{8}$ is less than $\frac{4}{5}$. 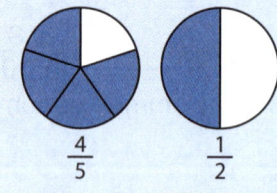 Nate should use the disk filled $\frac{3}{8}$ full. Step 4: Check Three is less than half of eight, so $\frac{3}{8} < \frac{1}{2}$. Four is greater than half of five, so $\frac{4}{5} > \frac{1}{2}$. So $\frac{3}{8} < \frac{4}{5}$.
Draw a Picture or Use a Model Drawing a number line can help you use a benchmark fraction to compare fractions. For proper fractions, label the number line from 0 to 1 and the location of the benchmark fraction. Then estimate the locations of the fractions you want to compare.	Step 2: Plan Draw a number line from 0 to 1. Estimate the location of $\frac{3}{8}$ and $\frac{4}{5}$ on the number line using $\frac{1}{2}$ as a benchmark fraction. Then use the number line to find the lesser of the two fractions. Step 3: Solve Find $\frac{3}{8}$ on the number line. Half of eight is four, so $\frac{3}{8} < \frac{1}{2}$. Therefore, $\frac{3}{8}$ must be located somewhere between 0 and $\frac{1}{2}$. Find $\frac{4}{5}$ on the number line. Four is greater than half of five. Therefore, $\frac{4}{5}$ must be located between $\frac{1}{2}$ and 1. 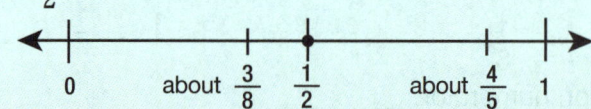 $\frac{3}{8}$ is to the left of $\frac{4}{5}$, so $\frac{3}{8}$ is less than $\frac{4}{5}$. Step 4: Check If you make models to show $\frac{3}{8}$ and $\frac{4}{5}$, a smaller portion of the first circle is shaded, so $\frac{3}{8} < \frac{4}{5}$.

YOUR TURN

Choose the Right Word

> benchmark fraction   common denominator
> common numerator   denominator

Fill in each blank with the correct word or phrase from the box.

1. The fractions $\frac{1}{2}$ and $\frac{1}{4}$ share a _____, but do not have a _____.

2. The _____ $\frac{1}{2}$ can be used to estimate the value of other fractions.

3. The _____ shows the total number of equal parts in a whole.

Choose a Strategy

Yes or No?

Answer these questions and be ready to explain your answers.

4. Does using the benchmark fraction $\frac{1}{2}$ help you compare $\frac{3}{14}$ and $\frac{5}{18}$? _____

5. Does a model always show a fraction greater than $\frac{1}{2}$ if there are more shaded parts than unshaded parts? _____

6. Is the fraction $\frac{12}{31}$ located between $\frac{1}{2}$ and 1 on the number line? _____

7. Is a fraction with a numerator of 10 always greater than a fraction with a numerator of one? _____

Show That You Know

Shade each model to show each fraction. Then use each model to compare each fraction to the benchmark fraction $\frac{1}{2}$.

8. $\frac{2}{7}$ ——— $\frac{1}{2}$

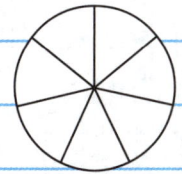

9. $\frac{9}{10}$ ——— $\frac{1}{2}$

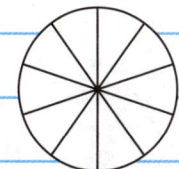

Estimate the location of each fraction. Then use the number line to compare the fractions.

10. $\frac{4}{9}$ ——— $\frac{3}{7}$

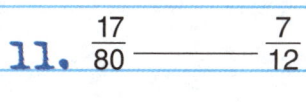

11. $\frac{17}{80}$ ——— $\frac{7}{12}$

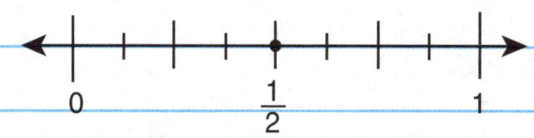

12. $\frac{2}{7}$ ——— $\frac{3}{4}$

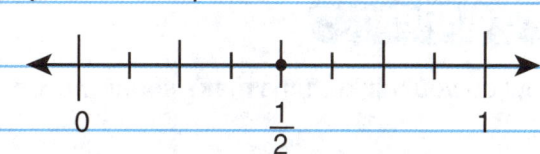

Unit 3, Lesson 12

Reading Comprehension

READ on Your Own

Reading Comprehension Strategy: Questioning

Sound Bites, *pages 20–22*

> **VOCABULARY**
>
> Watch for the words you are learning about.
>
> **tune:** to change the sound produced to a specific frequency
>
> **tuning fork:** a U-shaped piece of steel which produces a note of a certain pitch when struck
>
> **wavelength:** the distance from peak to peak in a wave
>
> **Fluency Tip**
>
> Identify words that you do not know. Find out how to pronounce them before reading.

Before You Read

Think about how the instruments in "Wind Instruments" produce sound. When have you used wind or your breath to make noise? How did you do it?

As You Read

Preview the pictures and captions of "How Sound Travels," pages 20–21.

Write a goal-setting question in the chart below.

Now read "How Sound Travels," pages 20–21.

Answer your question in the chart below.

Preview "How Sound Travels," page 22.

Write a goal-setting question.

Now read "How Sound Travels," page 22.

Answer your question in the chart below.

Goal-Setting Question	Answer
pages 20–21	
page 22	

After You Read

How do you think drums make sound waves?

_____

146 Unit 3, Lesson 12

Problem Solving

SOLVE on Your Own

Sound Bites, page 22

Organize the Information

Read You Do the Math in the magazine. Then use the number lines below to describe the movement of the wave from left to right and from right to left. Label each point with the drawing it represents.

Right to left:

|———————————————|
0   1

Left to right:

|———————————————————————————|
0   1

You Do the Math

Use the information in the number lines above to answer these questions. Write your answers in the space provided.

> Use benchmark fractions to describe each of the points in the drawings.

1. How did you divide the number lines above? Explain your reasoning.

   _____
   _____

2. How did benchmark fractions help you find the fraction represented by each drawing?

   _____
   _____
   _____

3. How do the locations in the drawings compare to the benchmark fractions below?

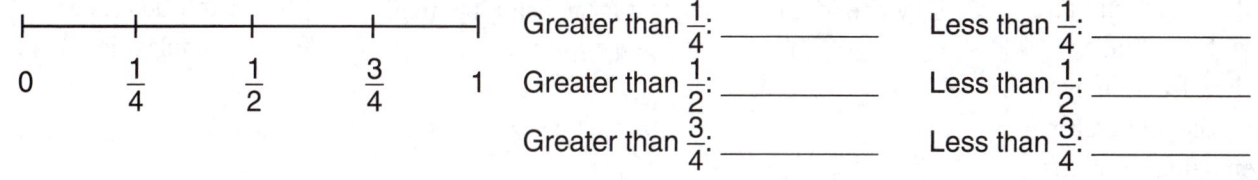

Greater than $\frac{1}{4}$: _____   Less than $\frac{1}{4}$: _____

Greater than $\frac{1}{2}$: _____   Less than $\frac{1}{2}$: _____

Greater than $\frac{3}{4}$: _____   Less than $\frac{3}{4}$: _____

4. Do any of the drawings appear to be equal to one of the benchmark fractions? Which one(s)?

   _____

After You Solve

What unanswered questions do you have about how sound travels?

_____

Learn the Skill

Equivalent Fractions and Simplest Form

Learn the SKILL

> **VOCABULARY**
>
> Watch for the words you are learning about.
>
> **common factor:** a number that divides evenly into the numerator and denominator
>
> **equivalent fractions:** fractions that represent the same value or amount
>
> **simplest form:** a fraction for which the only common factor for the numerator and denominator is one

Edward divided his backyard into 12 equal parts. He turned six out of the 12 parts into a flower garden. What are some different ways you can write a fraction to show how much of Edward's backyard is turned into a garden? How can you write the fraction in its simplest form?

SKILL	EXAMPLE	WRITE AN EXAMPLE
To find **equivalent fractions,** you can multiply the numerator and denominator by the same number. Another way to find equivalent fractions is to divide the numerator and denominator by a **common factor.**	To find an equivalent fraction for $\frac{6}{12}$, you can multiply the numerator and denominator by the same number. For example, $2 \times 6 = 12$; $2 \times 12 = 24$. So, $\frac{6}{12}$ and $\frac{12}{24}$ are equivalent fractions ($\frac{6}{12} = \frac{12}{24}$). You can also divide both the numerator and denominator by a common factor to find an equivalent fraction. For example: 3 is a common factor for 6 ($3 \times 2 = 6$) and 12 ($3 \times 4 = 12$). $6 \div 3 = 2$; $12 \div 3 = 4$. So, $\frac{6}{12}$ and $\frac{2}{4}$ are also equivalent fractions.	Write three equivalent fractions. _____ _____ _____
To write a fraction in its **simplest form,** find an equivalent fraction by dividing the numerator and denominator by the greatest common factor you can find. Check that the new numerator and denominator have no common factors except for the number 1.	To write $\frac{6}{12}$ in the simplest form, begin by finding the common factors of 6 and 12: $1 \times 6 = 6$ $1 \times 12 = 12$ $2 \times 3 = 6$ $2 \times 6 = 12$ $3 \times 4 = 12$ The greatest common factor for 6 and 12 is 6. Divide the numerator and denominator by 6: $6 \div 6 = 1$; $12 \div 6 = 2$. So, $\frac{6}{12}$ is equivalent to $\frac{1}{2}$. The only common factor for 1 and 2 is 1, so $\frac{6}{12}$ written in simplest form is $\frac{1}{2}$.	Write a fraction. Then find its simplest form. Fraction: _____ Simplest form: _____

YOUR TURN

Choose the Right Word

> common denominator   common factor
> equivalent fractions   simplest form

Fill in each blank with the correct word or phrase from the box.

1. Fractions that represent the same value or amount are _____.

2. A fraction is written in _____ when the only_____ for the numerator and denominator is 1.

3. Two fractions have a _____ _____ if their denominators are the same.

Learn the Skill

Yes or No?

Answer these questions and be ready to explain your answers.

4. Is the fraction $\frac{2}{3}$ written in simplest form?
_____

5. Are $\frac{4}{7}$ and $\frac{8}{14}$ equivalent fractions?
_____

6. Is 6 a common factor for 3 and 2?
_____

7. Can you find the simplest form of a fraction by multiplying the numerator and denominator by the same number?
_____

Show That You Know

Find the common factor(s) for each set of numbers.

8. 10 and 4

9. 6 and 18

10. 21 and 12

Write each fraction in simplest form.

11. $\frac{16}{18} =$

12. $\frac{4}{12} =$

13. $\frac{36}{39} =$

Unit 3, Lesson 13

Learn the Skill

SOLVE on Your Own

Skills Practice

Rewrite each fraction as an equivalent fraction.

If the numerator is a factor of the denominator, you can find the simplest form by dividing both numbers by the numerator.

1. $\frac{2}{3}$ = _____

2. $\frac{3}{4}$ = _____

3. $\frac{5}{7}$ = _____

4. $\frac{9}{11}$ = _____

5. $\frac{1}{4}$ = _____

9. 10 and 20 _____

10. 15 and 18 _____

Write the fractions in simplest form.

11. $\frac{5}{10}$ _____

12. $\frac{8}{12}$ _____

13. $\frac{3}{9}$ _____

14. $\frac{7}{28}$ _____

15. $\frac{8}{56}$ _____

Find the common factor(s) for each set of numbers.

6. 14 and 21 _____

7. 12 and 8 _____

8. 8 and 9 _____

Choose a Strategy

Equivalent Fractions and Simplest Form

Strategies

Make a List; Guess, Check, and Revise

Step 1: Read Shasta and James each make the same amount of lemonade. Shasta equally divides her lemonade into 27 cups but only sells 18 cups. James equally divides his lemonade into 24 cups but only sells 16. Shasta thinks they sold the same amount of lemonade. Is she right?

STRATEGY	SOLUTION
Make a List One way to check if two fractions are equivalent is to find their simplest forms. If the fractions are equivalent, then they will have the same simplest form. Making a list of the factors for both the numerator and denominator can help you identify the greatest common factor and write a fraction in simplest form.	**Step 2: Plan** Use a table to help write $\frac{18}{27}$ and $\frac{16}{24}$ in their simplest forms. Use the simplest forms to check if they are equivalent fractions. **Step 3: Solve** List the factors for the numerators and denominators for each fraction. Then circle the common factors. Use the tables to find the greatest common factors and write each fraction in its simplest form.

Factors of 18	Factors of 27	Factors of 16	Factors of 24
1, 2, 3, 6, 9, 18	1, 3, 9, 27	1, 2, 4, 8, 16	1, 2, 3, 4, 6, 8, 12, 24

Nine is the greatest common factor of 18 and 27. $18 \div 9 = 2$; $27 \div 9 = 3$. So, the simplest form of $\frac{18}{27}$ is $\frac{2}{3}$.

Eight is the greatest common factor of 16 and 24. $16 \div 8 = 2$; $24 \div 8 = 3$. So, the simplest form of $\frac{18}{27}$ is $\frac{2}{3}$. Both fractions are $\frac{2}{3}$ in their simplest forms, so $\frac{18}{27}$ and $\frac{16}{24}$ are equivalent fractions.

Step 4: Check Use multiplication to check your division: $2 \times 9 = 18$; $3 \times 9 = 27$. So, $\frac{2}{3} = \frac{18}{27}$. $2 \times 8 = 16$; $3 \times 8 = 24$. So, $\frac{2}{3} = \frac{16}{24}$.

| **Guess, Check, and Revise** Another way to find the simplest form of a fraction is to guess which common factor is the greatest and then check if the result is the simplest form. If not, you can repeat the process until the fraction is in its simplest form. | **Step 2: Plan** Use the Guess, Check, and Revise strategy until $\frac{18}{27}$ and $\frac{16}{24}$ are in their simplest forms. **Step 3: Solve** |

Guess: Divide 18 and 27 by 3:
$$\frac{18}{27} = \frac{6}{9}$$
Check: $\frac{6}{9}$ is not in simplest form.
Revise: Divide 6 and 9 by 3:
$$\frac{6}{9} = \frac{2}{3}$$
Check: $\frac{2}{3}$ is in simplest form.

Guess: Divide 16 and 24 by 4:
$$\frac{16}{24} = \frac{4}{6}$$
Check: $\frac{4}{6}$ is not in simplest form.
Revise: Divide 4 and 6 by 2:
$$\frac{4}{6} = \frac{2}{3}$$
Check: $\frac{2}{3}$ is in simplest form.

Step 4: Check Draw models to check if $\frac{18}{27} = \frac{16}{24}$.

Choose a Strategy

YOUR TURN

Choose the Right Word

> common factor   common numerator
> simplest form

Fill in each blank with the correct word or phrase from the box.

1. Three is a _____ of the numbers 9 and 6.
2. $\frac{1}{5}$ is the _____ of $\frac{5}{25}$.
3. Two fractions have a _____ if they both have the same number above the fraction bar.

Yes or No?

Answer these questions and be ready to explain your answers.

4. Can two fractions with different simplest forms be equivalent fractions? _____
5. A fraction's numerator and denominator are both even. Is it in simplest form? _____
6. Can comparing their simplest forms help you determine if two fractions represent the same amount? _____
7. Should you always stop revising your guess after two tries? _____

Show That You Know

Write the factors of the numerator and denominator. Circle the common factors.

8. $\frac{20}{30}$

   20:

   30:

9. $\frac{40}{56}$

   40:

   56:

10. $\frac{15}{75}$

    15:

    75:

Write each fraction in simplest form.

11. $\frac{33}{55} =$

12. $\frac{24}{36} =$

13. $\frac{21}{49} =$

14. $\frac{5}{125} =$

15. $\frac{30}{45} =$

Reading Comprehension

READ on Your Own

Reading Comprehension Strategy: Questioning

Fluency Tip
Skim the passage for words that are hard to pronounce. Practice reading those words ahead of time.

Sound Bites, pages 23–24

Before You Read

Think about high- and low-pressure waves in "How Sound Travels." How are they the same and how are they different?

As You Read

As you read "Wavelength," pages 23–24, think about how the information you are reading about fits together with what you already know about sound waves.

Use what you know to write a "between the lines" question for each page. Then write your answers.

Page	"Between the Lines" Question	Answer
23		
24		

After You Read

How do you think the amount of water in a glass changes the length of the sound wave to make different pitches?

_____

Unit 3, Lesson 14   153

Problem Solving

SOLVE on Your Own

Sound Bites, page 25

Organize the Information

Read You Do the Math in the magazine. Then complete the following table to help you organize possible sizes of cellos and corresponding string lengths.

String Length of 1st Cello	Distance Chosen on 1st Cello String	Fraction of 1st Cello String	String Length of 2nd Cello	Fraction of 2nd Cello String	Distance Chosen on 2nd Cello String

You Do the Math

Use the information in the table above to answer the questions. Write your answers in the space provided.

You can look for patterns and make lists to help you solve this problem.

1. How did you choose lengths of the cello string that would be simple fractions of the total length of the string?

   _____

   _____

2. What patterns do you see in the lengths of the strings for the larger cellos compared to the smaller ones to produce the same notes on both?

   _____

   _____

   _____

After You Solve

How might tightening and loosening the string on a violin change the pitch?

_____

The Four-Step Problem-Solving Plan

Step 1: Read	Step 2: Plan	Step 3: Solve	Step 4: Check
Make sure you understand what the problem is asking.	Decide how you will solve the problem.	Solve the problem using your plan.	Check to make sure your answer is correct.

Read the article below. Then answer the questions.

Nodes and Antinodes

When you tap the edge of a glass of water, you cause the glass, and the water in it, to vibrate. Some parts of the glass and water vibrate more than others. A part that vibrates the least is called a node. A part that vibrates the most is called an antinode. Any instrument that vibrates to produce music has these points. Many have more than one point.

When an artist makes a wind chime from a pipe, he or she drills the hole for the string at one of the pipe's nodes. The location of this node depends on the length of the pipe. For example, on a 50 centimeter pipe, the first node is about 10 centimeters from the end. On a 20 centimeter pipe, the first node is about 4 centimeters from the end. Since there is little vibration at the nodes, hanging the pipes from these points will not affect their sound.

The artist then hangs the chimes so they are hit at one of the antinodes when the wind blows. Because these are the points where the pipes vibrate the most, hitting a pipe at an antinode produces the best sound.

1. What do you think would happen if you touched a musical instrument at one of its nodes while it was being played? Why?

   _____
   _____

2. What fraction of the pipe's total length is 10 out of 50 cm? Write your answer in simplest form.

   _____

3. What fraction of the pipe's total length is 4 out of 20 cm? Write your answer in simplest form.

   _____

4. What do you notice about your answers to problems 2 and 3? What does this tell you about the location of the first nodes on the two pipes from the reading?

   _____
   _____

Application

YOUR TURN

Read the article below. Then answer the questions.

The Speed of Sound

Did you know that it takes time for sound to travel from the source to your ears? The reason we do not normally notice this is that sound moves very fast. In fact, in the air, sound can travel about 1,116 feet (or $\frac{1}{5}$ of a mile) in 1 second. If you think that is fast, sound travels almost 1 mile each second underwater. This is because water is much denser than air. The greater the density of a material, the faster sound travels through it.

If you want to experience the speed of sound in action, pay attention during the next thunderstorm. The farther away a lighting strike, the longer it takes to hear the thunder. In fact, you can estimate the distance of a storm by counting the number of seconds between a flash of lighting and the thunder. Sound travels through air about $\frac{1}{5}$ of a mile every second. So, dividing the number of seconds by five will tell you about how many miles away the storm is.

1. Does sound travel faster in air or water? Why?

   _____
   _____

2. According to the article, how can you estimate the distance of a storm?

   _____
   _____

3. Suppose you were standing $\frac{8}{10}$ of a mile away from a cannon when it was fired. How can you write the distance in its simplest form?

   _____

4. Using your answer to problem 3, about how long would it take for the sound to reach your ears after the cannon was fired?

   _____

Fluency Tip

Identify words that you do not know. Find out how to pronounce them before reading.

READ on Your Own

Reading Comprehension

Reading Comprehension Strategy: Questioning

Sound Bites, *pages 26–28*

VOCABULARY

Watch for the words you are learning about.

mallet: a stick with a wooden or plastic head

resonator: a part of a xylophone that helps increase the vibration of air, making the sound louder

wind chimes: hollow or solid tubes that strike each other or a striker and make sound when moved by wind

xylophone: a musical instrument made up of wooden or metal bars of various lengths

Fluency Tip

Reread sentences that you have trouble with. Rereading should help you read more smoothly.

Before You Read

Think about what you read in "Wavelength." Would a sound with a higher frequency have a longer or a shorter wavelength?

As You Read

Preview "Percussion," pages 26–28.

Write a "between the lines" question for pages 26–27. **Read about the xylophone on pages 26–27.**

Answer the question you have written in the chart below.

Write a "between the lines" question for page 28. **Read about wind chimes on page 28.**

Answer the question you have written in the chart below.

"Between the Lines" Question	Answer
The Xylophone	
Wind Chimes	

After You Read

What are some different places you might hear wind chimes?

Unit 3, Lesson 15   157

Problem Solving

SOLVE on Your Own

Sound Bites, page 29

Organize the Information

Read the Math Project in the magazine. Then complete the flowchart to help you plan how to find your solution to the Math Project.

Fraction strips can help you find nodes and antinodes.

Choose two lengths from the table on page 29. → Cut two paper strips of those lengths. → Fold the first strip into _____ to find the _____.

Then fold into _____ to find the _____. → Do the same for the second paper strip. → Use a meter stick to measure and record your results.

Math Project

Use the information in the flowchart above to answer these questions. Write your answers in the space provided.

1. What lengths did you choose for your model?

   _____

2. Where did you find the first node and antinode on your models?

   _____

   _____

   _____

3. Complete the model by drawing a hole where the string would go and an X where you would strike it to make a sound. Did you put the X at a node or antinode? Why?

   _____

After You Solve

If you have wind chimes available, use the third and fifth rule to find the location of a node and antinode. Strike the chime at these locations. How does the sound differ?

_____

158   Unit 3, Lesson 15

Ordering Fractions

Learn the SKILL

Sam ran $\frac{1}{10}$ of a mile, Susan ran $\frac{3}{5}$ of a mile, and Elliot ran $\frac{1}{2}$ of a mile. Order how far everyone ran from least to greatest.

VOCABULARY

Watch for the words you are learning about.

least common denominator (LCD): the least common multiple of two or more denominators

least common multiple (LCM): the least number that is a multiple of two or more other numbers

SKILL	EXAMPLE	COMPLETE THE EXAMPLE
To order fractions, the first step is to find the **least common denominator** (LCD). To find the LCD of the fractions, you must identify the **least common multiple** (LCM) of the fractions' denominators.	The denominators of $\frac{1}{10}$, $\frac{3}{5}$, and $\frac{1}{2}$ are: 10, 5, and 2. The LCM for all three numbers is 10: $10 \times 1 = 10$ $5 \times 2 = 10$ $2 \times 5 = 10$ So, the LCD of $\frac{1}{10}$, $\frac{3}{5}$, and $\frac{1}{2}$ is 10.	Find the LCD for the following fractions: $\frac{5}{6}, \frac{2}{3}, \frac{1}{4}$ _____ _____
Once you have found the LCD, change each fraction into an equivalent fraction with the LCD as a denominator. The fractions will then have a common denominator and can be ordered by comparing them directly.	$\frac{1}{10}$ already has the LCD for a denominator, so it does not need to be changed. Find equivalent fractions for $\frac{3}{5}$ and $\frac{1}{2}$ that have 10 for a denominator. $5 \times 2 = 10$, so multiply the numerator and denominator in $\frac{3}{5}$ by 2: $\frac{(3 \times 2)}{(5 \times 2)} = \frac{6}{10}$. So, $\frac{3}{5} = \frac{6}{10}$. $2 \times 5 = 10$, so multiply the numerator and denominator in $\frac{1}{2}$ by 5: $\frac{(1 \times 5)}{(2 \times 5)} = \frac{5}{10}$. So, $\frac{1}{2} = \frac{5}{10}$. Then compare the fractions: $\frac{1}{10} < \frac{5}{10} < \frac{6}{10}$, so $\frac{1}{10} < \frac{1}{2} < \frac{3}{5}$.	Find the numerators for the equivalent fractions. Then use the equivalent fractions to order the original fractions from least to greatest. $\frac{1}{2} = \frac{}{8}$ $\frac{3}{4} = \frac{}{8}$ $\frac{1}{8} = \frac{}{8}$ _____

Unit 3, Lesson 16

Learn the Skill

YOUR TURN

Choose the Right Word

> common factor   common numerator
> least common denominator
> least common multiple

Fill in each blank with the correct word or phrase from the box.

1. The least multiple shared by two or more numbers is called the _____ _____.

2. The _____ of $\frac{1}{3}$ and $\frac{1}{2}$ is 6.

3. Seven is a _____ of 14 and 21 because 7 × 2 = 14 and 7 × 3 = 21.

4. $\frac{4}{9}$ and $\frac{4}{81}$ share a _____.

Yes or No?

Answer these questions and be ready to explain your answers.

5. Is the fraction $\frac{2}{4}$ written in simplest form? _____

6. Is 5 the least common multiple of 2 and 10? _____

7. Do fractions have to be in simplest form before ordering? _____

8. If three fractions have a common denominator, does the one with the greatest numerator represent the greatest value? _____

Show That You Know

Find the least common denominator. Then use the LCD to rewrite the fractions with a common denominator.

9. Least common denominator:

   $\frac{2}{3} =$ $\frac{5}{6} =$ $\frac{1}{2} =$

10. Least common denominator:

    $\frac{3}{8} =$ $\frac{1}{2} =$ $\frac{3}{4} =$

11. Least common denominator:

    $\frac{1}{6} =$ $\frac{4}{15} =$ $\frac{2}{5} =$

Use your answers to 9–11 to write the original fractions in order from least to greatest.

12. 9:

13. 10:

14. 11:

160   Unit 3, Lesson 16

SOLVE on Your Own

Skills Practice

Find the least common denominator. Order the rewritten fractions from least to greatest.

If one denominator is a multiple of all the other denominators, then that denominator is the LCD.

1. $\frac{1}{2}, \frac{1}{4}, \frac{5}{8}$

   Least common denominator: _____

   Ordered fractions: _____

2. $\frac{2}{3}, \frac{7}{12}, \frac{3}{4}$

   Least common denominator: _____

   Ordered fractions: _____

3. $\frac{1}{2}, \frac{3}{4}, \frac{11}{16}$

   Least common denominator: _____

   Ordered fractions: _____

4. $\frac{3}{5}, \frac{1}{4}, \frac{7}{10}$

   Least common denominator: _____

   Ordered fractions: _____

5. $\frac{1}{2}, \frac{3}{4}, \frac{5}{8}$

   Least common denominator: _____

   Ordered fractions: _____

6. $\frac{8}{9}, \frac{2}{3}, \frac{5}{6}$

   Least common denominator: _____

   Ordered fractions: _____

7. $\frac{21}{50}, \frac{11}{20}, \frac{3}{10}$

   Least common denominator: _____

   Ordered fractions: _____

Use the answers from 1–7 to rewrite the original fractions in order from least to greatest.

8. 1: _____

9. 2: _____

10. 3: _____

11. 4: _____

12. 5: _____

13. 6: _____

14. 7: _____

Unit 3, Lesson 16

Choose a Strategy

Ordering Fractions

Strategies

Make a List, Draw a Picture or Use a Model

Step 1: Read A new electric drill comes with three different sized bits: $\frac{3}{8}$ in., $\frac{1}{4}$ in., and $\frac{5}{16}$ in. How can you rewrite the fractions so that all the bits have the same denominator? Which bit is the smallest? Which bit is the largest?

STRATEGY	SOLUTION
Make a List When finding the LCD for several fractions, making a list can help you organize the multiples of the numbers in each denominator and identify their LCM.	**Step 2: Plan** Use a table to organize the multiples for each denominator and identify the LCD. Then use the LCD to rewrite $\frac{3}{8}, \frac{1}{4}$, and $\frac{5}{16}$ with a common denominator. **Step 3: Solve** List the several multiples for each denominator. Then circle the multiples shared by all three numbers (the common multiples). <table><tr><th>Denominator</th><th>Multiples</th></tr><tr><td>8</td><td>8, ⑯ 24, ㉜, 40, 48</td></tr><tr><td>4</td><td>4, 8, 12, ⑯, 20, 24, 28, ㉜</td></tr><tr><td>16</td><td>⑯, ㉜, 48, 64, 80</td></tr></table> The least multiple shared by all three numbers is 16. So, the LCM of 8, 4, and 16 is 16 and the LCD of $\frac{1}{4}, \frac{3}{8}$, and $\frac{5}{16}$ is 16. Next, rewrite each fraction with the LCD as the denominator: $\frac{3}{8} = \frac{6}{16}$; $\frac{1}{4} = \frac{4}{16}$; $\frac{5}{16} = \frac{5}{16}$. $\frac{4}{16} < \frac{5}{16} < \frac{6}{16}$. The $\frac{1}{4}$ in. bit is the smallest and the $\frac{3}{8}$ in. bit is the largest. **Step 4: Check** Use repeated addition to check the multiples in the table.
Draw a Picture or Use a Model (number line) Finding fractions on a number line can help you order them. Use the rewritten fractions to locate each fraction on the number line. Label each point with both the original fraction and the rewritten fraction. Then use the number line to determine the order.	**Step 2: Plan** Use a number line to order the fractions. **Step 3: Solve** Draw a number line from 0 to 1 and divide the distance into equal parts; remember that the number of equal parts should be the same as the denominators of the fractions you are comparing. Then locate the position for each rewritten fraction. Label the point with both the rewritten fraction and the original fraction. 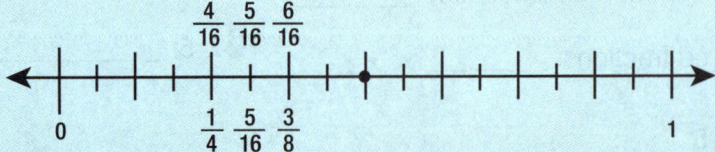 Use the number line to order the fractions from least to greatest: $\frac{4}{16}, \frac{5}{16}, \frac{6}{16}$ $\frac{1}{4}, \frac{5}{16}, \frac{3}{8}$ **Step 4: Check** Draw models of the original fractions. Compare the shaded parts to check the order.

YOUR TURN

Choose the Right Word

> common denominator
> least common denominator
> least common multiple

Fill in each blank with the correct word or phrase from the box.

1. A _____ is a denominator shared by two or more fractions.

2. The _____ is the _____ of two or more denominators.

Choose a Strategy

Yes or No?

Answer these questions and be ready to explain your answers.

3. Is 30 the least common multiple of 3 and 5? _____

4. Does $\frac{4}{8}$ represent a greater fraction than $\frac{1}{2}$? _____

5. Does multiplying the numerator and denominator by the same number change the value of a fraction? _____

6. Are $\frac{3}{4}$ and $\frac{3}{8}$ equivalent fractions? _____

Show That You Know

Rewrite each pair of fractions with a common denominator. Circle the greater fraction.

7. $\frac{2}{5} =$
   $\frac{3}{4} =$

8. $\frac{3}{7} =$
   $\frac{9}{14} =$

9. $\frac{9}{10} =$
   $\frac{3}{4} =$

10. $\frac{5}{8} =$
    $\frac{7}{10} =$

11. $\frac{1}{6} =$
    $\frac{7}{15} =$

12. $\frac{2}{9} =$
    $\frac{1}{4} =$

13. $\frac{2}{3} =$
    $\frac{5}{9} =$

14. $\frac{3}{7} =$
    $\frac{2}{5} =$

15. $\frac{5}{13} =$
    $\frac{1}{3} =$

Unit 3, Lesson 17

Reading Comprehension

READ on Your Own

Reading Comprehension Strategy: Questioning

Sound Bites, pages 30–31

Before You Read

Think about the instruments in "Percussion." Which instrument do you prefer: the xylophone or wind chimes? Why?

As You Read

Preview "The Amazing Ear," pages 30–31.

Write goal-setting questions for "The Inner Ear" and "Not Just for Hearing."

Read "The Amazing Ear," pages 30–31.

Write your answers in the chart below.

Before You Read	After You Read
The Inner Ear	
Not Just for Hearing	

After You Read

Why do you think sounds are harder to hear when you have water in your ears?

VOCABULARY

Watch for the words you are learning about.

cochlea: snail-shell-shaped structure in the inner ear containing the organ of hearing

hair cells: cells in the inner ear with hairs that sense changes in the fluid

saccule: a part of the inner ear that helps sense motion and position

utricle: a part of the inner ear that helps sense motion and position

Fluency Tip

If you find yourself reading so quickly that you are missing the meaning, slow down.

Problem Solving

SOLVE on Your Own

Sound Bites, page 32

Organize the Information

Read You Do the Math in the magazine. Then fill out the following table using the information from the magazine.

Comparing a fraction to a benchmark fraction can help you compare it to others.

Order	Species	Mass (grams)	Highest Frequency (Hz)	Mass / Frequency	Nearest Benchmark Fraction
	little brown bat				
	dog				
	elephant				
	cat				
	beluga whale				
	mouse				
	manatee				
	sea lion				

You Do the Math

Use the information in the table above to answer these questions. Write your answers in the space provided.

1. Fill in the Order column by numbering the animals from the smallest to the largest fraction. How did using the closest benchmark fraction make it easier to order the fractions?

   _____

2. What general pattern did you notice?

   _____

After You Solve

Humans can hear up to 10,000 Hz. The average adult weighs 80,000 g. Where are humans on the table?

_____

Unit 3, Lesson 17

Application

The Four-Step Problem-Solving Plan

Step 1: Read	Step 2: Plan	Step 3: Solve	Step 4: Check
Make sure you understand what the problem is asking.	Decide how you will solve the problem.	Solve the problem using your plan.	Check to make sure your answer is correct.

Read the article below. Then answer the questions.

Recorded Sound

"Mary had a little lamb, whose fleece was white as snow…" These words started the recording industry when, in 1877, Thomas Edison used them to test his new invention—the phonograph. Edison's phonograph was a very simple machine. When he spoke into the machine, the sound was recorded by a needle onto a tinfoil cylinder that was turned with a hand crank. When he placed a different needle on the cylinder and turned the crank again, the sound of Edison reciting the poem was played back.

Today, most music is sold on compact discs or CDs. Instead of a needle, a laser makes invisible marks on the underside of a CD. Another laser in your CD player "reads" the marks to recreate the music. A phonograph cylinder could only play for about 2 minutes, but a single CD can hold about 80 minutes of music. Still, it all started with Edison, Mary, and her little lamb.

1. What did Edison's first phonograph record his voice onto?

   _____

2. Jamal recorded 24 minutes of music onto a CD. How can you show the amount he recorded as a fraction of what a CD can hold? Write your answer in simplest form.

   _____

YOUR TURN

Application

Read the article below. Then answer the questions.

Are You Hurting Your Ears?

Some digital music players can hold up to tens of thousands of songs. In theory, you could listen to one for months without repeating a song or stopping. However, some doctors are worried that people are listening at too high a volume. They also think that people are listening at high volumes for too long. The reason to worry is that loud music can cause permanent hearing damage. Even somewhat loud sound can cause serious hearing damage if it lasts for a long period of time.

So what is so bad about digital music players? First, the "ear bud" style headphone that comes with many digital music players focuses the music directly into the ear. This can increase the risk of damage. Second, many people turn the volume up on their players to drown out street noises and other distractions. After a while, the ear adjusts to the new volume so you turn the volume up some more.

To be safe, experts suggest that you limit the volume to $\frac{3}{5}$ of the maximum. You should limit your listening time to 60 minutes. Taking action now will help you make sure you can hear your favorite songs for many years to come.

Fluency Tip

Remember to read smoothly. Try to read phrases instead of individual words.

1. What are two ways you can avoid hearing damage when using a digital music player?

   _____

   _____

   _____

   _____

2. Ron sets the volume at 13 out of 20. Is $\frac{13}{20}$ greater than $\frac{3}{5}$ of the maximum volume? Show your work.

   _____

   _____

3. In a poll, $\frac{1}{12}$ of the voters thought hearing loss was a big health problem, $\frac{1}{2}$ said smoking, and about $\frac{1}{3}$ said being overweight. Write the fractions in order from least to greatest. Which health issue did the fewest voters realize was a big health problem?

   _____

Unit 3, Lesson 18   167

Reading Comprehension

READ on Your Own

Reading Comprehension Strategy: Questioning

Sound Bites, *pages 33–35*

VOCABULARY

Watch for the words you are learning about.

decibel (dB): a unit for measuring the intensity of sound

intense: strong

intensity: the strength of a sound

loudness: how intense a sound seems to a human ear

Fluency Tip

Emphasize certain words and phrases that you think are important.

Before You Read

Consider your hearing, which you read about in "The Amazing Ear." Why is it important to protect your ears from too much sound?

As You Read

Preview "Louder and Louder," pages 33–35. 🛑

Write a goal-setting question or questions.

_____
_____

Read "Louder and Louder," pages 33–35. 🛑

Answer your goal-setting question(s).

_____
_____

Did you have to change your goal-setting question as you read? Why or why not?

_____
_____
_____

After You Read

What did you learn in this article that you could apply to your own life? Explain your answer.

_____
_____
_____
_____

168   Unit 3, Lesson 18

SOLVE on Your Own

Problem Solving

Sound Bites, page 36

Organize the Information

Read the Math Project in the magazine. Then use the information to complete the table.

Sound	Decibel Level	Number of Decibels Higher or Lower than Conversation Intensity	Intensity as Fraction of Conversation Intensity
jet engine at 150 meters	120		
alarm clock	80	20 (higher)	
normal conversation at 1 meter	60		
rustle of paper	30		
whisper	20	40 (lower)	
rustle of leaves in a light breeze	10		
threshold of hearing	0		

Math Project

Use the information in the table above to answer these questions. Write your answers in the space provided.

1. What problems might you have if the numbers of decibels were not multiples of 10?

   _____

   _____

> Each increase of 10 dB increases the intensity of a sound 10 times.

2. What would you want to set as an upper decibel limit for your sound system? Why?

   _____

   _____

After You Solve

What kinds of noises might you want to avoid in order to protect your hearing?

_____

Unit 3, Lesson 18

Put It Together

Introducing Accuracy and Precision

When measuring a length, precision is important. Precision, in technical terms, means that you would get the same length if you measured again. Accuracy is similar to precision, but a little different. Accuracy is how close a measurement is to the actual length. For example, if a necklace is almost exactly 11 inches long, rounding the length to 1 foot would be less accurate than rounding it to 11 inches. This is because the smaller the unit, the more accurately you can measure something with it.

Before you measure a length, you must decide how accurate your measurement should be. In general, the longer or taller something is, the less accurate you need to be. For example, you might use yards to measure the height of a tall tree, because you generally do not need to be know the height of something so tall to the nearest foot or inch. When measuring something small, like the length of a piece of chalk, you would use inches because the length of a piece of chalk is too short to measure accurately with feet or yards.

Practicing Accuracy and Precision

For each length, choose the unit you would use—inches, feet, or yards—to measure the length with an appropriate amount of accuracy.

1. The length of a pencil _____
2. The length of a car _____
3. The distance you walk to a friend's house _____
4. The width of an envelope _____
5. The height of a mug of hot chocolate _____
6. The height of a bookshelf _____
7. The length of a school hallway _____
8. The width of the hollow tube in a wind chime _____

Connections

Thinking About Accuracy and Precision

One way to increase the accuracy of a measurement is to use fractions. For example, inches can be divided into halves, fourths, or eighths. Measuring the length of something to the nearest half inch is more accurate than measuring to the nearest inch because half an inch is smaller than a whole inch. Likewise, measuring to the nearest fourth (or quarter) of an inch is more accurate than measuring to the nearest half an inch.

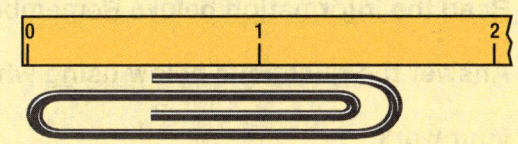

1. Use the first ruler to measure the paper clip. Round the length to the nearest whole inch.

   _____

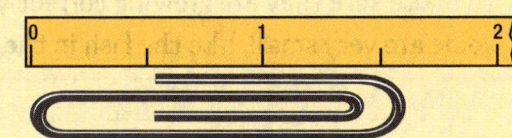

2. Use the second and third rulers to measure the paper clip. Round the length to the nearest half of an inch or fourth of an inch. Write your answer as a mixed number.

   _____

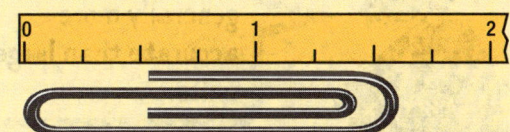

3. How many equal parts is each inch on the fourth ruler divided into? Use the ruler to measure the paper clip as accurately as you can.

   _____

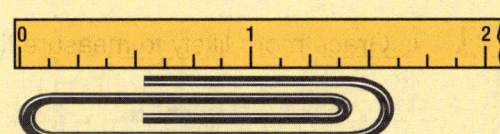

4. Which ruler allowed you to make the most accurate measurement? Why?

   _____

   _____

   _____

Unit 3, Lesson 19   171

Connections

Show That You Know

Read the information below. Remember what you have learned about accuracy and precision. Answer the questions below using what you have learned. Use the space provided to show your work.

> Grace is a veterinarian for a zoo. Part of her job is to measure the height and length of the animals to make sure they are growing correctly. Some of the animals are quite large, like a giraffe, and some are very small, like the fish in the picture below.

Remember that smaller units are generally more accurate than larger units.

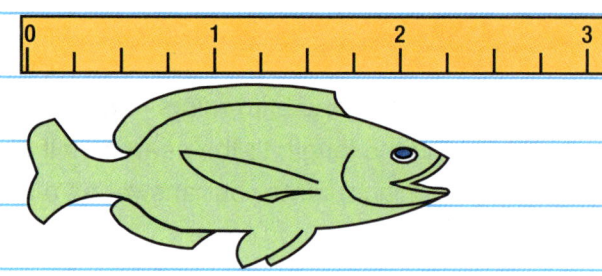

1. Is Grace more likely to measure the height of a giraffe in inches or feet? Explain your answer.

2. If Grace wants to watch the animals' growth closely, should she use larger or smaller units? Why?

3. How long is the fish to the nearest inch?

4. How could you make your answer to the last question more accurate?

Connections

Show That You Know (continued)

5. Grace measures the fish using the most accurate markings on the ruler. What part of an inch does each of these markings represent? What length should she record?

6. Grace measures another fish with a different ruler. The second fish is $2\frac{3}{8}$ inches long. Which fish is longer? How do you know? (Hint: Use the LCD to compare the fractional parts.)

7. How are fractions on a ruler like fractions on a number line?

Review What You've Learned

8. What have you learned in this Connections lesson about the size of the units used to measure length?

9. What have you learned in this Connections lesson that you did not already know?

10. How will this lesson help you measure the length of things more accurately?

Review and Practice

Skills Review

Common denominators and common numerators

If two fractions have a common denominator, the one with the greater numerator is the greater fraction.

$\frac{2}{7} > \frac{1}{7}, \frac{5}{8} < \frac{7}{8}$

If two fractions have a common numerator, the one with the greater denominator represents the lesser amount.

$\frac{2}{3} > \frac{2}{13}, \frac{4}{7} < \frac{4}{5}$

Benchmark fractions

If two fractions have different numerators and denominators, you can sometimes compare them by using a benchmark fraction to estimate their values.

$\frac{3}{7}$: Three out of seven equal parts is less than $\frac{1}{2}$.

$\frac{7}{9}$: Seven out of nine equal parts is greater than $\frac{1}{2}$.

Therefore, $\frac{3}{7} < \frac{7}{9}$.

Equivalent fractions

Equivalent fractions represent the same value or amount. To find equivalent fractions, you can multiply a fraction's numerator and denominator by the same number.

$\frac{2}{3} = \frac{2 \times 4}{3 \times 4} = \frac{8}{12}$

You can also find equivalent fractions by dividing a fraction's numerator and denominator by a common factor.

$\frac{3}{9} = \frac{(3 \div 3)}{(9 \div 3)} = \frac{1}{3}$

Fractions in simplest form

In simplest form, the numerator and denominator of a fraction have no common factors except for 1.

To rewrite a fraction in its simplest form, divide the numerator and denominator by the greatest common factor they share.

$\frac{3}{6} = \frac{(3 \div 3)}{(6 \div 3)} = \frac{1}{2}$

The numerator and denominator in $\frac{1}{2}$ have no common factors except for 1.

So, $\frac{3}{6}$ written in simplest form is $\frac{1}{2}$.

Least common denominators (LCD)

To find the LCD of two or more fractions, you must find the least multiple that the denominators all share (the LCM).

For example, $\frac{3}{5}$ and $\frac{1}{4}$: Some multiples of 5 are: 5, 10, 15, 20, 25, and 30. Some multiples of 4 are: 4, 8, 12, 16, 20, 24, and 28. The LCM of both numbers is 20, so the LCD for $\frac{3}{5}$ and $\frac{1}{4}$ is 20.

Ordering fractions

To order a group of fractions, first rewrite them using the least common denominator. Then compare their numerators to determine which fractions have the greatest value.

$\frac{2}{33} = \frac{4}{66} \qquad \frac{4}{11} = \frac{24}{66} \qquad \frac{5}{22} = \frac{15}{66}$

$\frac{4}{66} < \frac{15}{66} < \frac{24}{66}$

In order from least to greatest: $\frac{2}{33}, \frac{5}{22}, \frac{4}{11}$.

Strategy Review

- Making an organized list of the numerator's and denominator's factors can help you find the greatest common factor.
- Listing the multiples of two or more numbers and then circling the common multiples can help you find the LCM of the numbers.
- When writing a fraction in simplest form, you can guess which common factor is the greatest and then check and revise the rewritten fraction until it is in simplest form.
- Drawing a number line can help you order fractions.

Review and Practice

Skills and Strategies Practice

Complete the exercises below.

1. Write $\frac{4}{16}$ in simplest form. _____

2. Draw a rectangle and divide it into nine equal parts. Then shade four parts. What fraction of the rectangle is shaded? _____

   What fraction of the rectangle is not shaded? _____

3. Which fraction is greater, $\frac{7}{10}$ or $\frac{11}{30}$? _____

4. What is the least common denominator of $\frac{3}{7}$ and $\frac{4}{21}$? _____

5. Write three equivalent fractions for each fraction.

   $\frac{1}{6}$ _____

   $\frac{5}{12}$ _____

   $\frac{3}{11}$ _____

6. Write the following fractions in order from least to greatest.

   $\frac{5}{8}, \frac{9}{16}, \frac{3}{4}$

   _____

Test-Taking tip

Be sure you understand what a test question is asking. Read it twice if necessary, replacing symbols with the words they represent. For example, if a question states "$\frac{3}{13} < ?$", say to yourself, "$\frac{3}{13}$ is less than..." Also make sure that when a question asks you to put fractions in order, you know whether that order is from least to greatest (such as $\frac{1}{4}, \frac{2}{4}, \frac{3}{4}$) or greatest to least (such as $\frac{3}{4}, \frac{2}{4}, \frac{1}{4}$).

Unit 3, Lesson 20

Review and Practice

Unit Review

Circle the letter of the correct answer.

1. What is $\frac{3}{30}$ in simplest form?
   - A. $\frac{1}{10}$
   - B. $\frac{1}{30}$
   - C. $\frac{3}{10}$
   - D. $\frac{1}{100}$

2. What is the least common denominator of $\frac{2}{3}$ and $\frac{3}{7}$?
   - A. 7
   - B. 14
   - C. 21
   - D. 42

3. $\frac{3}{19} <$ _____
   - A. $\frac{6}{19}$
   - B. $\frac{1}{19}$
   - C. $\frac{3}{20}$
   - D. $\frac{3}{22}$

4. Order $\frac{1}{3}, \frac{4}{5},$ and $\frac{2}{5}$ from least to greatest.
   - A. $\frac{2}{5}, \frac{1}{3}, \frac{4}{5}$
   - B. $\frac{1}{3}, \frac{2}{5}, \frac{4}{5}$
   - C. $\frac{4}{5}, \frac{2}{5}, \frac{1}{3}$
   - D. $\frac{1}{3}, \frac{4}{5}, \frac{2}{5}$

5. What is $\frac{14}{49}$ in simplest form?
   - A. $\frac{1}{7}$
   - B. $\frac{3}{7}$
   - C. $\frac{4}{7}$
   - D. $\frac{2}{7}$

6. Use the least common denominator to rewrite $\frac{7}{27}$ and $\frac{1}{3}$.
   - A. $\frac{7}{27}$ and $\frac{9}{27}$
   - B. $\frac{15}{54}$ and $\frac{18}{54}$
   - C. $\frac{7}{27}$ and $\frac{12}{27}$
   - D. $\frac{21}{27}$ and $\frac{9}{27}$

7. What is $\frac{10}{12}$ in simplest form?
   - A. $\frac{5}{12}$
   - B. $\frac{5}{6}$
   - C. $\frac{10}{6}$
   - D. $\frac{6}{6}$

8. $\frac{5}{27} <$ _____
   - A. $\frac{5}{31}$
   - B. $\frac{6}{27}$
   - C. $\frac{4}{27}$
   - D. $\frac{5}{28}$

9. What is the least common denominator of $\frac{1}{4}$ and $\frac{3}{2}$?
   - A. 8
   - B. 2
   - C. 4
   - D. 6

10. Order $\frac{5}{14}, \frac{3}{28},$ and $\frac{2}{7}$ from greatest to least.
    - A. $\frac{3}{28}, \frac{5}{14}, \frac{2}{7}$
    - B. $\frac{2}{7}, \frac{5}{14}, \frac{3}{28}$
    - C. $\frac{5}{14}, \frac{2}{7}, \frac{3}{28}$
    - D. $\frac{2}{7}, \frac{5}{14}, \frac{3}{28}$

11. $\frac{9}{12} =$ _____
    - A. $\frac{1}{4}$
    - B. $\frac{2}{3}$
    - C. $\frac{3}{4}$
    - D. $\frac{6}{8}$

12. Which fraction is greater than $\frac{1}{2}$?
    - A. $\frac{1}{1}$
    - B. $\frac{1}{3}$
    - C. $\frac{1}{4}$
    - D. $\frac{2}{4}$

Review and Practice

13. What is the least common denominator of $\frac{2}{5}$ and $\frac{2}{3}$?
 A. 10 　　C. 20
 B. 8 　　D. 15

14. What is $\frac{8}{40}$ written in simplest form?
 A. $\frac{2}{20}$ 　　C. $\frac{1}{5}$
 B. $\frac{4}{10}$ 　　D. $\frac{1}{8}$

15. What is the least common denominator of $\frac{3}{4}, \frac{3}{8},$ and $\frac{1}{32}$?
 A. 16 　　C. 8
 B. 2 　　D. 32

16. $\frac{4}{9} >$ _____
 A. $\frac{7}{18}$ 　　C. $\frac{39}{81}$
 B. $\frac{18}{27}$ 　　D. $\frac{8}{9}$

17. $\frac{6}{80}$ in simplest form is _____.
 A. $\frac{3}{40}$ 　　C. $\frac{2}{40}$
 B. $\frac{2}{27}$ 　　D. $\frac{3}{4}$

18. $\frac{5}{15}$ in simplest form is _____.
 A. $\frac{1}{10}$ 　　C. $\frac{1}{5}$
 B. $\frac{1}{2}$ 　　D. $\frac{1}{3}$

19. $\frac{3}{51} =$ _____
 A. $\frac{2}{17}$ 　　C. $\frac{3}{17}$
 B. $\frac{1}{17}$ 　　D. $\frac{1}{48}$

20. The simplest form of $\frac{3}{24}$ is _____.
 A. $\frac{1}{6}$ 　　C. $\frac{1}{8}$
 B. $\frac{1}{12}$ 　　D. $\frac{1}{9}$

21. What is the least common denominator of $\frac{2}{8}$ and $\frac{3}{10}$?
 A. 20 　　C. 80
 B. 10 　　D. 40

22. $\frac{3}{4} =$ _____
 A. $\frac{5}{8}$ 　　C. $\frac{4}{8}$
 B. $\frac{7}{8}$ 　　D. $\frac{6}{8}$

23. What is the least common denominator of $\frac{9}{4}, \frac{3}{9},$ and $\frac{1}{12}$?
 A. 12 　　C. 3
 B. 36 　　D. 9

24. $\frac{1}{12} >$ _____
 A. $\frac{1}{13}$ 　　C. $\frac{1}{4}$
 B. $\frac{1}{6}$ 　　D. $\frac{1}{3}$

25. 22 is the least common denominator of _____.
 A. $\frac{1}{44}$ and $\frac{5}{22}$ 　　C. $\frac{1}{4}$ and $\frac{2}{5}$
 B. $\frac{1}{22}$ and $\frac{3}{11}$ 　　D. $\frac{1}{5}$ and $\frac{3}{17}$

Unit 3, Lesson 20

Unit 3 Reflection

MATH SKILLS

The easiest part about working with fractions is

Fractions are helpful for

Sound Bites

MATH STRATEGIES & CONNECTIONS

For me, the math strategies that work the best are

Using fractions in measurements makes it easier to

READING STRATEGIES & COMPREHENSION

The easiest part about questioning is

One way that questioning helps me with reading is

The vocabulary words I had trouble with are

INDEPENDENT READING

My favorite part of <u>Sound Bites</u> is

I read most fluently when

UNIT 4
Decimals

MATH SKILLS & STRATEGIES
After you learn the basic **SKILLS**, the real test is knowing when to use each **STRATEGY**.

AMP LINK MAGAZINE
You Do the Math and Math Projects: After you read each magazine article, apply what you know in real-world problems.
Fluency: Make your reading smooth and accurate, one tip at a time.

READING STRATEGY
Learn the power of **Previewing and Predicting**.

VOCABULARY
MATH WORDS:
Know them!
Use them!
Learn all about them!

CONNECTIONS
You own the math when you make your own connections.

Reading Comprehension Strategy

Reading Comprehension Strategy: Previewing/Predicting

How to Preview and Predict

Preview the article by reading the **title** and **subtitles**.	Look at the **photos**. Read the **captions**.	Think about **what you already know** about the topic or related topics.	Now **predict** what you think the article is about. What will you learn about as you read?	As you read, use what you learn to **check your prediction**. You may change it at any time.

To **preview**, you look through the pages you are going to read. Read the **title, subtitles,** and **captions.** Study the **photos.** Look at the last paragraph of the article to see how it ends. Are there review questions? They can tell you what you should look for while reading. When you preview, also look for **bold** words.

Amazing Animal Abilities

Humans can do many things that no other living things can do. People can write and read, create art, and build skyscrapers. However, other living things have their own surprising abilities.

1. What does the title tell you about the subject of the article?
   _____
   _____
   _____

Before you read, look at photos and read their captions. Use what you see and read to **predict** something about the article. Try to add to your prediction by using details from the photos.

Grasshoppers: Powerful Jumpers

Strength gives the grasshopper its hop. First, it crouches to the ground. Then it pushes quickly away from the ground with 10 times more power than human leg muscles can produce. A grasshopper can hop upward 10 times its length and forward 20 times its length. With the help of a springy pole, top human athletes can jump about fifteen feet up. If they jumped like grasshoppers do, they could soar right over a five-story building. They could also go from one end of a football field to the other in three easy hops.

2. What do you already know about grasshoppers? How did this help you as you read?
   _____
   _____
   _____
   _____

A grasshopper's legs are 10 times more powerful than human legs.

You have previewed the text and made predictions based on titles, subtitles, and photos. Before you read, think about **what you already know** about the topic. You can use your knowledge and experience to predict what the article will tell you.

180 Unit 4

Reading Comprehension Strategy

Cheetahs: Sensational Sprinters

Flexibility, rather than strength, is the force behind the cheetah's legendary speed. A cheetah's spine can bend like a spring. This allows the cheetah's legs to stretch on each step. Although a cheetah can outrun a human in a sprint, a human can run much farther than a cheetah. Cheetahs can run only a little way before needing to rest. So even while humans cannot run faster than cheetahs, they could beat them to the finish line of a marathon or other long race.

A cheetah is off the ground for more than half its stride.

3. Look at the photograph, caption, and heading. Make a detailed prediction about what the article will tell you about cheetahs.
   _____
   _____
   _____
   _____
   _____

Now you are ready to read the whole article. As you read, check the predictions you have made. Make new predictions as you read. Check them as you learn more.

Falcons: Fastest Creatures on Earth

The Peregrine Falcon, like the owl and the eagle, is a raptor, or bird of prey. These birds rely on great vision and speed to find and capture their meals. Speed has never been a problem for the Peregrine Falcon. The fastest animals on Earth, falcons typically soar at speeds up to 55 miles per hour. When diving to catch its prey, the falcon can reach speeds over 200 miles per hour.

4. What did you think you would learn from this passage? Was your prediction accurate?
   _____
   _____
   _____
   _____

When you **predict,** you make smart guesses about what an article will tell you. You add your knowledge and experience to what you read to **make and check predictions.** Making predictions helps you understand and remember more of what you read.

There are many different kinds of animals and insects on the planet. Despite the amazing abilities they may have, animals are not always able to outrun the dangers of human activities. Animals and their habitats need human help. By learning how to help them, you can make sure these creatures continue to amaze people for many years to come.

5. Look at the predictions you have made so far. Were you right? How can you add to or change your prediction so that it is correct?
   _____
   _____
   _____
   _____
   _____

6. What is the most useful strategy for predicting? Explain your answer.
   _____
   _____
   _____

Use the Strategies

Use the reading comprehension strategies you have learned to answer questions about the article below.

Arranging an Orchestra

Sections of an Orchestra

An orchestra commonly has four sections of musicians. Each section plays one type of instrument.

- strings (violin, viola, cello, bass)
- percussion (timpani, bass drum, cymbals, triangle, gong)
- woodwind (flute, oboe, clarinet, bassoon)
- brass (trumpet, trombone, tuba, French horn)

The number of musicians in each section depends on the orchestra. The largest part of an orchestra is made up of the strings. Here is the breakdown in a typical orchestra.

45 strings	12 woodwinds
11 brass	4 percussion

Placement of the Sections

Each section sits in a different area of the orchestra. String instruments sit closest to the conductor. Violins and violas are on one side and cellos and basses are on the other. Woodwinds sit in the center, with brass on either side and behind them. Since the timpani and bass drum make the loudest noise, the percussion instruments are in the back.

Bands and Orchestras

What is the difference between a band and an orchestra? It is not the size. Full-sized bands and orchestras can both have more than a hundred members. The difference is in the instruments. An orchestra has most of the instruments you hear in a band: brass, woodwinds, and percussion. Yet there is one type of instrument found only in an orchestra, the strings. An example of a band instrument not usually found in an orchestra is the saxophone.

1. Based on the title, what might this article be about?
   _____
   _____

2. How can you preview the information on this page?
   _____
   _____

3. After you have previewed the page, make a prediction about what the article is about. Write your prediction below.
   _____
   _____

4. What goal-setting question could you ask about the last paragraph? Write an answer to your question.
   _____
   _____
   _____

5. Summarize the last paragraph in one sentence.
   _____
   _____
   _____

Use the Strategies

Reading Strategies: Summarizing, Questioning, Previewing/Predicting
Use the reading comprehension strategies you have learned in this and previous units to answer the questions below.

1. How do the headings help you figure out what the article is about?
   _____

2. What knowledge did you already have about orchestras before you read this piece? How did it help you understand what you read?
   _____
   _____

3. Write a question that you still have about this article. Reread the article and answer your question.
   _____
   _____

4. Write a summary for the whole article.
   _____
   _____
   _____
   _____

Problem-Solving Strategies:
Draw a Picture or Use a Model, Find a Pattern, Make a List
Use these problem-solving strategies to answer the questions below.

5. There are four different sections in an orchestra. How many different ways can two of the four sections be grouped together? The order of the sections does not matter.
   _____

6. Draw a picture of the orchestra as it is described in the second paragraph. How does drawing the orchestra help you better understand what you have read?
   _____

7. How could you use graph paper to make a model of the orchestra? Would this activity add to your understanding? Explain why or why not.
   _____
   _____
   _____

8. In one orchestra, there are 36 strings, 12 woodwinds, and four percussion players. What is the rule for the pattern these numbers make?
   _____

Unit 4   183

Learn the Skill

Decimals

Learn the SKILL

Not everyone weighs exactly the same amount. Sometimes two people can weigh about the same amount. For example, Phil and Fred both weigh about 180 pounds. However, Phil really weighs 180.4 pounds and Fred really weighs 180.1 pounds. How can you tell who is heavier?

VOCABULARY

Watch for the words you are learning about.

decimal: a number with digits to the right of the decimal point

decimal point: the dot in a decimal number, which separates numbers less than one from numbers greater than or equal to one

SKILL	EXAMPLE	COMPLETE THE EXAMPLE
Decimals are numbers that contain a **decimal point**. Numbers to the left of the decimal point are one or more. Numbers to the right of the decimal point are less than one but more than zero. You may be familiar with decimals from using money. The amount $3.56 has two decimal places. The 5 is in the tenths place and the 6 is in the hundredths place. To the right of the hundredths place is the thousandths place, and so on.	Use the chart below to find the place value of each digit. | Hundred-thousands | Ten-thousands | Thousands | Hundreds | Tens | Ones | . | Tenths | Hundredths | Thousandths | | 3 | 2 | 5 | 7 | 0 | 4 | . | 1 | 8 | 6 |	Find the place value of each digit in the number 1,790.35. _____ _____ _____ _____ _____ _____
To compare decimal numbers, write one number above the other to line up the decimal points. Compare each lined-up pair of digits, going from left to right, even past the decimal point, if necessary. When you find digits that do not match, choose the number with the greater digit. That decimal number is greater.	Compare 180.4 and 180.1. The numbers to the left of the decimal point are all the same. Compare the numbers after the decimal point. 4 > 1 180.4 > 180.1 180.4 is greater than 180.1 because the digit in the tenths place is greater. If the digits in the tenths place of both numbers had been equal, you would need to continue comparing digits.	Compare the following pairs of numbers. Which is greater? 197.35 or 197.45? _____ Which is lesser? 67.9 or 182.1? _____

YOUR TURN

Choose the Right Word

> compare   decimal   decimal point   place value

Fill in each blank with the correct word or phrase from the box.

1. A number with digits to the right of the decimal point is a _____.
2. The _____ depends on where a digit is located in a number.
3. To _____ two decimals, start with the largest place value.
4. The _____ is written as a dot in the middle of a number.

Yes or No?

Answer these questions and be ready to explain your answers.

5. Is the tenths place value the same as the tens? _____
6. Is 86.9 greater than 86.88? _____
7. In the number 86.52, is the digit 2 in the hundreds place? _____
8. Is one hundred greater than one hundredth? _____

Learn the Skill

Show That You Know

Complete the sentences.

9. What is the place value of the 2 in 39.2?

10. What is the place value of the 1 in 100,000.00?

11. What is the place value of the 3 in 1.593?

Compare the decimals below. Write > or <.

12. 0.05   0.5

13. 1.32   0.32

14. 4.7   7.4

15. 1,000.1   100.1

16. 5.55   4.66

Unit 4, Lesson 1

Learn the Skill

SOLVE on Your Own

Remember to compare numbers by reading left to right.

Give the place value of the underlined digit in the numbers below.

1. <u>6</u>0.6 _____

2. <u>4</u>75.2 _____

3. 0.0<u>8</u> _____

4. <u>1</u>,000 _____

5. 0.10<u>5</u> _____

6. <u>1</u>00,000 _____

7. 2,<u>8</u>72 _____

8. 6.<u>5</u>22 _____

9. <u>9</u>.57 _____

10. 78.6<u>8</u>5 _____

Compare the following decimals. Circle the greater decimal.

11. 0.1 and 0.4

12. 0.42 and 0.24

13. 0.045 and 0.44

14. 0.37 and 0.73

15. 0.891 and 0.8911

16. 18.9 and 16.2

17. 56.8 and 56.5

18. 872.87 and 82.87

19. 462 and 426.9

20. 6,584.8 and 6,499.9

Decimals

Strategies

Make a Table or a Chart, Draw a Picture or Use a Model

Step 1: Read The table shows the lengths of three bugs. However, the lengths are missing three decimal points and some zeros. You know that Bug A is longer than Bug B, and Bug C is longer than Bug A. Use a place-value chart to decide where you can place decimal points and zeros to make the lengths of each ant correct.

Bug	Bug Length
A	25 inch(es)
B	62 inch(es)
C	16 inch(es)

STRATEGY: Make a Table or a Chart (place-value chart)

Place-value charts can be used to write out and compare decimals. Make sure to line up the numbers at the decimal point. If there is no digit on the left side of the decimal point, add a zero as a placeholder in the ones column. The value of the decimal in this case is always less than 1.

SOLUTION

Step 2: Plan Draw a place-value chart from ones to thousandths. The lengths must each have a decimal point. I can use a place-value chart to write the three numbers. I can move the decimal point around so that Bug C is the largest bug and Bug B is the smallest bug.

Step 3: Solve Place each number into the place-value chart in a way that satisfies the conditions of the problem.

Bug	Ones	.	Tenths	Hundredths	Thousandths
A	0	.	2	5	
B	0	.	0	6	2
C	1	.	6		

Bug A is 0.25 inch, Bug B is 0.062 inch, and Bug C is 1.6 inches.

Step 4: Check Compare the numbers in each column to make sure that Bug A is longer than Bug B and Bug C is longer than Bug A.

Draw a Picture or Use a Model (decimal model)

Decimal models can be similar to models for representing whole numbers. For example, the 100-unit square can also be used to show decimals that include hundredths. Each square is equal to one hundredth.

Step 2: Plan Use decimal models to represent decimals visually. Fill in the number of squares that represent each decimal. If the number goes down into the thousandths, fill in one more square on the hundredths model to model the thousandth place. Use the models to compare possible sizes visually.

Step 3: Solve

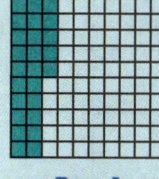 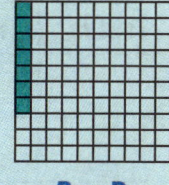 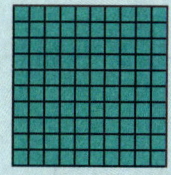 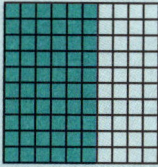

Bug A   Bug B   Bug C

Now compare the three models. Bug A is 0.25 inch, Bug B is 0.062 inch, and Bug C is 1.6 inches.

Step 4: Check Place the three numbers on a number line. The length of Bug B is between 0.06 and 0.07, which is less than Bug A at 0.25. The length of Bug C is 1.6 and is longer than both.

Choose a Strategy

YOUR TURN

Choose the Right Word

> hundredths   place value   tenths

Fill in each blank with the correct word or phrase from the box.

1. The _____ that is immediately to the left of the decimal is called the ones place.

2. The number 0.095 has a 9 in the _____ place.

3. The place value that is immediately to the right of the decimal is called the _____ place.

Yes or No?

Answer these questions and be ready to explain your answers.

4. Does adding zeros to the right of the last number of a decimal affect the decimal? _____

5. Is the number 0.06 written as "six hundredths" in word form? _____

6. Are numbers to the right of the decimal less than numbers to the left of the decimal? _____

7. Is a tenth less than a hundredth? _____

Show That You Know

Write each number in standard decimal form.

8. sixty-seven ten-thousandths

9. one and five tenths

10. nine and three hundredths

11. four hundred two thousandths

Place the numbers in 8–11 in the place-value chart below.

	Ones	.	Tenths	Hundredths	Thousandths	Ten-thousandths
12. #8						
13. #9						
14. #10						
15. #11						

Reading Comprehension

READ on Your Own

Reading Comprehension Strategy: Previewing/Predicting

Animals in Action, pages 3–4

VOCABULARY

Watch for the words you are learning about.

colony: a group of living things that depend on each other

environment: an animal's surroundings

species: a group of plants, animals, or insects that share many common characteristics

Fluency Tip

Everyone reads at a different pace. Practice until you can read at a pace that is comfortable for you.

Before You Read

Think about the largest and smallest ants you have ever seen. How could you estimate their length?

As You Read

Preview "How Big Is an Ant?", pages 3–4.

Then read page 3.

Based on what you have read, predict what this section will be about. Write your predictions in the chart below.

Now read page 4.

Complete the chart.

Preview, Read, and Predict	Read and Check
I predict "How Big Is an Ant?" will be about _____ _____ _____	Did your prediction match what you read, or did you have to revise it? _____ _____ _____

After You Read

Choose the most interesting part of the reading. Explain why you think it was the most interesting.

_____
_____
_____

Unit 4, Lesson 2   189

Problem Solving

SOLVE on Your Own

Animals in Action, *page 5*

Organize the Information

Read You Do the Math in the magazine. Then use the table on page 4 and the place-value chart below to compare the lengths of several different ants. Order from greatest to least.

Ant	Ones	.	Tenths	Hundredths	Thousandths	Ten-thousandths

You Do the Math

Use the information in the table above to answer these questions. Write your answers in the space provided.

1. Are the largest carpenter ant and the largest grease ant the same size? Explain why or why not.

   _____

   _____

2. Which ant did you choose? Which seed sizes did you choose? Were they able to fit through the tunnel?

   _____

   _____

After You Solve

Since ants are often less than an inch long, it is helpful to measure them using decimals. What else that is less than an inch long could you measure using decimals?

_____

Fractions and Decimals

Learn the SKILL

VOCABULARY

Watch for the words you are learning about.

rename: to show a number in another way

Mrs. Williams asked her sixth-grade class how much homework they were able to finish. Marcia said she completed $\frac{1}{2}$ of her homework. Nikki said she would express the amount of homework she did as the decimal 0.5. Which girl finished more of her homework?

SKILL	EXAMPLE	COMPLETE THE EXAMPLE
A decimal can be **renamed** as a fraction. The place value of the last digit shows you how many parts there are in a whole. Use this number as the denominator. Use the number to the right of the decimal point as the numerator.	Write 0.5 as a fraction. The digit 5 is in the tenths place, so the denominator is 10. The digit 5 is to the right of the decimal point, so 5 is the numerator. $0.5 = \frac{5}{10}$ Simplified, $\frac{5}{10} = \frac{1}{2}$.	Write 0.4 as a fraction in simplest form. _____
To change a fraction to a decimal, first rewrite it as an equivalent fraction with a denominator of 10, 100, or 1,000. Use the denominator to identify the place value of the decimal. Then write the decimal, placing the numbers in the numerator to the right of the decimal point.	Write $\frac{1}{2}$ as a decimal. $\frac{1}{2} = \frac{1 \times 5}{2 \times 5} = \frac{5}{10} = 0.5$ Write $\frac{3}{100}$ as a decimal. The place value of the denominator is hundredths, so $\frac{3}{100}$ is written as 0.03.	Write $\frac{24}{25}$ as a decimal. _____
If you rewrite a decimal as a mixed number, the number to the left of the decimal point becomes the whole number in the mixed number. When you change a mixed number to a decimal, the whole number becomes the number to the left of the decimal point.	Write 3.75 as a fraction. The whole number is 3 and the fractional part is 0.75. Since $0.75 = \frac{3}{4}$, you can write 3.75 as $3\frac{3}{4}$. Write $2\frac{1}{2}$ as a decimal. The whole number is 2 and the decimal part is $\frac{1}{2}$. Since $\frac{1}{2} = 0.5$, you can write $2\frac{1}{2}$ as 2.5.	Write 5.25 as a fraction. _____ Write $1\frac{2}{5}$ as a decimal. _____

Unit 4, Lesson 3

Learn the Skill

YOUR TURN

Choose the Right Word

> decimal   decimal point   rename

Fill in each blank with the correct word or phrase from the box.

1. To show a number in another way is to _____ it.

2. The number to the left of the _____ _____ becomes the whole number in a mixed number.

3. The _____ equivalent of the fraction $\frac{1}{4}$ is 0.25.

Yes or No?

Answer these questions and be ready to explain your answers.

4. Can a fraction be renamed as a decimal? _____

5. In 86.9, is 9 the whole number? _____

6. In the number 79.52, is the place value of the 5 the tens place? _____

7. Are 0.5 and $\frac{1}{2}$ equivalent? _____

Show That You Know

Write each decimal as a fraction. Simplify if possible.

8. 0.1 =

9. 0.6 =

10. 0.49 =

11. 0.70 =

12. 1.12 =

13. 2.25 =

Write each fraction as a decimal.

14. $5\frac{1}{2}$ =

15. $6\frac{3}{4}$ =

16. $3\frac{4}{5}$ =

17. $1\frac{45}{50}$ =

18. $\frac{1}{100}$ =

19. $\frac{12}{25}$ =

Learn the Skill

SOLVE on Your Own

Skills Practice

Now you know all about equivalent fractions and decimals. Show it by completing these exercises.

Write each decimal as a fraction. Simplify if possible.

Write each fraction as a decimal.

1. 0.33 = _____

2. 0.8 = _____

3. 0.29 = _____

4. 0.11 = _____

5. 0.111 = _____

6. 0.891 = _____

7. 1.7 = _____

8. 5.6 = _____

9. 3.75 = _____

10. 2.24 = _____

11. $\frac{1}{4}$ = _____

12. $\frac{1}{2}$ = _____

13. $6\frac{3}{4}$ = _____

14. $\frac{1}{10}$ = _____

15. $3\frac{1}{2}$ = _____

16. $10\frac{1}{20}$ = _____

17. $\frac{9}{10}$ = _____

18. $\frac{13}{25}$ = _____

19. $\frac{999}{1,000}$ = _____

20. $\frac{111}{500}$ = _____

Unit 4, Lesson 3

Choose a Strategy

Fractions and Decimals

Strategies

Draw a Picture or Use a Model,
Try a Simpler Form of the Problem

Step 1: Read Different animals can travel at different speeds. For example, an elephant travels $\frac{2}{5}$ mile each minute and an antelope travels $1\frac{1}{100}$ miles each minute. A pig travels 0.1 mile each minute and a lion travels 0.83 mile each minute. Which animal travels the fastest?

STRATEGY	SOLUTION
Draw a Picture or Use a Model (number line) Both fractions and decimals can be ordered using a number line.	**Step 2: Plan** Place the fractional and decimal speeds on a number line. The number that is the farthest to the right is the largest number. That animal travels the fastest. **Step 3: Solve** 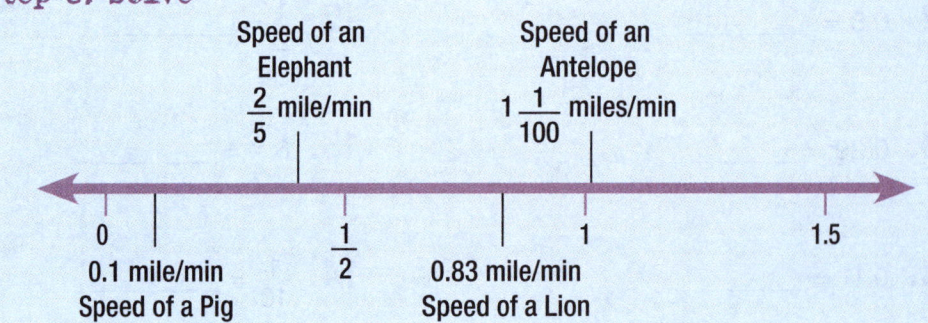 Looking at the number line, the speed of the antelope is the farthest to the right. This means the antelope travels the fastest. **Step 4: Check** Compare the fractions $\frac{2}{5}$ and $1\frac{1}{100}$. Since $1\frac{1}{100}$ is a mixed number, it is greater than $\frac{2}{5}$. Now change $1\frac{1}{100}$ to a decimal, 1.01. Since it has a whole number part, it is greater than both 0.1 and 0.83.
Try a Simpler Form of the Problem It can be easier to compare fractions and decimals by changing them all into fractions or all into decimals.	**Step 2: Plan** Change all the numbers to fractions or to decimals. Compare and order the numbers once they are all in the same form. **Step 3: Solve** Change all the numbers to fractions with the same denominator. Order the fractions. $0.83 = \frac{83}{100}$ $\frac{2}{5} = \frac{40}{100}$ $\frac{10}{100} < \frac{40}{100} < \frac{83}{100} < \frac{101}{100}$ $0.1 = \frac{1}{10} = \frac{10}{100}$ $1\frac{1}{100} = \frac{101}{100}$ The antelope is the fastest. **Step 4: Check** You can compare these numbers using models. Create decimal models for the decimals and divide up blocks of the same size to model the fractions. The antelope's speed will take up more than one block, so it is the fastest.

YOUR TURN

Choose the Right Word

denominator   fractions   number line

Fill in each blank with the correct word or phrase from the box.

1. Writing fractions and decimals on a _____ is one way to compare them.

2. When comparing numbers that are both decimals and fractions, it can be easier to first rename them all as _____.

3. To compare fractions, they all need to have the same _____.

Choose a Strategy

Yes or No?

Look at the fractions and decimals below. Are they equal? Write *yes* or *no* and be ready to explain your answers.

4. $\frac{1}{10}$ and 0.01 _____

5. 0.75 and $\frac{3}{4}$ _____

6. $\frac{75}{100}$ and $\frac{1}{25}$ _____

7. 1.008 and 1.00800 _____

8. 0.5 and $\frac{1}{5}$ _____

Show That You Know

Below are the speeds of four animals in miles per minute.

Change each fraction into a decimal.

9. Wild turkey: $\frac{1}{4}$

10. Giraffe: $\frac{53}{100}$

Change each decimal into a fraction.

11. Elk: 0.75

12. Cheetah: 1.16

Place your answers from exercises 9–12 on the number line.

0      $\frac{1}{2}$ 1   1.5

Unit 4, Lesson 4

Reading Comprehension

READ on Your Own

Reading Comprehension Strategy: Previewing/Predicting

Animals in Action, *pages 6–7*

VOCABULARY

Watch for the words you are learning about.

predators: animals that live by eating other animals

prey: animals that are eaten by other animals

resistance: a force that slows a moving object

Fluency Tip

Pay attention to punctuation marks. Punctuation marks tell you when to pause and when to raise your voice for a question or an exclamation.

Before You Read

Think about the information you read about in "How Big Is an Ant?" What did you learn that you did not know before about the different sizes of ants?

As You Read

Read "Animal Races," page 6.

Use what you know to make a prediction about why certain animals are much faster than others. Write your prediction in the chart below.

Read the rest of the article on page 7. 🛑

Complete the two remaining boxes in the chart.

Page 6
I predict
_____
_____

Page 7	
Information I predicted that was on the page	**Information that was on the page that I did not predict**
_____	_____
_____	_____

After You Read

How might the "bodies" of cars, boats, or planes be designed to help them move faster?

_____

_____

196   Unit 4, Lesson 4

Problem Solving

SOLVE on Your Own

Animals in Action, page 8

Organize the Information

Read You Do the Math in the magazine. Place the animals' 100-meter-race finish times on the number line below.

You Do the Math

Use the information in the number line above to answer these questions. Write your answers in the space provided.

1. Which two animals have the same speed? What is different about their speeds?

   _____

   _____

2. Arrange the animals from fastest to slowest in the chart below.

Racing on Land	Swimming	Flying

3. Which animal would win overall? Which would come in last?

   _____

   _____

After You Solve

Is it easier to compare speeds as fractions or as decimals? Explain your reasoning.

_____

_____

Unit 4, Lesson 4

Application

The Four-Step Problem-Solving Plan

Step 1: Read	Step 2: Plan	Step 3: Solve	Step 4: Check
Make sure you understand what the problem is asking.	Decide how you will solve the problem.	Solve the problem using your plan.	Check to make sure your answer is correct.

Read the article below. Then answer the questions.

Brains and Intelligence

Some people think that the bigger your brain is, the smarter you are. Could they be right? Scientists have measured and compared the brains of all kinds of animals, including people. You might be surprised by some of their results.

It turns out that total brain size does not tell you a lot about intelligence. An average man has a brain that weighs about 3 pounds. An elephant's brain weighs about 10 pounds and a whale's brain weighs about 15 pounds. It would take about 10 regular-sized birds to have even 1 ounce of brains.

A better number is the ratio, or fraction, comparing brain weight to body weight. People, for example, have a ratio of about $\frac{1}{50}$. Cats have a ratio of about $\frac{1}{100}$. Do not think that a larger ratio always means more intelligence, however. Small birds have a ratio of about $\frac{1}{12}$, and mice have the same ratio as people. Also, when people lose or gain weight, their ratio changes, but that does not mean they become more or less intelligent.

1. If bigger is not smarter when it comes to brains, what does a bigger brain usually show?

   _____

   _____

2. Jamie weighs 100 pounds. Using the ratio of human brain weight to human weight, about how many pounds does Jamie's brain weigh? Explain your answer.

   _____

   _____

   _____

   _____

   _____

   _____

198 Unit 4, Lesson 5

YOUR TURN

Application

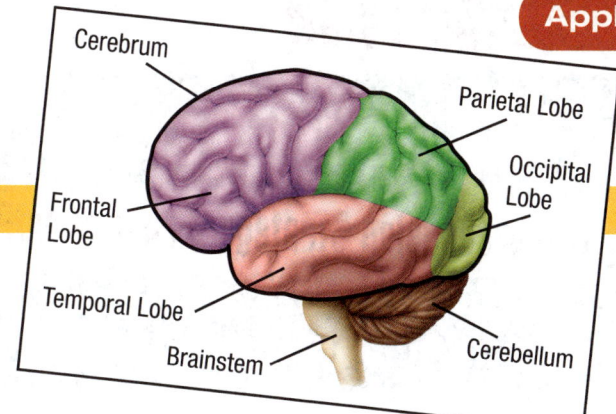

Read the article below. Then answer the questions.

Brain Anatomy

The brain is made up of several parts: the cerebrum (suh REE bruhm), the cerebellum, and the brainstem. The big difference between people and other animals is in the relative size of the different parts. The cerebrum controls intelligence. In humans, it takes up over $\frac{3}{4}$ of the brain, but it takes up less than $\frac{1}{3}$ of a rat's brain.

Inside the cerebrum are four lobes, or rounded sections. The occipital (ahk SIHP uh tuhl) lobe is mostly for vision and recognition of shapes. The frontal lobe is used for planning and problem solving. The temporal lobe is used for memory, and the parietal (puh RY uh tuhl) lobe is used for language. Animals have a well-developed occipital lobe, but people have a much larger frontal lobe. If one lobe is relatively bigger, it also can make a big difference in intelligence.

Fluency Tip
Skim the passage for words that are hard to pronounce. Practice reading those words ahead of time.

1. What part of the brain makes humans different from other animals?

   _____
   _____
   _____

2. Why might animals need a large occipital lobe?

   _____
   _____

3. The frontal lobe is equal to 0.41 of the total mass of a human brain. The fraction of the brain that is the cerebellum is $\frac{11}{100}$. Which relative amount is greater?

   _____
   _____
   _____

Unit 4, Lesson 5

Reading Comprehension

READ on Your Own

Reading Comprehension Strategy: Previewing/Predicting

Animals in Action, pages 9–11

VOCABULARY

Watch for the words you are learning about.

arteries: tubes that carry blood away from the heart

hibernation: the long winter period when some animals sleep

mammal: warm-blooded animals

marine: of or relating to the sea

veins: tubes that carry blood toward the heart

Fluency Tip

As you read and reread, pay attention to punctuation marks that are clues to correct phrasing.

Before You Read

Consider the animals you read about in "Animal Races." What do the fastest animals have in common?

As You Read

Read "Keep the Blood Flowing," page 9.

Use what you know to predict what you will learn about the heartbeats of animals. Write your prediction in the first column of the chart below.

Read pages 10–11.

Answer the question in the second column of the chart.

Keep the Blood Flowing	
Prediction Large animals: _____ _____ _____ Smaller animals: _____ _____ _____	**Did your prediction match what you read, or did you need to revise it?** _____ _____ _____ _____ _____ _____

After You Read

How might a person slow down his or her heart rate? Explain your answer.

_____

_____

Problem Solving

SOLVE on Your Own

Animals in Action, *page 12*

Organize the Information

Read the Math Project in the magazine. Use the table below to organize the animals from lightest to heaviest.

Mammal										
Weight (kg)										
Time Between Heartbeats (sec)										

Math Project

Try to decide if the heartbeat increase keeps pace with the increase in weight.

Use the information in the table above to answer these questions. Write your answers in the space provided.

1. What is the best way to figure out where one of the animals you are examining would fit into the pattern?

   _____

   _____

2. What assumption do you have to make when estimating the time between heartbeats for animals that you are examining?

   _____

3. What time between heartbeats would you predict for the Guinea pig, large dog, and hippopotamus? Explain your reasoning.

   _____

   _____

   _____

After You Solve

How else could you express the same information in the table?

_____

Unit 4, Lesson 5

Learn the Skill

Ordering and Rounding Decimals

Learn the SKILL

Three students in Mr. Dell's art class walk home from school. Lucia walks 1.228 miles, Candace walks 1.221 miles, and Joshua walks 1.256 miles. Who walks the farthest? Can you order how far each person walks from least to greatest?

SKILL	EXAMPLE	COMPLETE THE EXAMPLE
A decimal has a whole number part and a decimal part. The number to the left of the decimal is the whole number, and to the right is the decimal part. To compare decimals, first look at the whole number part. If those are the same, compare the decimal part. Compare the decimal numbers from left to right.	Compare 1.228 and 1.221. First compare the whole number part. Both whole numbers are 1, which means they are equal. Then compare the digits of the decimal part from left to right. The tenths digit of 1.228 is 2 and of 1.221 is 2. They are equal. The hundredths digit of both is also 2, so they are equal. Now look at the thousandths place. Since 8 > 1, 1.228 > 1.221.	Compare 1.56 and 1.48. Whole number part: _____ Decimal parts: _____ 1.56 ____ 1.48
To order decimals, first compare them in pairs. Once you have compared all of the decimals, write them in order. The question will tell you whether they need to be in order from least to greatest or greatest to least.	Order 1.228, 1.221, and 1.256 from least to greatest. From the previous example, 1.228 > 1.221. Compare 1.228 and 1.256. The whole number parts of both are 1, so they are equal. The tenths digit in both is 2. The hundredths digits are 2 and 5. Since 2 < 5, 1.228 < 1.256. In order from least to greatest: 1.221, 1.228, 1.256	Order 1.3, 1.1, and 1.7 from least to greatest. _____
To round a decimal, look at the digit to the right of the place you wish to round to. If this digit is less than 5, leave the number as it is. If the digit is equal to or greater than 5, increase the number by 1. Then drop all numbers to the right of the place.	Round to the hundredths place. 1.228: The number in the thousandths place is 8. Since 8 > 5, 1.228 rounds to 1.23. 1.256: The number in the thousandths place is 6. Since 6 > 5, 1.256 rounds to 1.26.	Round the following numbers to the tenths place. 3.45 _____ 3.41 _____

YOUR TURN

Choose the Right Word

> compare   ordering   round

Fill in each blank with the correct word or phrase from the box.

1. Placing decimals according to their numerical value is known as _____.

2. When you _____, you decide if a number is equal to, greater than, or less than another number.

3. One way of making comparing easier is to _____ the decimals before comparing them.

Yes or No?

Answer these questions and be ready to explain your answers.

4. If the decimal parts are equal, do you still need to compare the whole numbers when comparing decimals? _____

5. When ordering decimals, do you compare the decimal from right to left? _____

6. In the number 6.92, is 2 the first number you look at when comparing it to another number? _____

7. Is 7 the whole number in the decimal 7.88? _____

Learn the Skill

Show That You Know

Compare. Write > or <.

8. 0.4 _____ 0.23

9. 1.89 _____ 3.0

10. 7.94 _____ 0.35

Order the decimals from least to greatest.

11. 0.75, 0.8, 0.245

12. 1.9, 2.8, 0.7

13. 5.6, 5.5, 5.39

Round the following decimals to the place given.

14. 12.345, hundredths

15. 7.62, tenths

16. 0.4567, thousandths

Unit 4, Lesson 6

Learn the Skill

SOLVE on Your Own

Skills Practice

Make sure you compare and order the decimals by reading them left to right.

Compare. Write > or <.

1. 0.33 _____ 0.32
2. 0.6 _____ 1.6
3. 0.2 _____ 0.178
4. 1.29 _____ 1.92
5. 6.8 _____ 6.68
6. 0.891 _____ 0.9
7. 5.6 _____ 8.1

Order the decimals from least to greatest.

8. 1.4, 1.89, 0.4 _____
9. 0.25, 1.15, 1.25 _____
10. 1.11, 1.079, 1.111 _____
11. 9.9, 9.99, 8.52 _____
12. 3.5, 1.5, 9.1 _____

Round the following sets of decimals to the place given.

13. 3.27, 1.23, 2.25; tenths _____
14. 0.988, 0.972, 9.929; hundredths _____
15. 1.2345, 1.2444, 1.2327; thousandths _____
16. 5.032, 5.051, 5.222; tenths _____

204   Unit 4, Lesson 6

Choose a Strategy

Ordering and Rounding Decimals

Strategy

Draw a Picture or Use a Model

Step 1: Read The marine animals listed in the chart eat squid to survive. At what depth might a squid be caught by any of the animals?

Animal	Deepest Dive
Killer Whale	0.85 km
Elephant Seal	1.52 km
Weddell Seal	0.54 km
Beaked Whale	1.89 km

STRATEGY	SOLUTION
Draw a Picture or Use a Model (number line) Number lines can be used to compare decimals visually. Numbers increase on a number line as you move from left to right.	**Step 2: Plan** Draw a number line from 0 km to 2 km. Arrange the depths of each dive on a number line. Use the number line to the depth at which all of the animals have access to squid. **Step 3: Solve** Arrange the animals on a number line from the shallowest diver to the deepest diver. 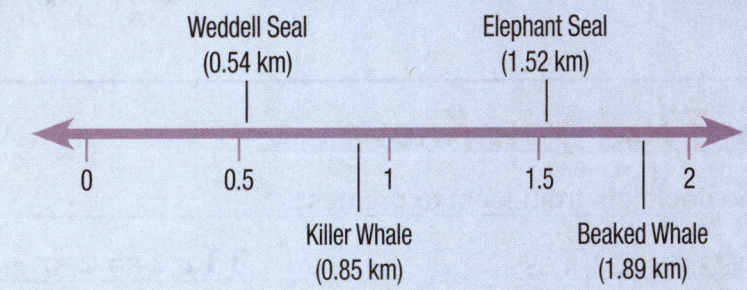 The Weddell seal is the shallowest diver. Any squid that swims above 0.54 km will be a target for all of the animals. **Step 4: Check** Compare the decimal values for the dives of the four animals. Choose the least value as your answer.
Draw a Picture or Use a Model (decimal model) Decimal models can be used to compare decimal amounts visually. Each box equals one hundredth.	**Step 2: Plan** Use shaded decimal grids to show the depth of each animal's deepest dive. **Step 3: Solve** Look at the models to see which is the smallest. 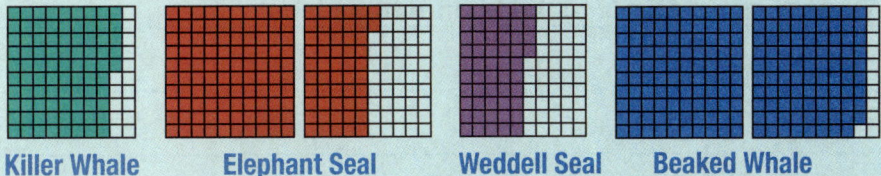 Killer Whale Elephant Seal Weddell Seal Beaked Whale Any squid that swims higher than a Weddell seal can dive (0.54 km) could by caught by any of these animals. **Step 4: Check** Arrange each decimal model from largest to smallest to make sure the Weddell seal has the shallowest dive.

Unit 4, Lesson 7

Choose a Strategy

YOUR TURN

Choose the Right Word

greater than   less than   equal to

Fill in each blank with the correct word or phrase from the box.

1. 0.85 km is _____ 1.52 km.

2. 1.09 km is _____ 1.090 km.

3. 0.32 km is _____ 0.09 km.

Yes or No?

Answer these questions and be ready to explain your answers.

4. Is 0.13 km equal to 0.1300 km? _____

5. Is 0.46 km greater than 1.46 km? _____

6. Is 0.31 km greater than 0.29 km? _____

7. Is 0.7 km less than 0.70 km? _____

8. Is it easier to compare distances when they are in the same units? _____

Show That You Know

Order the decimals from least to greatest.

9. 2.3, 2.13, 2.23, 1.33

10. 1.09, 1.009, 0.19, 1.19

11. 4.56, 4.57, 4.48, 4.39, 3.69

12. 8.88, 8.01, 1.08, 1.88, 8.08

Round each decimal to the hundredths place.

13. 1.656

14. 3.283

Reading Comprehension

READ on Your Own

Reading Comprehension Strategy: Previewing/Predicting

Animals in Action, *pages 13–14*

VOCABULARY

Watch for the words you are learning about.

depth: the distance below a given level

pressure: the application of a force on an object

Fluency Tip

Reread sentences that you have trouble with. Rereading should help you read more smoothly.

Before You Read

You learned in "Keep the Blood Flowing" that a bear's heart rate slows when it hibernates. Do you think your heart rate changes when you sleep? Explain your answer.

As You Read

**Preview "Into the Deep," pages 13–14.
Then read the first sentence of each paragraph on pages 13–14.**

Based on what you have read, predict what this magazine will be about. Write your predictions in the chart below.

Now read pages 13–14.
Complete the chart.

Preview, Read, and Predict	Read and Check
After reading the first sentence of each paragraph, I predict "Into the Deep" will be about _____	What is one main idea from the magazine that was not included in your prediction? _____

After You Read

What is one thing you learned from the magazine that you would like to learn more about?

_____
_____
_____

Unit 4, Lesson 7

Problem Solving

SOLVE on Your Own

Animals in Action, page 15

Organize the Information

Read You Do the Math in the magazine. Arrange the depths of each dive of the marine mammals in the graphic organizer below.

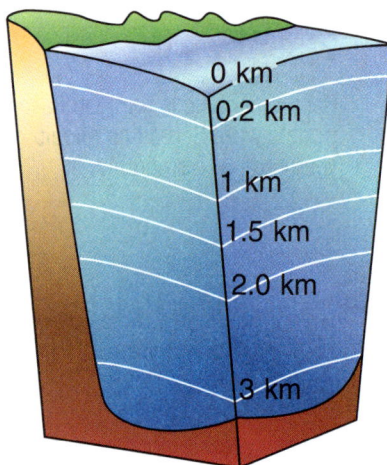

Use the depths on the graphic organizer like the ticks on a number line.

You Do the Math

Use the information in the graphic organizer above to answer these questions. Write your answers in the space provided.

1. A squid is traveling in the ocean. What is a depth at which the squid would be safe from one predator? Two predators? Three predators?

   _____
   _____

2. At what depths will the squid be safe from all predators?

   _____
   _____

After You Solve

Marine mammals have to go to great lengths to catch their favorite food. What do you have to do to get your favorite food?

_____

208   Unit 4, Lesson 7

Solve It!

Application

The Four-Step Problem-Solving Plan

Step 1: Read	Step 2: Plan	Step 3: Solve	Step 4: Check
Make sure you understand what the problem is asking.	Decide how you will solve the problem.	Solve the problem using your plan.	Check to make sure your answer is correct.

Read the article below. Then answer the questions.

Food for the Oceans

One of the smallest creatures in the sea is also one of the most important. Krill are tiny, shrimp-like creatures that can grow to be up to 5 cm long. Although small, krill play a big part in the ocean's food chain. They keep the ocean's plant life in check by eating plankton, tiny marine plants. They also become food for some of the largest animals in the seas.

For some whales, krill is the major part of their diet. Fish, squid, penguins, and seals also snack on krill. Krill swim in large groups called schools. There can be as many as 10,000 to 30,000 krill in a cubic meter of water. Schools of krill can stretch for kilometers. These schools of krill may live near the surface. Other kinds of krill spend part of the day near the surface and part of the day deep in the ocean. This is why krill is the favorite food of so many sea animals.

How important are krill? Many scientists believe that many larger animals depend on krill. If the number of krill available decreased, the entire system of whales, penguins, seals, and fish could also collapse. That is why so many scientists study the krill in summer and winter. They are watching the populations of krill to see if the krill are in danger.

1. Why do scientists study the krill so carefully?

   _____
   _____
   _____
   _____

2. If the population of krill decreased from 25,000 per cubic meter to 3,000 per cubic meter, do you think scientists would be concerned? Why?

   _____
   _____
   _____
   _____

Unit 4, Lesson 8   209

Application

YOUR TURN

Read the article below. Then answer the questions.

The Voyage of the RRS *James Clark Ross*

The United Kingdom has several ships used only for ocean research. The Royal Research Ship *James Clark Ross* spends a season in Antarctica, in part to study krill.

The *JCR*, as it is known, travels to Antarctica and back every year, researching the animal life in the water and in the air. The weather is often bad. While this might be uncomfortable for the sailors, it is much worse for the birds. The crew frequently finds exhausted birds on board the ship. These birds have often landed there to avoid a storm or strong winds.

One of the research jobs is to replace and recover specially equipped buoys. These buoys float a few hundred meters below the surface. They have cameras and other instruments that keep a record of the water above them. The buoys are placed in the same spot each time. This creates a record of conditions at that spot over several years.

Fluency Tip
Reread sentences that you find difficult. Change your expression as you read.

1. One of the research jobs performed is called catch and count. The scientists catch all the krill they can, and then count how many they have. Is this an accurate way of keeping track of the krill population?

   _____
   _____
   _____

2. Each adult krill weighs about 2 g. If there are 10,000 krill in a cubic meter of water, what is the total weight of these krill?

   _____
   _____

3. Why is it important that the buoys go back in the same places they came from?

   _____
   _____
   _____

Reading Comprehension

READ on Your Own

Reading Comprehension Strategy: Previewing/Predicting

Animals in Action, pages 16–18

VOCABULARY

Watch for the words you are learning about.

biologists: scientists who study living things

hydrothermal vents: places on the sea floor where very hot water flows from under rocks

submersible: a boat that can travel underwater

Fluency Tip

As you read and reread, pay attention to punctuation marks that are clues to correct phrasing.

Before You Read

Think back to what you read in "Into the Deep." What fact did you find the most unusual? Explain.

As You Read

Read "Looking Below the Surface," pages 16–17.

In the chart below, predict what you think you will learn about in the section "Deeper and Deeper." Be sure to expand on your prediction.

Read page 18.

Answer the question in the chart.

Pages 16–17	Page 18
Prediction	**Did your prediction match what you read, or did you need to revise it?**
_____	_____
_____	_____
_____	_____
_____	_____

After You Read

How is *Nereus* different from other robotic submersibles? Why might this be an advantage?

_____
_____
_____

Unit 4, Lesson 8   211

Problem Solving

SOLVE on Your Own

Animals in Action, page 19

Organize the Information

Read the Math Project in the magazine. Complete the Venn diagram by filling in the missing submersibles.

Bottom of Pacific Ocean

Bottom of South China Sea

Jason

Alvin

Bottom of Sea of Japan

Math Project

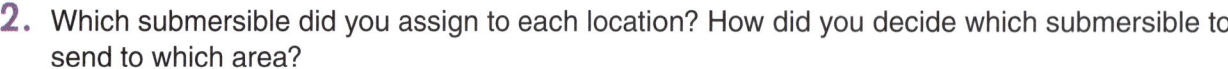

How might you use a chart to compare the depths instead?

Use the information in the magazine to answer these questions. Write your answers in the space provided.

1. Imagine that the *SeaBED* broke down. Which other submersibles could you send to do its job?

   _____
   _____

2. Which submersible did you assign to each location? How did you decide which submersible to send to which area?

   _____
   _____

3. How might you have sent out the submersibles differently?

   _____

After You Solve

What are some recent deep-sea discoveries made by a submersible?

_____

Put It Together

Connections

Introducing Using Decimals to Find Equivalent Fractions

You have learned how to change decimals to equivalent fractions. First, read the decimal with its place value, and then write the fraction.

Sometimes the fraction is already in simplest form. $0.3 = \frac{3}{10}$

$$0.47 = \frac{47}{100}$$

Sometimes the fraction can be reduced. $0.8 = \frac{8}{10} = \frac{4}{5}$

$$0.24 = \frac{24}{100} = \frac{12}{25}$$

Look what happens when a decimal ends in zero.

$$0.800 = \frac{800}{1,000} = \frac{80}{100} = \frac{8}{10} = \frac{4}{5}$$

$$0.80 = \frac{80}{100} = \frac{8}{10} = \frac{4}{5}$$

$$0.8 = \frac{8}{10} = \frac{4}{5}$$

These are all equivalent fractions: $\frac{800}{1,000}, \frac{80}{100}, \frac{8}{10},$ and $\frac{4}{5}$.

What are some equivalent fractions and decimals for 0.25?

$$0.25 = \frac{25}{100} = \frac{5}{20} = \frac{1}{4}$$

$$0.250 = \frac{250}{1,000} = \frac{25}{100} = \frac{5}{20} = \frac{1}{4}$$

$$0.2500 = \frac{2,500}{10,000} = \frac{250}{1000} = \frac{25}{100} = \frac{5}{20} = \frac{1}{4}$$

Practicing Using Decimals to Find Equivalent Fractions

Use what you have learned to complete the following exercises.

1. Write 0.4 as a fraction. _____

2. Write three decimals equivalent to 0.3. _____

3. Write three fractions equivalent to 0.3. _____

4. Write $0.75 as a fractional part of a dollar. _____

Unit 4, Lesson 9

Connections

YOUR TURN

Thinking About Using Decimals to Find Equivalent Fractions

When decimals are renamed as fractions, the denominator is originally a multiple of 10. This includes 10, 100, 1,000, or another multiple of 10. Think about reducing these fractions to simplest form. All multiples of 10 have factors of 2 and 5. When you rename a decimal as a fraction, the fraction can only be reduced if the numerator also has a factor of 2 or 5.

Look at this example: $0.16 = \frac{16}{100}$. The numerator (16) is an even number (divisible by 2). The fraction can be reduced: $\frac{16}{100} = \frac{8}{50}$.

Because 8 and 50 are both even numbers, the fraction can be reduced again: $\frac{8}{50} = \frac{4}{25}$.

The remaining denominator is 25, or 5×5. The numerator, 4, is not divisible by 5. The fraction cannot be reduced again. It is in simplest form.

The decimals 0.20, 0.34, and 0.628 are all divisible by 2. When they are renamed as fractions, they can be reduced because the denominator will also be divisible by 2.

The decimals 0.95 and 0.475 are both divisible by 5. You can tell because they end in 5. When they are renamed as fractions, they can be reduced because the denominator will also be divisible by 5.

1. Show how you would write 0.60 as a fraction. Then reduce it to simplest form.
   _____

2. How do you know that when you rename the decimals 0.15, 0.25, 0.35, 0.45, and 0.75 as fractions that the fractions will not be in simplest form?
   _____

3. What have you learned about decimals and writing decimals as fractions that would help you write 0.50000000000 as a fraction?
   _____
   _____
   _____

Tip Sometimes, it is easier to find equivalent fractions using decimals. Other times, it is easier to find equivalent fractions by multiplying the numerator and denominator by the same number. Use the method that works best for you.

Show That You Know

Read the information below. Use what you read about rewriting fractions as decimals to answer the questions. Use the space provided to show your work.

> Audrey is completing her report on the weight of birds and needs to order her list from least to greatest. It will be easier if the weights are all reported as fractions or all reported as decimals.

> Is it easier for you to change fractions to decimals or decimals to fractions? When comparing, use what works best for you.

A	Yellow-headed blackbird	$2\frac{3}{10}$ ounces
B	Brown-headed cowbird	$1\frac{1}{2}$ ounces
C	European starling	2.9 ounces
D	Red-winged blackbird	1.8 ounces
E	Gray jay	2.5 ounces
F	Rusty blackbird	$2\frac{1}{10}$ ounces
G	Brewers blackbird	$2\frac{1}{5}$ ounces

1. Change the weight of the European starling to a fraction.

2. Change the weight of the brown-headed cowbird to a decimal.

3. Rename $\frac{1}{5}$ as a fraction with a denominator of 10.

   How would you write the weight of the Brewers blackbird as a decimal?

4. Change any remaining fractional values from the chart to decimals.

Connections

Unit 4, Lesson 9

Connections

Show That You Know (continued)

5. Change the remaining decimal values (the weights for *D* and *E*) to fractions.

6. Is it easier to compare and order these numbers as fractions or decimals?

7. Writing these numbers as decimals is the same as writing them as fractions using what common denominator?

8. Order the birds from least to greatest weight. Write their letters.

Review What You've Learned

9. What have you learned in this Connections lesson about renaming decimals as fractions?

10. What have you learned in this Connections lesson that you did not already know?

11. How will this lesson help you compare fractions and decimals?

Review and Practice

Skills Review

Place values

The position of a digit in a number is its place value.
In 235.796:
2 is in the hundreds place, 3 is in the tens place, 5 is in the ones place, 7 is in the tenths place, 9 is in the hundredths place, and 6 is in the thousandths place.

Renaming decimals as fractions

A fraction is part of a whole. A decimal is also part of a whole. Use the place value of the digits in a decimal to find how many parts of the whole it is.

In 0.42, the digit 2 is in the hundredths spot.
$0.42 = 42$ parts out of $100 = \frac{42}{100}$ or $\frac{21}{50}$

Equivalent decimals and fractions

Decimals and fractions that show the same value are equivalent.

$0.3 = \frac{3}{10}$ $0.33 = \frac{33}{100}$

$0.437 = \frac{437}{1,000}$ $0.6 = \frac{6}{10} = \frac{3}{5}$

Comparing decimals

Decimals are compared by first comparing the whole number part of the number, and then comparing the decimal part. For the decimal part, first compare the digits in the tenths place, then those in the hundredths place, thousandths place, and so on.
143.9829 is greater than 143.9827.
2,349.33 is less than 2,349.38.

Ordering decimals

To put numbers into order, first compare the decimals and then list them from least to greatest or greatest to least.
In order from greatest to least, 0.34, 0.399, 2.49, and 3.947 is: 3.947, 2.49, 0.399, 0.34.

Rounding decimals

To round, look at the digit to the right of the place you wish to round to. If this number is less than 5, leave the digit as it is. If the number is equal to or greater than 5, increase the digit by 1. After you have done this, drop all numbers to the right of the place you rounded.

Strategy Review

- Organize digits into a place-value chart to help compare and order decimals. Start comparing the digits in the place values farthest to the left in the chart.
- Number lines and decimal grids are useful tools when you order decimals.
- Changing all fractions to decimals or all decimals to fractions can help you order numbers more easily.

Review and Practice

Skills and Strategies Practice

Complete the exercises below.

1. What digit is in the tens place in 124.35? _____
   What is the place value of the 1?
   _____

   What is the digit in the hundredths place? _____
   What is the place value of the 3?
   _____

2. Put the following numbers into a place-value chart.
   1.342
   0.338
   3.72

Ones	.	Tenths	Hundredths	Thousandths

3. Identify the number of lesser value in each pair.
   1.309, 1.310 _____
   43.327, 43.227 _____
   34.998, 35 _____

4. Change each of the following numbers from decimals to fractions or from fractions to decimals.

   0.45 = _____

   $\frac{22}{50}$ = _____

5. Put these numbers in order from least to greatest.
   2.38, 1.39, 2.93, 2.39, 6.1
   _____

6. Round the following numbers to the tenths place.
   5.333, 24.670, 8.811
   _____

Studying in small groups and asking each other questions is a good way to review for tests. For example, one person could be asked to name the digits in the various place values of a given number, like 234.56. He or she would say "the digit 2 is in the hundreds place, the digit 3 is in the tens place," and so on. If the person has trouble, other students in the group can help him or her out. This exercise helps everyone to learn and review together.

Mid-Unit Review

Circle the letter of the correct answer.

1. Which digit is in the tenths place in the number 249.80?

   A. 0   C. 9
   B. 8   D. 4

2. Which number is greater than 9.73?

   A. 9.71   C. 9.73
   B. 9.72   D. 9.74

3. What is the whole number in 53.2?

   A. 50   C. 53
   B. 3   D. 0.2

4. The first digit to the left of a decimal point is in the _____ place.

   A. tens   C. tenths
   B. ones   D. hundredths

5. The place value of 6 in the number 134.786 is _____.

   A. thousandths   C. hundredths
   B. tenths   D. ones

6. What is $23\frac{1}{2}$ written as a decimal?

   A. 23   C. 23.05
   B. 23.5   D. 25.3

7. What is 0.34 written as a fraction in simplest form?

   A. $\frac{34}{1,000}$ C. $\frac{34}{50}$
   B. $\frac{17}{100}$ D. $\frac{17}{50}$

8. What number is smaller than 97.3?

   A. 97.3
   B. 97.4
   C. 97.1
   D. 98.3

9. What is $\frac{9}{100}$ written as a decimal?

   A. 0.09
   B. 0.9
   C. 0.009
   D. 0.0009

10. What is the decimal part of 433.90?

    A. 0.09
    B. 433
    C. 0.90
    D. 43

11. What is $\frac{2}{20}$ written as a decimal?

    A. 0.1
    B. 0.2
    C. 0.3
    D. 0.4

12. What is 0.444 written as a fraction in simplest form?

    A. $\frac{11}{25}$ C. $\frac{44}{100}$
    B. $\frac{111}{250}$ D. $\frac{444}{1,000}$

Unit 4, Lesson 10

Review and Practice

Mid-Unit Review

13. Which shows the decimals in order from greatest to least?

A. 41.5, 40.22, 40.3, 40
B. 40.3, 40.22, 41.5, 40
C. 40, 40.22, 40.3, 41.5
D. 41.5, 40.3, 40.22, 40

14. Which number is greater than 3.334?

A. 3.33   C. 3.335
B. 3.32   D. 3.333

15. Which shows the decimals in order from least to greatest?

A. 4.332, 4.323, 4.221, 4.234
B. 4.332, 4.323, 4.234, 4.221
C. 4.221, 4.234, 4.332, 4.323
D. 4.221, 4.234, 4.323. 4.332

16. What place value is the underlined digit in 32.3<u>8</u>5?

A. ones   C. hundredths
B. tenths   D. thousandths

17. Which number is the greatest?

A. 63.22   C. 61.2
B. 7.12   D. 59.6

18. Which number is the least?

A. 0.9   C. 0.89
B. 1.2   D. 0.99

19. Which number is less than 1.011?

A. 10.1   C. 1.1
B. 1.0   D. 1.02

20. Which number is greater than 3.99?

A. 3.899   C. 3.999
B. 3.990   D. 3.909

21. Which shows the decimals in order from least to greatest?

A. 30.2, 30.4, 30.33, 31.2, 33.5
B. 30.2, 30.33, 30.4, 31.2, 33.5
C. 30.2, 30.33, 30.4, 33.5, 31.2
D. 31.2, 30.33, 30.4, 33.5, 30.2

22. Round 32.245 to the tenths place.

A. 30
B. 32
C. 32.3
D. 32.2

23. Round 1.3573 to the thousandths place.

A. 1.3573
B. 1.357
C. 1.356
D. 1.36

24. Round 8.989 to the hundredths place.

A. 8.99
B. 8.98
C. 8.97
D. 8.96

25. Which number is greatest when rounded to the tenths place?

A. 1.11
B. 1.23
C. 1.35
D. 1.32

Comparing and Ordering Decimals and Fractions

Learn the SKILL

Larissa, Tom, and Angela each bring a bottle of water to their soccer game. Larissa drinks $\frac{3}{4}$ of her water, Tom drinks 0.79 of his water, and Angela drinks $\frac{1}{2}$ of her water. Who drinks the most water? Can you show the order of who drinks the least amount of water to who drinks the greatest amount?

SKILL	EXAMPLE	COMPLETE THE EXAMPLE
Decimals and fractions can be compared. First, convert the fractions into decimals or convert the decimals into fractions. Then use the methods you already know for comparing decimals or comparing fractions.	Compare $\frac{3}{4}$ to 0.79. $\frac{3}{4} = 0.75$ $0.75 < 0.79$ So, $\frac{3}{4} < 0.79$. Compare $\frac{2}{5}$ to 0.2. $\frac{2}{5} = \frac{4}{10} = 0.4$ $0.4 > 0.2$ So, $\frac{2}{5} > 0.2$.	Compare 0.5 and $\frac{2}{3}$. _____ _____ Compare $\frac{11}{20}$ and 0.56. _____ _____
Decimals and fractions can be ordered. First, convert all the numbers into decimals or all the numbers into fractions. Then order the numbers from greatest to least or least to greatest.	Order $\frac{3}{4}$, 0.79, and $\frac{1}{2}$ from least to greatest. $\frac{3}{4} = 0.75, \frac{1}{2} = 0.5$ Ordered: 0.5, 0.75, 0.79 In their original form: $\frac{1}{2}, \frac{3}{4}$, 0.79	Order $\frac{1}{4}$, 0.9, and $\frac{3}{4}$ from least to greatest by changing them all to decimals. Then order the originals. _____ _____
There are some fractions that cannot easily be changed to decimals, such as $\frac{2}{3}$ or $\frac{4}{7}$. When comparing decimals to fractions like these, it is easier to change the decimal to a fraction.	Order $\frac{7}{9}$, 0.3, and $\frac{5}{6}$ from least to greatest. $0.3 = \frac{3}{10}$; denominators: 6, 9, 10 Least common denominator is 90. $\frac{7}{9} = \frac{70}{90}; \frac{3}{10} = \frac{27}{90}; \frac{5}{6} = \frac{75}{90}$ $\frac{27}{90} < \frac{70}{90} < \frac{75}{90}$ So, $0.3 < \frac{7}{9} < \frac{5}{6}$.	Order $\frac{1}{3}$, 0.3, and $\frac{2}{5}$ from least to greatest by changing them all to fractions with a common denominator. Then order the originals. _____ _____

Unit 4, Lesson 11

Learn the Skill

YOUR TURN

Choose the Right Word

> compare   decimal   fractions   ordering

Fill in each blank with the correct word or phrase from the box.

1. Some _____ may not easily be changed to decimals.

2. To _____ decimals and fractions, all of the numbers should first be changed to the same form.

3. The easiest way to change a _____ with hundredths to a fraction is to put the digits over 100.

4. Placing decimals and fractions according to their value is _____ them.

Yes or No?

Answer these questions and be ready to explain your answers.

5. Is it easier to compare numbers by first changing them into the same form—either all decimals or all fractions? _____

6. Can all fractions be changed to a decimal with two decimal places? _____

7. Is a fraction always greater than a decimal? _____

8. If a mixed number has 7 as its whole number and a decimal has 8 as its whole number, is the decimal greater? _____

Show That You Know

Compare. Write >, <, or =.

9. 0.4 _____ $\frac{1}{2}$

10. 1.89 _____ $1\frac{3}{4}$

11. 0.1 _____ $\frac{1}{10}$

12. $\frac{8}{9}$ _____ 0.9

Convert all the numbers into decimals. Then order the decimals from least to greatest.

13. $0.4, \frac{3}{4}, \frac{1}{2}$

14. $1\frac{9}{10}, 1\frac{1}{2}, 1.2$

15. $3\frac{3}{4}, 3.7, 3\frac{1}{4}$

SOLVE on Your Own

Skills Practice

Okay, you know how to compare and order decimals and fractions. Show it by completing these exercises.

Compare. Write >, <, or =.

1. 0.33 _____ $\frac{1}{2}$

2. $1\frac{1}{4}$ _____ 1.6

3. 0.75 _____ $\frac{3}{4}$

4. 0.2 _____ $\frac{1}{10}$

5. $1\frac{3}{4}$ _____ 1.92

6. 1.1 _____ $1\frac{1}{10}$

7. $\frac{11}{100}$ _____ 0.111

8. 0.11 _____ $\frac{10}{100}$

9. 6.8 _____ $6\frac{4}{5}$

10. $1\frac{1}{4}$ _____ 0.9

11. $\frac{1}{2}$ _____ 1.5

12. 9.5 _____ $8\frac{1}{2}$

13. 3.75 _____ $3\frac{1}{4}$

14. 1.111 _____ $1\frac{100}{1,000}$

15. 2.25 _____ $2\frac{1}{4}$

Convert all the numbers to decimals. Then order the decimals from least to greatest.

16. 1.4, $\frac{1}{4}$, $1\frac{1}{10}$ _____

17. $\frac{3}{4}$, 0.11, 1.4 _____

18. 1.11, $1\frac{100}{1,000}$, 1.111 _____

19. 9.9, $9\frac{3}{4}$, $9\frac{2}{10}$ _____

20. 6.5, $4\frac{1}{2}$, $7\frac{3}{4}$ _____

Choose a Strategy

Comparing and Ordering Decimals and Fractions

Strategies

Make a Table or a Chart, Draw a Picture or Use a Model

Step 1: Read The shutter speed of a camera determines how much light is let in. A large hawk flaps its wings for 0.48 seconds per stroke. Your camera has shutter speeds of 2 seconds, 1 second, $\frac{1}{2}$ second, $\frac{1}{4}$ second, and $\frac{1}{8}$ second. To get the clearest picture of the bird's wings, you must choose a shutter speed that is equal to or less than the time it takes for the wings to flap. Which shutter speed should you choose?

STRATEGY	SOLUTION
Make a Table or a Chart Tables can be used to organize related information, such as decimal representations of different fractions.	**Step 2: Plan** Find the decimal equivalents of each shutter speed. Compare the decimals to find out which exposure times take less than 0.48 second. **Step 3: Solve** | Fraction	Decimal Equivalent
2	2.0
1	1.0
$\frac{1}{2}$	0.5
$\frac{1}{4}$	0.25
$\frac{1}{8}$	0.125 | $2.0 > 0.48$ $1.0 > 0.48$ $0.5 > 0.48$ $0.25 < 0.48$ $0.125 < 0.48$ A shutter speed of either $\frac{1}{4}$ or $\frac{1}{8}$ second will work. **Step 4: Check** Round 0.48 second to the nearest tenth, then change the decimal to a fraction and compare it to the shutter speeds.
Draw a Picture or Use a Model (number line) Number lines can be used to compare fractions and decimals without converting one to the other.	**Step 2: Plan** Draw a number line from 0 to 2. Imagine the number line is a time line. Make a tic mark to represent 0.48, the time of the wing flapping. Find the shutter speeds that are less than 0.48 second. **Step 3: Solve** 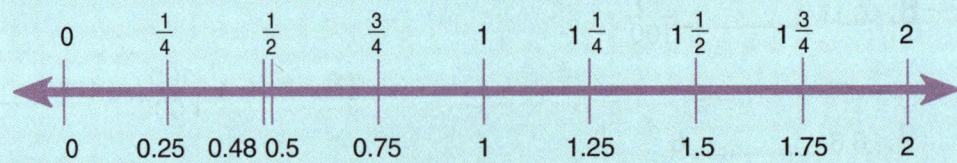 Shutter speeds to the left of 0.48 are shorter than the time it takes for the hawk to flap its wings. You can choose a shutter speed of $\frac{1}{4}$ or $\frac{1}{8}$ second to take the picture. **Step 4: Check** Change all the shutter speeds to decimals and compare them to 0.48.

YOUR TURN

Choose a Strategy

Choose the Right Word

equal to   greater than   less than

Fill in each blank with the correct word or phrase from the box.

1. When comparing fractions with the same denominator, a fraction with a larger numerator is _____ one with a smaller numerator.

2. Equivalent fractions are _____ each other.

3. When comparing decimals with the same whole number, a decimal with a smaller fractional part is _____ one with a larger fractional part.

Yes or No?

Answer these questions and be ready to explain your answers.

4. Can decimals and fractions both be compared visually? _____

5. Will a mixed number always be larger than a decimal with no whole number part? _____

6. If $\frac{1}{10}$ is equal to 0.1, does that mean that $\frac{1}{20}$ is equal to 0.2? _____

7. Can all fractions be written easily as decimals? _____

Show That You Know

Order the fractions listed below from least to greatest. Then write the equivalent decimals.

8. $\frac{9}{10}, \frac{3}{4}, \frac{1}{2}, \frac{3}{5}$

   Ordered fractions:

   Equivalent decimals:

Order the decimals listed below from greatest to least. Then write the equivalent fractions in simplest form.

9. 0.002, 0.125, 0.008, 0.25, 0.004, 0.5

   Ordered decimals:

   Equivalent fractions:

Unit 4, Lesson 12

Reading Comprehension

READ on Your Own
Reading Comprehension Strategy: Previewing/Predicting

Animals in Action, pages 20–21

VOCABULARY

Watch for the words you are learning about.

shutter: the part of a camera that lets light into the camera

shutter speed: the amount of time the shutter stays open to allow light into the camera

updraft: a wind that blows up from the ground

Fluency Tip

Remember to preview a text and look up the meanings of unfamiliar words.

Before You Read

The record depth for a human dive without breathing equipment is 172 meters. However, humans were able to explore the depths of the Mariana Trench at 10.9 kilometers. How is this possible?

As You Read

Skim page 20 of "Moving Pictures."

Write a prediction in the first column for what this page is about. Then read the page and complete the first column.

Skim page 21.

Write a prediction in the second column for what this page is about. Then read the page and complete the second column.

Page 20	Page 21
Prediction: _____ _____ _____	Prediction: _____ _____ _____
Information I predicted that was on the page: _____ _____ _____	Information I predicted that was on the page: _____ _____ _____
Information on the page that I did not predict: _____ _____ _____	Information on the pages that I did not predict: _____ _____ _____

After You Read

What is another way cameras can be used to study bird flight?

_____

Problem Solving

SOLVE on Your Own

Animals in Action, *page 22*

Organize the Information

Read You do the Math in the magazine. Use the information about time between wing beats to make a bar graph.

You Do the Math

Use the information in the graph to answer these questions. Write your answers in the space provided.

1. Write equivalent fractions for each time between wing beats.

   _____
   _____

2. To find the shutter speeds you are looking for, is it easier to convert all the speeds to decimals or to compare the fractional speeds to the answers in exercise 1?

   _____
   _____

3. Which shutter speed would you choose for each bird? Explain your answers.

   _____
   _____
   _____

After You Solve

What is something else you do that could be measured in a fraction of a second?

_____
_____

Estimating Decimal and Fractional Amounts

Learn the SKILL

Candace and Robert each surveyed their classmates on what type of music they like best. Candace showed her results as a decimal and Robert showed his results as a fraction. Candace found that 0.252 of the class liked jazz music the best. Robert found that $\frac{8}{33}$ of the class liked classical music the best. How can you easily compare these two numbers?

> **VOCABULARY**
>
> Watch for the words you are learning about.
>
> **compatible number:** a number that is close to the original number and easier to work with
>
> **estimate:** to give an answer that is close to the correct answer

SKILL	EXAMPLE	COMPLETE THE EXAMPLE
Rounding can be used to find numbers that are easier to work with. Rounding can also help you compare numbers more easily. By rounding a decimal to a number that is easily changed to a fraction, you can compare the decimal to a known fraction.	Round 0.252 to the nearest hundredth. 0.252 rounds to 0.25, which is easily changed to the fraction $\frac{1}{4}$.	Round 1.375 to the nearest tenth. Find the fraction that represents this number. _____
Fractions can be **estimated** by changing either the numerator or denominator to a **compatible number**. Then the fraction can be simplified and easily changed into a decimal.	Estimate the decimal value of $\frac{8}{33}$. The closest compatible fraction would be $\frac{8}{32} = \frac{1}{4} = 0.25$.	Estimate the decimal value of $\frac{22}{28}$. _____
The decimal value of fractions can also be estimated by using a number line. Find decimal values for the nearest easy fractions. Put them on the number line. Place the given fraction on the number line and estimate its decimal value. Find the actual value using a calculator.	Estimate the decimal value of $\frac{3}{8}$. $\frac{3}{8}$ is between $\frac{2}{8}$ and $\frac{4}{8}$. $\frac{2}{8} = \frac{1}{4} = 0.25$ and $\frac{4}{8} = \frac{1}{2} = 0.50$ Put $\frac{3}{8}$ on the number line. Its value is between 0.25 and 0.50. The actual value is 0.375. ← 0.25 0.3 0.35 $\frac{3}{8}$ 0.4 0.45 0.5 →	Estimate the decimal value of $\frac{7}{8}$. Then find its actual decimal value. _____

228 Unit 4, Lesson 13

YOUR TURN

Choose the Right Word

> compatible number   estimate
> number line   rounding

Fill in each blank with the correct word or phrase from the box.

1. Simplifying a number to the nearest tenth, hundredth, or so on is called _____.

2. A number that is easier to work with mentally is a _____.

3. Numbers that are shown as points on a line make a _____.

4. To _____ is to give an answer that is close to the correct answer.

Learn the Skill

Yes or No?

Answer these questions and be ready to explain your answers.

5. Can you use a number line to estimate the decimal value of a fraction? _____

6. Is 0.3 an estimate for 0.253? _____

7. If you round 1.375 to the nearest tenth, is the answer 1.38? _____

8. Is $\frac{7}{35}$ the best compatible number for $\frac{7}{45}$? _____

Show That You Know

Round to the nearest tenth.

9. 0.475

10. 1.8936

Round to the nearest hundredth.

11. 0.11111

12. 0.899

Estimate the nearest decimal amount by using a number line or by using compatible numbers.

13. $\frac{5}{8}$

14. $\frac{17}{32}$

Unit 4, Lesson 13

Learn the Skill

SOLVE on Your Own

Remember, round up if the digit to the right is 5 or higher.

Round each decimal to a number that is easily changed to a fraction.

1. 0.33 _____

2. 1.7665 _____

3. 0.752 _____

4. 0.21 _____

5. 1.929292 _____

6. 1.494 _____

Find compatible numbers for each fraction. Then write the equivalent decimal.

Estimate the decimal amount using a number line.

7. $\frac{23}{100}$ _____

8. $\frac{3}{9}$ _____

9. $\frac{17}{20}$ _____

10. $\frac{9}{13}$ _____

11. $\frac{45}{89}$ _____

12. $\frac{12}{29}$ _____

13. $\frac{6}{7}$ _____

14. $\frac{5}{9}$ _____

15. $\frac{6}{19}$ _____

230   Unit 4, Lesson 13

Estimating Decimal and Fractional Amounts

Strategy
Make a Table or a Chart

Step 1: Read A museum has many specimens of large birds. One measure of such birds is their wingspans. Some of the specimens include the California condor ($8\frac{1}{2}$ feet), bald eagle ($6\frac{3}{8}$ feet), turkey vulture (5.73 feet), raven ($3\frac{3}{4}$ feet), osprey ($6\frac{1}{8}$ feet), and pelican (9.26 feet). A museum director wants to re-label the birds so they can be compared more easily. How should he do this?

STRATEGY

Make a Table or a Chart
By listing the measurements, you can examine them easily to decide how to revise them. Since the measurements include both fractions and decimals, you will want to decide which type of number to use.

It may also help to use estimation to find the approximate wingspan of birds that do not have easily comparable wingspans.

SOLUTION

Step 2: Plan Look at the wingspan measurements above. Using estimation, the decimal values will be easy to convert into fractions. Convert the decimal values to fractions, and then convert all of the fractions to fractions with a common denominator, 8.

Step 3: Solve Keep track of your information in an organized chart or table.

Bird	Wingspan	Conversion	New Labels
bald eagle	$6\frac{3}{8}$ ft	none needed	$6\frac{3}{8}$ ft
California condor	$8\frac{1}{2}$ ft	$\frac{1}{2} = \frac{2}{4} = \frac{4}{8}$	$8\frac{4}{8}$ ft
osprey	$6\frac{1}{8}$ ft	none needed	$6\frac{1}{8}$ ft
pelican	9.26 ft is about 9.25 ft	$\frac{25}{100} = \frac{1}{4} = \frac{2}{8}$	$9\frac{2}{8}$ ft
raven	$3\frac{3}{4}$ ft	$\frac{3}{4} = \frac{6}{8}$	$3\frac{6}{8}$ ft
turkey vulture	5.73 ft is about 5.75 ft	$\frac{75}{100} = \frac{3}{4} = \frac{6}{8}$	$5\frac{6}{8}$ ft

Step 4: Check Recheck changes into equivalent fractions with the denominator 8. Check the reasonableness of decimal conversions. For example, according to the chart, 9.26 is close to 9.25. Both 9.26 and 9.25 round up to the same decimal, 9.3. They must be reasonably close if they round to the same number.

Choose a Strategy

YOUR TURN

Choose the Right Word

> estimate   rounding   tenths

Fill in each blank with the correct word or phrase from the box.

1. The number 4.3 is a(n) _____ of the number 4.2583.

2. If you rewrite the number 6.429 as 6.43, you are _____ to the hundredths place.

3. To estimate a number to the _____ place, you must look at the number in the hundredths place.

Yes or No?

Answer these questions and be ready to explain your answer.

4. If you just need an estimate, should you try to find the exact answer? _____

5. When rounding, should you look at the number to the left of the place you are rounding? _____

6. Is rounding helpful when an exact answer is not necessary? _____

Show That You Know

Convert each fraction to a decimal equivalent or decimal approximation.

7. $\frac{24}{32}$

8. $\frac{8}{17}$

Round each decimal number to the underlined digit.

11. 8.3<u>1</u>08

12. 104.23<u>8</u>7

Convert each decimal to a fractional equivalent. Reduce fractions to simplest form.

9. 0.422

10. 0.875

Reading Comprehension

READ on Your Own

Reading Comprehension Strategy: Previewing/Predicting

Animals in Action, *pages 23–24*

Fluency Tip
To help you read with expression, pretend you are reading aloud to a friend.

Before You Read

You learned in "Moving Pictures" that the shutter controls the amount of light that enters the camera. Which lets in more light, a shutter speed of $\frac{1}{15}$ s or $\frac{1}{125}$ s? Explain your answer.

As You Read

Preview all the text in "Winging Through the Air."

Predict what you will read on pages 23–24. Complete the first two sentences in the chart.

Then read pages 23–24.

Answer the last question.

Winging Through the Air
I predict this article will be about _____ _____
To make my prediction, I looked at _____ _____
Did your prediction help you to think about the main idea of the article? Why or why not? _____ _____

After You Read

After reading the article, which bird did you find the most interesting? Why?

_____
_____

Unit 4, Lesson 14   233

Problem Solving

SOLVE on Your Own

Animals in Action, *page 25*

Organize the Information

Read You Do the Math in the magazine. Use the table below to help you organize information from the magazine. Order the birds by the decimal value, from least to greatest.

Bird	Decimal Equivalent of $\frac{\text{Length}}{\text{Wingspan}}$	Fractional Equivalent of $\frac{\text{Length}}{\text{Wingspan}}$

You Do the Math

Use the information in the table to answer these questions. Write your answers in the space provided.

1. How do the drawings in the magazine relate to the actual sizes of the birds?

   _____

2. Write a compatible number for the length/wingspan fraction for each bird you drew. How might these compatible numbers help you determine which of the birds you have seen?

   _____
   _____

3. Which birds might you have seen? How can you tell?

   _____
   _____

After You Solve

If you could fly, which bird would you most want to resemble? Why?

_____

234   Unit 4, Lesson 14

Solve It!

Application

The Four-Step Problem-Solving Plan

Step 1: Read	Step 2: Plan	Step 3: Solve	Step 4: Check
Make sure you understand what the problem is asking.	Decide how you will solve the problem.	Solve the problem using your plan.	Check to make sure your answer is correct.

Read the article below. Then answer the questions.

Buoyant Force

Archimedes was an ancient Greek mathematician and inventor. He was once asked how to tell if the gold crown given to the king was really made of gold. The story is that he solved the problem in his bath. When he got into the tub, the water level rose. He figured that his body displaced, or moved, its volume, or the space it took up, in water. This idea became Archimedes' Principle: an object placed in water will feel a buoyant, or lifting, force. This force is equal to the weight of the water displaced. He measured how much water the crown displaced, which gave him its volume. Then he weighed the crown. If the crown was not real gold, it would have a different weight per volume.

This principle has some important uses. An aircraft carrier weighs about 97 million kilograms. However, it displaces about 1.9 billion kilograms of water. Because the amount of water it displaces weighs more than the aircraft carrier itself, the carrier floats.

1. How does an object float in water?

   _____
   _____
   _____
   _____

2. Different substances have different weights per volume. If a substance has a higher weight per volume than water, will it float or sink? Why?

   _____
   _____
   _____

Unit 4, Lesson 15   235

Application

YOUR TURN

Read the article below. Then answer the questions.

Iceberg Ahoy!

The next time you enjoy a glass of ice water, observe the ice cubes. Your ice cubes will float because they are less dense than water. If one type of matter is denser than another, the difference creates a buoyant force. This force helps keep the other object afloat.

The buoyant force from displacing the same volume of water is greater than the weight of the ice cubes. Each cube only displaces as much water as is needed to cancel out its weight. How much is that? The density, or mass per volume, of solid ice is 0.9. Only nine-tenths of the volume needs to be displaced.

Icebergs are like enormous ice cubes, or floating mountains of solid ice. Since nine-tenths of the volume displaces enough water to float the iceberg, that means only a tenth of the iceberg shows above water. This was important to the RMS *Titanic* in 1912. It ran into an iceberg that seemed small. Since nine-tenths of the iceberg was underwater, a large part of the bottom of the boat was torn open. The boat sank $2\frac{1}{2}$ hours later.

Fluency Tip
Reread sentences that you have trouble with. Rereading should help you read more smoothly.

1. The density of cork is 0.24. The density of ice is 0.9. Will cork or ice float higher in the water?

   _____
   _____
   _____

2. Adding salt makes water denser. Which gives more buoyant force, plain water or salt water?

   _____
   _____
   _____

3. Draw a conclusion based upon what happened to the *Titanic*. Did the collision with the iceberg increase or decrease the ship's buoyancy? What do you think caused this change?

   _____
   _____
   _____
   _____
   _____

READ on Your Own

Reading Comprehension Strategy: Previewing/Predicting

Animals in Action, pages 26–28

VOCABULARY

Watch for the words you are learning about.

flightless: not able to fly

gland: a group of cells that control the flow of some chemicals in the body

streamlined: shaped so as to move through air or water more easily

Fluency Tip

Look for any unfamiliar words in a selection. Find out how to pronounce these words before you read.

Before You Read

Which of the birds in "Winging Through the Air" move by soaring? What is the advantage of soaring?

As You Read

Skim pages 26–28.

Use what you previewed to predict how birds will be described and how penguins find their food. Write your predictions in the first column of the chart below.

Read pages 26–28.

Complete the second column of the chart.

Preview and Predict	Read and Check
I predict animals will be described by _____ _____ _____	Did your prediction match what you read, or did you have to revise it? _____ _____ _____
I predict that penguins will find their food _____ _____ _____	Did your prediction match what you read, or did you have to revise it? _____ _____ _____

After You Read

Why do you think that only some bird species are divers?

_____

Problem Solving

SOLVE on Your Own

Animals in Action, page 29

Organize the Information

Read the Math Project in the magazine. Use the information in the magazine to find the average diving speed of each penguin species, and then order them.

> Speed is equal to distance divided by time.

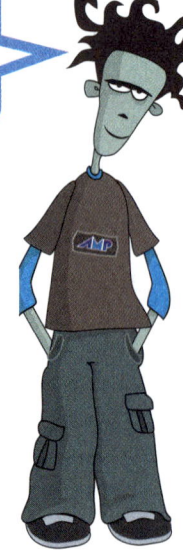

Order	Type of Bird	Average Diving Speed (m/s)
	Emperor penguin	
	Chinstrap penguin	
	Adelie penguin	
	Gentoo penguin	

Math Project

Use the information in the table above to answer these questions. Write your answers in the space provided.

1. How did you find the average speed of each penguin species? Did you find the problem-solving strategy helpful? Explain.

   _____
   _____
   _____

2. Do you see any relationship between a penguin's weight and its average speed?

   _____
   _____
   _____

After You Solve

Which penguin would win a 500-meter race if they were not allowed to come up for air? Explain.

   _____

238   Unit 4, Lesson 15

Decimals in Graphs

Learn the SKILL

Holly bikes on four different trails. If Holly bikes each day for two weeks, it can be difficult to keep track of how many miles she has biked. However, there are several ways to represent this information in a way that is easy to study.

VOCABULARY

Watch for the words you are learning about.

frequency table: a table that shows how often a value occurs

line plot: a graph with marks above the number to show the frequency of the data

SKILL

A **frequency table** shows how frequently, or often, a certain value occurs. The number of times a value occurs can be shown by a number or by tally marks such as lines.

EXAMPLE

Distances Holly biked (in miles): 1.6, 5.6, 5.6, 10.1, 3.4, 3.4, 5.6, 1.6, 3.4, 10.1, 10.1, 5.6, 3.4

Distances Biked in Two Weeks		
Trail	Times	Tally Marks
1.6 miles	2	II
3.4 miles	5	IIIII
5.6 miles	4	IIII
10.1 miles	3	III

COMPLETE THE EXAMPLE

Distances Holly biked (in miles): 2.0, 4.25, 8.75, 6.5, 6.5, 6.5, 4.25, 2.0, 6.5, 8.75, 8.75, 2.0, 2.0, 2.0

Distances Biked in Two Weeks		
Trail	Times	Tally Marks
2.0 miles		
4.25 miles		
6.5 miles		
8.75 miles		

A **line plot** is a graph that uses marks above numbers to show the frequency of the data. This can be used to show the information in a frequency table visually.

Show the information in the table as a line plot.

Number of Miles Biked Each Day

```
              X
              X       X
              X       X
      X       X       X       X
      X       X       X       X
    1.6 mi  3.4 mi  5.6 mi  10.1 mi
```

Show the information in the table as a line plot.

Decimals can be shown in bar graphs the same way whole numbers are shown in bar graphs. Rather than having each line represent an increase of a whole number, it can represent an increase of a tenth or a hundredth. A bar can also be shown as stopping between two lines to show a fractional or decimal amount.

Show the information in a bar graph.

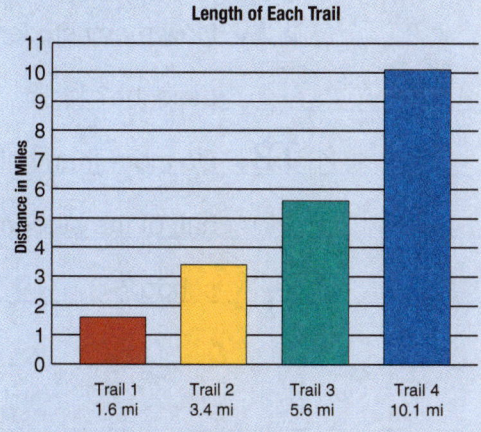

Show the information in a bar graph.

Unit 4, Lesson 16   239

Learn the Skill

YOUR TURN

Choose the Right Word

bar graph   frequency table   line plot

Fill in each blank with the correct word or phrase from the box.

1. In a _____, the heights of bars can be used to show data with decimals.

2. A student could use a _____ to show how often they record a certain value.

3. A _____ is similar to a frequency table in that it uses marks to show how often a value occurs.

Yes or No?

Answer the questions below and be ready to explain your answers.

4. Are all tables frequency tables? _____

5. Does a line connect dots on a line plot? _____

6. Can a bar graph show fractional and decimal values? _____

7. Can the frequency be shown in a frequency table without using numbers? _____

Show That You Know

Construct a bar graph from the data below. Then answer the questions.

Some friends compared how far away they each live from school. They recorded the data below.

Shawn: 6.3 miles, Beth: 13.2 miles, Garth: 2.7 miles, Gail: 4.6 miles

8. Draw a bar graph to show the data.

9. Who lives the farthest from school?

10. Who lives the closest to school?

11. How many students does the data describe?

12. Do more than half, exactly half, or less than half of the students live at least 5 miles from school?

240   Unit 4, Lesson 16

SOLVE on Your Own

Skills Practice

Use the given data for the amount of ingredients in a bread recipe to make the indicated graph. Use your graph to answer the question below it.

Recipe for bread: 2 cups water, 0.25 cups oil, 0.75 cups honey, 5.5 cups flour, and 0.15 cups yeast.

Use what you know about decimals in graphs to show the information below and answer any questions.

In a muffin cookbook, there are three recipes that require 1 cup of flour, five recipes that require 2 cups of flour, three recipes that require 3 cups of flour, and one recipe that requires 4 cups of flour.

1. Draw a bar graph showing each of these amounts. Make sure to label the bars, label the scale, and title the graph.

3. Draw a frequency table organizing the information above.

4. Draw a line plot describing the information in the frequency table. Make sure to include labels and a title.

2. How many ingredients have at least 1 cup?

    _____

5. Of the graphs and table, which would be the best way to compare the temperatures for baking four different pies?

    _____
    _____
    _____

Unit 4, Lesson 16 241

Choose a Strategy

Decimals in Graphs

Strategies

Guess, Check, and Revise; Try a Simpler Form of the Problem

Step 1: Read The frequency table below organizes how much money people donated at a school fund-raiser last year. The possible donation amounts were $1, $2, $5, or $10. This year, the possible donation amounts are $1, $3, $5, and $8. If people donate the same total amount of money this year, how many people donated each amount?

Amount	Number of People Donating
$1	10
$2	15
$5	20
$10	15

STRATEGY	SOLUTION
Guess, Check, and Revise Use this strategy to make a guess about a possible answer. Check your answer to see whether it is correct. Then revise if the answer is incorrect.	**Step 2: Plan** Guess how many people will donate each amount. Check what the total amount donated is. Revise your answer if the total is not what you are looking for. **Step 3: Solve** The total amount donated in the frequency table above is $290. The donations for this year must add up to the same amount. | $1 | $3 | $5 | $8 | Total | |---|---|---|---|---| | 10 | 15 | 20 | 15 | $275 | | 15 | 15 | 22 | 15 | $290 | The numbers in the second row are one possible answer. **Step 4: Check** Check each total amount by subtracting each of the amounts donated from the total. You should end up with zero.

Try a Simpler Form of the Problem
 	
Solving a simpler form of the problem can make a difficult problem easier to understand.
	Step 2: Plan Start with one of the columns and see how many people must donate that amount of money to get the desired total. You may need to include several donation amounts to get the correct total.
	
	Step 3: Solve
	A Divide 290 by 5: 290 ÷ 5 = 58
	       Therefore, 58 × $5 = $290
	B Divide 290 by 8: 290 ÷ 8 = 36.25
	       8 does not divide evenly into 290
	       36 × $8 = $288
	       Add 2 × $1 = $2 to reach total of $290
	
	Possible answers: 58 people contributing $5 *or* 36 people contributing $8 plus two people contributing $1
	
	Step 4: Check Use division to check your multiplication.

Choose the Right Word

bar graph   frequency table   line plot

Fill in each blank with the correct word or phrase from the box.

1. A _____ is different from other tables because it shows the number of times a value occurs.

2. When drawing a _____, you should make sure that the tops of the bars are the correct height.

3. In a _____, you can count the marks above a baseline number to find the frequency of that value.

Choose a Strategy

Yes or No?

Answer these questions and be ready to explain your answer.

4. Could the information in the frequency table in the Choose a Strategy problem be shown as a line plot? _____

5. Could a frequency table show what temperatures were measured on which days during the course of a week? _____

6. Could you have displayed the information in a frequency table with a bar graph? _____

Show That You Know

Answer the following questions about the frequency table shown below.

Class Scores on a 20-Point Test	
Score	Number of Students
1–5	3
6–10	6
11–15	11
16–20	10

7. How many students took the test?

8. Can you tell what the highest score was? Explain.

9. What was the range of scores with the most students?

Unit 4, Lesson 17

Reading Comprehension

READ on Your Own

Reading Comprehension Strategy: Previewing/Predicting

Animals in Action, pages 30–31

Before You Read

Think back to what you read in "Diving Birds." What are some special characteristics the birds have that help them swim and dive? What are some actions they take that help them stay underwater?

As You Read

Read page 30 of "Dinosaurs."

On the lines below, make a prediction about what information you will learn on page 31.

I predict that page 31 will be about

_____

_____

Read page 31.

On the lines below, tell if your prediction matched the text or if you read anything that you did not expect.

_____

_____

_____

_____

After You Read

What fact about dinosaurs did you find the most interesting?

_____

_____

VOCABULARY

Watch for the words you are learning about.

carnivores: animal eaters

extinct: no longer existing on Earth; when there are no members of a species left

fossils: the remains from ancient plants or animals

herbivores: plant eaters

paleontologists: people who study fossils

Fluency Tip

Reread difficult paragraphs until you are comfortable with pronunciation, phrasing, and punctuation.

Problem Solving

SOLVE on Your Own

Animals in Action, page 32

Organize the Information

Read You Do the Math in the magazine. Use the information to complete the table below.

Eggs per Nest	Number of Nests	Total Eggs
4	4	
5	3	
6	6	
7	2	

What other information would be good to add to the table?

You Do the Math

Use the information in the table above to answer these questions. Write your answers in the space provided.

1. What might be a good last column to add to the table? Explain your reasoning.

   _____
   _____

2. What might the paleontologists need to take into account when making their estimate of the total number of eggs?

   _____

3. How would you recommend the paleontologists explain the number of eggs at the site in their letter? Explain.

   _____
   _____
   _____

After You Solve

How does the number of eggs dinosaurs laid compare to modern-day lizards?

_____

Unit 4, Lesson 17

Application

The Four-Step Problem-Solving Plan

Step 1: Read	Step 2: Plan	Step 3: Solve	Step 4: Check
Make sure you understand what the problem is asking.	Decide how you will solve the problem.	Solve the problem using your plan.	Check to make sure your answer is correct.

Read the article below. Then answer the questions.

Ancient Humans

What were ancient humans like? Scientists have looked across the world for answers to this question. In 1850, workers digging for limestone in the Neander Valley in Germany came across the skull and bones of an ancient near-human. That skeleton is an example of what is now known as Neanderthal man. Neanderthals are now thought to have lived in Europe from 350,000 to 22,000 years ago. They grew to a height of between 5 and 5.5 feet.

Not long after the discovery of Neanderthals, workers in Cro-Magnon in France discovered the skeleton of another more modern near-human. The Cro-Magnon are thought to have appeared about 40,000 years ago. They closely resemble modern humans.

Paleontologists working in Africa found even older skeletons. These became known as the Australopithecines. The oldest bones are about 4 million years old, while the youngest are only 1 million years old.

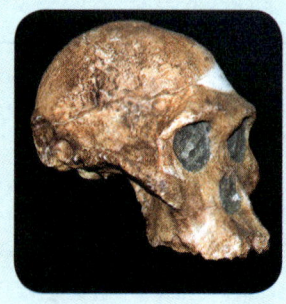

1. Were Australopithecine, Neanderthal, and Cro-Magnon humans different only because of the different places they lived? Explain.

   _____
   _____
   _____
   _____

2. The oldest Australopithecines are about 4 feet tall, while they later grew to about 4.5 feet tall. How do their heights compare to the Neanderthals?

   _____
   _____
   _____
   _____

246 Unit 4, Lesson 18

YOUR TURN

Application

Read the article below. Then answer the questions.

The Brain Game

When scientists study the bodies of ancient humans, the skull is one of the most important bones. Overall brain size is usually estimated from the size of the skull. From the shape of the skull, scientists can also guess at the shape of the brain.

The earliest humans had a brain with a volume of 380 to 450 cubic centimeters. A cubic centimeter is the amount of space that fits in a cube that is 1 centimeter on each side. Modern humans have a brain that is about 1,400 cubic centimeters. Brain volume did not always increase over time. The Cro-Magnon had a brain volume of almost 1,600 cubic centimeters, larger than a modern human's.

Total brain size is not the whole story, however. The ratio of brain size to body size is one indicator of intelligence. How much of the brain is taken up by the parts that control thinking also makes a difference. This part increases in size as you get closer to modern humans, and it is very small in most animals.

Fluency Tip
Practice reading aloud with a partner. Take turns listening and speaking.

1. One ancient human had a brain volume of 705.53 cubic centimeters. Another had a brain volume of 705.4 cubic centimeters. Which one had the greater brain volume?

   _____
   _____
   _____

2. Write the volume of a modern human's brain as a fraction of the Cro-Magnon man's brain. What is a decimal estimate of this fraction?

   _____
   _____
   _____

3. A cubic centimeter is 0.000001 of a cubic meter. A cubic decimeter is 0.001 of a cubic meter. Which is larger?

   _____

Reading Comprehension

READ on Your Own

Reading Comprehension Strategy: Previewing/Predicting

Animals in Action, pages 33–35

VOCABULARY

Watch for the words you are learning about.

habitat: the place or type of place where a plant or animal lives

pollution: anything that fouls the air, water, or land

Fluency Tip

As you read and reread, pay attention to punctuation marks that are clues to correct phrasing.

Before You Read

Think back to what you read in "Diving Birds." Why might birds not be able to dive as deeply as seals or whales?

As You Read

Preview all the text features in "Extinction" to predict what you will read about on pages 33–35.

Write the information you used to make your prediction. Then use the second column to make a prediction about what causes extinction.

Read pages 33–35.

Use what you read to answer the questions in the last column.

Preview	Predict	Reflect
To make my prediction I looked at _____ _____ _____ _____	I predict that three causes of extinction are _____ _____ _____ _____	Did your prediction help you to think about the ideas in this passage? Why or why not? _____ _____ _____

After You Read

Do you think large or small animals are more likely to become extinct? Explain.

_____

_____

_____

Problem Solving

SOLVE on Your Own

Animals in Action, *page 36*

Organize the Information

Read the Math Project in the magazine. Use the number line below to create a timeline showing the times of extinction for the different species in the article.

|—————————————————————————|
0 (Current day)   12,000 years ago

Math Project

Use the information in the timeline above to answer these questions. Write your answers in the space provided.

You may want to find the fractions first and use them to place the animals on the timeline.

1. How would you divide the timeline? Explain your reasoning.

   _____
   _____

2. Did you have trouble placing any of the four animals on the timeline? Explain.

   _____
   _____

3. List the fractional and decimal estimates of the positions on the timeline. Which animal's fractional location is closest to the decimal 0.8?

   _____
   _____
   _____

After You Solve

How would the number line change if dinosaurs were added to the timeline?

_____
_____

Unit 4, Lesson 18

Connections

Put It Together

Introducing Decimals and Stem-and-Leaf Plots

You have learned about bar graphs, frequency tables, and line plots.

Each of these methods can be used to display data. The bar graph is used for comparison. The frequency table uses rows and columns to organize data. The line plot uses a labeled line to show differences among data. Here is another method.

> A stem-and-leaf plot is a data display that helps you to see how data are distributed.
>
> Each data value is separated into a leaf (the last digit, to the right of the line) and a stem (the remaining digits, to the left of the line).
>
> The data set {104, 111, 113, 129, 93, 104, 102, 127, 116} is shown in the stem-and-leaf plot below.
>
> | Stem | Leaf |
> |------|------|
> | 9 | 3 |
> | 10 | 2 4 4 |
> | 11 | 1 3 6 |
> | 12 | 7 9 |
>
> Key: 9 | 3 = 93
>
> In a stem-and-leaf plot, the leaves for each stem are listed in order from least to greatest. You can use a stem-and-leaf plot to order data. In this stem-and-leaf plot, the leaf represents the ones place. The stem represents the remaining digits in the tens and hundreds places.

Practicing Decimals and Stem-and-Leaf Plots

Use this data set to answer the following questions. {32, 45, 47, 53, 74, 54, 53, 66, 75, 44}

1. What digits would go in the stem? _____

2. How many leaves will be in your plot? _____

3. Will the leaves be on the left or right side of the vertical line? _____

4. What value in the data is repeated? _____

5. How are the digits in the stem ordered? _____

Connections

Thinking About Decimals and Stem-and-Leaf Plots

Think about how the stem-and-leaf plot was constructed using whole numbers. The same rules apply to a stem-and-leaf plot displaying decimals. If the last digit of the numbers is the tenths place, then that becomes the leaf and the whole number becomes the stem. The data set {7.3, 7.8, 9.2, 10.3, 8.0, 8.5, 11.3, 5.2} is shown in the stem-and-leaf plot below.

Stem	Leaf
5	2
6	
7	3 8
8	0 5
9	2
10	3
11	3

Key: 10 | 3 = 10.3

Stem-and-leaf plots are used in a wide variety of situations. Like frequency tables and line plots, they are another way to show how frequently a certain value occurs. If a leaf is repeated in one row, it is because the number is repeated in the data set.

1. Why do you think the digit 6 was included in the stem?
   _____

2. How is the number of leaves related to the number of pieces of data?
   _____

3. Where can you find the largest value in your stem-and-leaf plot?
   _____

4. Why is it important to have a key for your stem-and-leaf plot?
   _____

5. Does a 0 leaf mean there is no number?
   _____

> **Tip** Make sure to include the key when you make a stem-and-leaf plot. This will let the reader know the place value of the leaf and whether or not it is a decimal.

Unit 4, Lesson 19

Connections

Show That You Know

Read the information below. Use what you read about stem-and-leaf plots to answer the questions. Use the space provided to show your work.

> Lee researched data about her state's average monthly temperature for January and February for the last 10 years.
> She is studying how changes in temperature affect wildlife in her state. Her project is not concerned with the change from year to year, but is looking for patterns over a 10-year period. She wants to combine the data for both months into a single stem-and-leaf plot for her science fair project.
>
> January   34.5   36.4   29.4   31.0   32.4   February   30.5   34.1   36.1   32.4   27.1
>   22.2   34.6   30.4   29.2   33.9   26.9   28.5   30.9   36.0   35.3

Try this: Order the numbers before making a stem-and-leaf plot.

1. What two-digit numbers should she put in the stem?

2. How many pieces of data will be in the plot?

3. Why is it important for Lee to give a key for the data in the plot?

4. What numbers in the stem will not have leaves?

Connections

Show That You Know (continued)

5. Construct the stem-and-leaf plot for Lee's data.

6. What are the least and greatest temperatures?

7. Do any months have the same average temperature?

Review What You've Learned

8. List two situations in which you could use stem-and-leaf plots.
   _____
   _____
   _____

9. How will this lesson help you order data?
   _____
   _____
   _____

Review and Practice

Skills Review

Comparing decimals and fractions

To compare decimals and fractions, convert all the numbers into fractions or all into decimals.
Compare $\frac{1}{8}$ and 0.10.
$0.10 = \frac{10}{100} = \frac{1}{10}$
$\frac{1}{8} > \frac{1}{10}$

Ordering decimals and fractions

Converted fractions and decimals can be placed in order from least to greatest:
$\frac{1}{8}$, 0.10, 0.25.
$0.10 = \frac{1}{10}$, $0.25 = \frac{1}{4}$
$\frac{1}{10} < \frac{1}{8} < \frac{1}{4}$

Estimating decimal amounts of fractions using a number line

$\frac{7}{16}$ is about halfway between $\frac{4}{16}$ and $\frac{12}{16}$.
$\frac{4}{16} = \frac{1}{4} = 0.25$; $\frac{12}{16} = \frac{3}{4} = 0.75$, so $\frac{7}{16}$ is approximately 0.5.

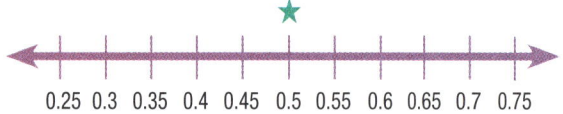

Estimating decimal or fractional amounts using compatible numbers

To estimate the decimal value of $\frac{7}{16}$, find compatible numbers, changing the fraction to $\frac{8}{16}$.
$\frac{8}{16} = \frac{1}{2} = 0.5$, so $\frac{7}{16}$ is about 0.5.
To estimate the fractional value of 0.21, round to the nearest tenth.
$0.21 \rightarrow 0.2$ $0.2 = \frac{2}{10} = \frac{1}{5}$, so 0.21 is about $\frac{1}{5}$.

Frequency tables and line plots

Frequency tables organize data on how often something occurs. Line plots can be used to show the information found in frequency tables.

Result	Number of Times
1	1
2	2
3	1
4	3
5	2
6	1

Results of Rolling a Six-Sided Number Cube 10 Times

```
                    X
          X         X    X
    X  X  X   X  X  X
    1  2  3   4  5  6
```

Bar graphs and decimals

Bar graphs show data with different heights of bars. They can be used to show amounts in whole numbers, fractions, and decimals.

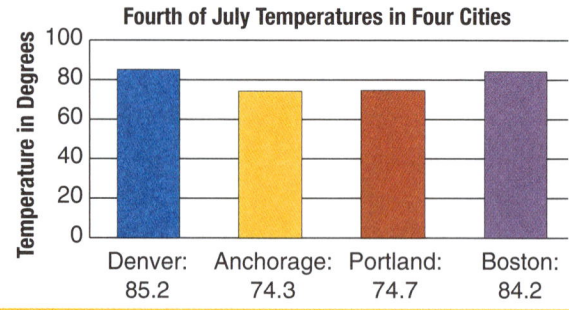

Strategy Review

- Arrange equivalent fractions and decimals in a table to help compare and order fractions.
- When rounding decimals or comparing two decimals, use a place-value chart to organize the digits.
- Use a number line to compare and order fractions and decimals.

Review and Practice

Skills and Strategies Practice

Complete the exercises below.

1. Which has the greater value, $\frac{1}{3}$ or 0.5?
   _____

2. Write the equivalent decimals for these fractions. Then order them from least to greatest.
   $\frac{2}{5}, \frac{1}{4}, \frac{3}{4}, \frac{7}{10}$
   _____
   _____

3. Place these in order from least to greatest: $1\frac{1}{2}$, 1.3, $1\frac{3}{4}$.
   _____

4. Estimate the decimal value of $\frac{8}{33}$.
   _____

5. Round each decimal to the underlined digit.
   9.34<u>2</u>51
   _____

   11.8<u>2</u>3
   _____

6. Which city had the highest temperature?

   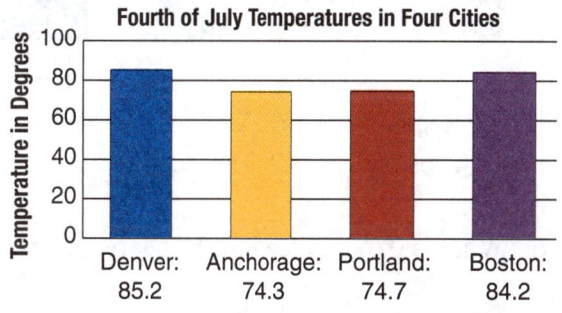

   Fourth of July Temperatures in Four Cities
   Denver: 85.2   Anchorage: 74.3   Portland: 74.7   Boston: 84.2

   _____

Test-Taking tip: When taking a test, be sure you understand what a test question is asking. Several questions can be asked about the data in a frequency table, bar graph, pictograph, or line plot. Read the question carefully before you answer.

Unit 4, Lesson 20   255

Review and Practice

Unit Review

Circle the letter of the correct answer.

1. 0.39 _____ $\frac{2}{5}$

   A. > C. =
   B. < D. cannot be compared to

2. The decimal value of $\frac{9}{17}$ is closest to _____.

   A. 0.75 C. 0.9
   B. 0.5   D. 0.65

3. 0.2 _____ $\frac{4}{10}$

   A. < C. >
   B. = D. cannot be compared to

4. On which day did the least amount of snow fall?

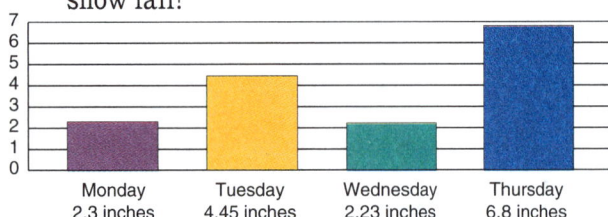

   A. Monday   C. Wednesday
   B. Tuesday   D. Thursday

5. What is 0.37 rounded to the nearest tenth?

   A. 0.3   C. 0.4
   B. 0.38 D. $\frac{3}{10}$

6. 1.74 _____ $1\frac{3}{4}$

   A. < C. =
   B. > D. cannot be compared to

7. 3.6 is equal to _____.

   A. $3\frac{3}{5}$ C. $3\frac{4}{5}$
   B. $\frac{36}{100}$ D. $3\frac{1}{2}$

8. What are $\frac{1}{3}$, 0.25, $\frac{1}{6}$, and 0.10 in order from least to greatest?

   A. $\frac{1}{3}$, 0.25, $\frac{1}{6}$, 0.10
   B. 0.10, $\frac{1}{6}$, 0.25, $\frac{1}{3}$
   C. 0.10, $\frac{1}{6}$, $\frac{1}{3}$, 0.25
   D. $\frac{1}{3}$, $\frac{1}{6}$, 0.10, 0.25

9. The estimated decimal value of $\frac{4}{7}$ is _____.

   A. 0.7   C. 0.4
   B. 0.47 D. 0.5

10. Which day of the week was the hottest day?

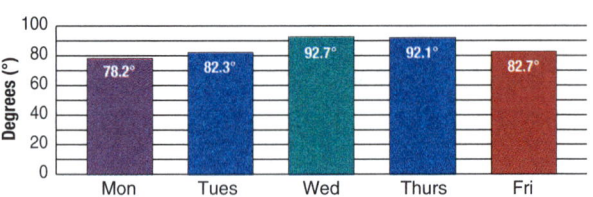

    A. Wednesday C. Thursday
    B. Sunday   D. Monday

11. $\frac{34}{100}$ _____ 0.34

    A. < C. >
    B. = D. cannot be compared to

12. The decimal value of $\frac{22}{80}$ is closest to _____.

    A. 0.3 C. 0.5
    B. 0.4 D. 0.6

13. 0.2 _____ $\frac{1}{20}$

    A. > C. =
    B. < D. cannot be compared to

Review and Practice

14. Which of these is greatest in value: 0.7, $\frac{8}{10}$, $\frac{3}{5}$, or 0.9?

A. 0.7 C. $\frac{3}{5}$
B. $\frac{8}{10}$ D. 0.9

15. $11\frac{1}{5}$ is equal to _____.

A. 11.5 C. 11.51
B. 11.15 D. 11.2

16. The estimated fractional value of 0.62 is _____.

A. $\frac{3}{5}$ C. $\frac{7}{10}$
B. $\frac{3}{4}$ D. $\frac{3}{10}$

17. What are $\frac{2}{4}$, 0.24, 0.51, and $\frac{5}{100}$ in order from least to greatest?

A. $\frac{5}{100}$, 0.24, $\frac{2}{4}$, 0.51
B. 0.51, $\frac{2}{4}$, 0.24, $\frac{5}{100}$
C. $\frac{5}{100}$, $\frac{2}{4}$, 0.24, 0.51
D. 0.24, 0.51, $\frac{2}{4}$, $\frac{5}{100}$

18. How many more households had one car than had four cars?

Cars per Household

1	2	3	4
X	X		
X	X	X	
X	X	X	
X	X	X	X

A. 2 C. 4
B. 3 D. 5

19. The estimated decimal value of $\frac{3}{9}$ is _____.

A. 0.3 C. 0.9
B. 0.2 D. 0.4

20. 7.3 _____ $7\frac{2}{3}$

A. = C. <
B. > D. cannot be compared to

21. How much money did the most students spend at the school store today?

Today's School Store Sales

$0.50	$1.25	$1.75	$2.50
			X
	X		X
	X	X	X
X	X	X	X

A. $0.50 C. $1.75
B. $1.25 D. $2.50

22. 2.45 is equal to _____.

A. $2\frac{1}{2}$ C. $2\frac{9}{20}$
B. $24\frac{5}{1}$ D. $2\frac{4}{5}$

23. The estimated decimal value of $\frac{4}{17}$ is _____.

A. 0.33 C. 0.4
B. 0.25 D. 0.5

24. The estimated fractional value of 0.74 is _____.

A. $\frac{7}{10}$ C. $\frac{3}{4}$
B. $\frac{4}{5}$ D. $1\frac{3}{4}$

25. Jan is 5.75 feet tall, Kelly is $5\frac{2}{3}$ feet tall, Mona is $5\frac{7}{12}$ feet tall, and Andrea is 5.5 feet tall. Who is the shortest?

A. Jan B. Kelly C. Mona D. Andrea

Unit 4, Lesson 20

Unit 4 Reflection

MATH SKILLS

The most useful thing I learned about decimals is

To order fractions and decimals, I like to first

MATH STRATEGIES & CONNECTIONS

For me, the math strategies that work the best are

Stem-and-leaf plots can be used to

READING STRATEGIES & COMPREHENSION

The easiest part about previewing/predicting is

One way that previewing/predicting helps me with reading is

The vocabulary words I had trouble with are

INDEPENDENT READING

My favorite part of <u>Animals in Action</u> is

I read most fluently when

Animals in Action

GLOSSARY UNITS 1-4

A

addend (AD-end): a number being added (p. 24)

area model (EHR-ee-uh MAHD-ul): a model that uses rectangles to represent multiplication (p. 27)

array (uh-RAY): an arrangement of objects in rows and columns (p. 27)

associative property (uh-SOH-shuh-tiv PRAHP-ur-tee): the grouping of addends or factors does not affect the sum or product (p. 31)

B

bar graph (bahr graf): a way of comparing information using rectangular bars (p. 18)

benchmark fraction (BENCH-mahrk FRAK-shun): a common fraction that can be used to estimate the value of other fractions. (p. 141)

C

circle graph (SUR-kul graf): a graph shaped like a circle that shows a whole broken into parts (p. 18)

combination (kahm-buh-NAY-shun): a group of objects in which order does not matter (p. 8)

common denominator (KAHM-un dee-NAHM-uh-nayt-ur): a denominator shared by two fractions (p. 141)

common factor (KAHM-un FAK-tur): a number that divides evenly into the numerator and denominator (p. 148)

common numerator (KAHM-un NOO-mur-ayt-ur): a numerator shared by two fractions (p. 141)

commutative property (kuh-MYOO-tuh-tiv PRAHP-ur-tee): when adding or multiplying numbers, the order does not matter (p. 31)

compatible number (kum-PAT-uh-bul NUM-bur): a number that is close to the original number and easier to work with (p. 228)

concept map (KAHN-sept map): a graphic organizer showing a main topic and related ideas (p. 10)

coordinate grid (koh-AWR-duh-nit grid): a grid showing ordered pairs (p. 18)

D

data (DAYT-uh): the information from a survey (p. 79)

decimal (DES-uh-mul): a number with digits to the right of the decimal point (p. 184)

decimal point (DES-uh-mul poynt): the dot in a decimal number, which separates numbers less than one from numbers greater than or equal to one (p. 184)

denominator (dee-NAHM-uh-nayt-ur): the bottom number in a fraction; shows the number of equal parts the whole is divided into (p. 104)

difference (DIF-ur-uns): the number that results from subtracting one number from another number (p. 61)

digit (DIJ-it): any numeral between 0 and 9 used to show a number (p. 42)

distributive property (dih-STRIB-yoo-tiv PRAHP-ur-tee): when a sum is multiplied by a factor, you can add first and then multiply, or multiply each addend by the factor and then add (p. 31)

divide (duh-VYD): to subtract a number many times (p. 61)

dividend (DIV-uh-dend): the number being divided (p. 61)

division (duh-VIZH-un): repeated subtraction (p. 61)

divisor (duh-VY-zur): the number you divide by (p. 61)

GLOSSARY continued

E

equivalent fractions (ee-KWIV-uh-lunt FRAK-shunz): fractions that represent the same value or amount (p. 148)

estimate (ES-tuh-mayt): to give an answer that is close to the correct answer (p. 228)

expanded notation (ek-SPAN-did noh-TAY-shun): a number shown as a sum of the number's digits multiplied by their place value (p. 42)

expression (ek-SPRESH-un): a mathematical statement including numbers and symbols (p. 4)

F

factor (FAK-tur): a number multiplied by another number (p. 24)

flowchart (FLOH-chahrt): a diagram that can be used to show the steps in a process (p. 10)

fraction (FRAK-shun): a part of a whole (p. 104)

frequency table (FREE-kwun-see TAY-bul): a table that shows how often a value occurs (p. 239)

I

improper fraction (im-PRAHP-ur FRAK-shun): a fraction with a numerator that is greater than or equal to its denominator (p. 111)

inverse operations (IN-vurs ahp-uh-RAY-shunz): operations that undo each other, such as addition and subtraction (p. 68)

K

key (kee): a chart that explains the parts of a graph (p. 79)

L

least common denominator (LCD) (leest KAHM-un dee-NAHM-uh-nayt-ur): the least common multiple of two or more denominators (p. 159)

least common multiple (LCM) (leest KAHM-un MUL-tuh-pul): the least number that is a multiple of two or more other numbers (p. 159)

line plot (lyn plaht): a graph with marks above the number to show the frequency of the data (p. 239)

M

mixed number (mikst NUM-bur): a whole number and a proper fraction together (p. 111)

multiple (MUL-tuh-pul): the product of a whole number and any other whole number (p. 34)

multiply (MUL-tuh-ply): to add a number many times (p. 24)

N

number line (NUM-bur lyn): a line with points representing numbers, increasing from left to right (p. 34)

numerator (NOO-mur-ayt-ur): the top number in a fraction; shows the number of parts in the fraction (p. 104)

O

operation (ahp-uh-RAY-shun): addition, subtraction, multiplication, or division (p. 68)

ordered pair (AWR-durd pehr): a pair of numbers that names one point on a coordinate grid (p. 18)

P

partitioning (pahr-TISH-un-ing): separating a group of objects into smaller equal groups (p. 64)

pattern (PAT-urn): objects, designs, or numbers that change in a specific way (p. 6)

perimeter (puh-RIM-uh-tur): the distance around the outside of a shape (p. 16)

physical model (FIZ-ih-kul MAHD-ul): a real-life representation of an object (p. 4)

pictograph (PIK-tuh-graf): a graph that uses pictures to represent data (p. 79)

place value (plays VAL-yoo): the value assigned to each position in a number (p. 42)

place-value chart (plays VAL-yoo chahrt): a chart that shows the place value of each digit in a number (p. 45)

plot (plaht): to find and mark the point named by an ordered pair (p. 18)

product (PRAHD-ukt): the number that results from multiplying two or more numbers together (p. 24)

proper fraction (PRAHP-ur FRAK-shun): a fraction with a numerator that is less than the denominator (p. 104)

Q

quotient (KWOH-shunt): the number that results from dividing one number by another number (p. 61)

R

range (raynj): the difference between the greatest data value and the least data value in a set (p. 82)

rename (ree-NAYM): to show a number in another way (p. 191)

represent (rep-rih-ZENT): to show an idea using drawings or models (p. 27)

rule (rool): a description of the way a pattern works (p. 6)

S

scale (skayl): numbers that are the units used on a bar graph (p. 18)

simplest form (SIM-plist fawrm): a fraction for which the only common factor for the numerator and denominator is one (p. 148)

skip-counting (skip KOWN-ting): counting by numbers other than 1 (p. 34)

standard notation (STAN-durd noh-TAY-shun): a number written as a group of digits (p. 42)

strategy (STRAT-uh-jee): a plan or way of doing something (p. 4)

sum (sum): the number that results from adding two or more numbers together (p. 24)

T

three-column chart (three KAHL-um chahrt): a chart that can be used to take notes or organize ideas (p. 10)

tree diagram (tree DY-uh-gram): a diagram that shows possible combinations branching off each other (p. 8)

V

Venn diagram (ven DY-uh-gram): overlapping circles used to compare and contrast ideas (p. 10)

W

whole number (hohl NUM-bur): a number such as 0, 1, 2, 3, 4, and so on (p. 34)

STAFF CREDITS

Josh Adams, Amanda Aranowski, Mel Benzinger, Karen Blonigen, Carol Bowling, Sarah Brandel, Kazuko Collins, Nancy Condon, Barb Drewlo, Sue Gulsvig, Daren Hastings, Laura Henrichsen, Ruby Hogen-Chin, Becky Johnson, Julie Johnston, Jody Manderfeld, Carol Nelson, Heather Oakley-Thompson, Carrie O'Connor, Deb Rogstad, Marie Schaefle, Julie Theisen, LeAnn Velde, Mike Vineski, Peggy Vlahos, Charmaine Whitman, Sue Will

PHOTO AND ILLUSTRATION CREDITS

Cover: background, © Andi Hazelwood/Shutterstock; top, © Rob Ahrens/Shutterstock; bottom, © Dwight Smith/Shutterstock; p. 1: background, © Jack Hollingsworth/Stockbyte/Getty Images; left, © Andi Hazelwood/Shutterstock; top left, © Rob Ahrens/Shutterstock; middle, © Dwight Smith/Shutterstock; p. 20: upper right background, © Andi Hazelwood/Shutterstock; top, © Rob Ahrens/Shutterstock; middle, © Dwight Smith/Shutterstock; lower right, © JuiceDrops; p. 21: background, © Jack Hollingsworth/Stockbyte/Getty Images; foreground, © Rob Ahrens/Shutterstock; p. 38, © Frances Roberts / Alamy; p. 39, © Sylvaine Thomas/Shutterstock; p. 50, © Andrei Volkovets/Shutterstock; p. 55, © JuiceDrops; p. 76, © WITTY234/Shutterstock; p. 87, © Tomo Jesenicnik/Shutterstock; p. 98: top, © Rob Ahrens/Shutterstock; bottom, © JuiceDrops; p. 99: background, © Jack Hollingsworth/Stockbyte/Getty Images; foreground, © Andi Hazelwood/Shutterstock; p. 100, © Sascha Burkard/Shutterstock; p. 101, © Tebenkova Svetlana/Shutterstock; p. 119, © Maja Schon/Shutterstock; p. 129, © Carlos E. Santa Maria/Shutterstock; p. 166, Library of Congress/Wikipedia; p. 178: top, © Andi Hazelwood/Shutterstock; bottom, © JuiceDrops; p. 179: background, © Jack Hollingsworth/Stockbyte/Getty Images; foreground, © Dwight Smith/Shutterstock; p. 180, © Peter Wey/Shutterstock; p. 181, © Getty Images; p. 182, © James Steidl/Shutterstock; p. 199, © Pearson Learning Group; p. 209, © DK Images; p. 235, © Kenneth Vincent Summers/Shutterstock; p. 246, © photobar/Shutterstock; p. 252, © Ron Hilton/Shutterstock; p. 258: top, © Dwight Smith/Shutterstock; bottom, © JuiceDrops; Back Cover: top, © Rob Ahrens/Shutterstock; middle, © Andi Hazelwood/Shutterstock; bottom, © Dwight Smith/Shutterstock

All coach characters: KATMO